AF351392

ISBN:978-1-970254-02-0

This book is intended as a practical resource and informational guide. It is not a substitute for professional counseling or therapy. The author and publisher assume no liability for outcomes related to the use of this book.

THE STOIC ENTREPRENEUR

CALM MASTERY IN THE AGE OF CHAOS

by

Ethan Starke

Introduction

The Candle, Not the Sword

We live in a time that worships acceleration. The world rewards the entrepreneur who scales quickly, pivots instantly, and chases opportunity with a kind of restless urgency. Speed is treated as intelligence; expansion is treated as destiny. But what is celebrated in the moment often collapses under its own momentum. Many modern enterprises operate less like structures and more like explosions; spectacles of force that produce temporary light before fading into irrelevance. In this climate, the builder who rejects speed, who values depth over visibility and structure over sensation, appears almost subversive. Yet it is this quieter figure; not the conqueror, not the disruptor; who builds what truly lasts.

This book is written for the builder who feels the pull toward another way. For the entrepreneur who suspects that business is something more than strategy, performance, or personal glory. For the person who senses that an enterprise, when built with intention, becomes a vessel rather than a weapon; an offering rather than a conquest. Building in this way requires not only skill but character. It demands restraint, clarity, rhythm, and the willingness to serve something larger than the self. It is an approach that often runs counter to the noise of modern ambition, yet it is the only approach that produces structures capable of enduring.

To build is to enter into a covenant with the work. It is not merely the act of assembling parts or executing a vision; it is the acceptance of responsibility for what the creation becomes. What is built without inner discipline eventually collapses from within. What is erected without purpose decays into spectacle. The true builder understands that an enterprise is not a fortress for self-protection or a monument to personal legacy. It is a space of gathering; a system meant to elevate the lives it touches. And because it is meant to serve, it demands that the builder grow smaller than the work, refining their ego so that clarity and steadiness can guide the structure.

This path is not gentle. Every serious builder will face failure, fatigue, betrayal, and uncertainty. These wounds are not signs that the builder is inadequate. They are the initiation. They carve out the humility, seriousness, and precision necessary to build without illusion. Over time, these wounds become the builder's only real credentials; not the trophies earned in victory, but the resilience earned in struggle.

The strength required for this work is not the loud, posturing strength so often celebrated. It is a quieter strength; one grounded in rhythm rather than intensity. Nature teaches this rhythm. The tide advances and retreats. The heart contracts and expands. Growth cycles through seasons of motion, reflection, rest, and renewal. When an entrepreneur violates these rhythms; when they attempt perpetual expansion, perpetual effort, perpetual visibility; their structure becomes brittle. When they honor these rhythms, they develop the capacity to endure.

Endurance, not victory, is the goal. Victory is momentary; endurance is structural. The builder's task is not to outshine competitors or dominate markets, but to illuminate steadily over time; to build something that retains integrity through chaotic seasons and evolving circumstances. This requires a shift from conquest to communion, from force to stewardship, from spectacle to service. It is the movement from the sword to the candle.

This book is not a manual of tactics or trends. It will not teach you growth hacks, shortcuts, or methods for outmaneuvering rivals. Strategies shift with every cycle of technology and culture. What endures are principles: clarity, humility, stewardship, rhythm, stillness, disciplined presence. These qualities do not become obsolete. They are the foundation upon which enduring enterprises are built.

Each chapter offers a meditation on one such principle, drawn from the psychology of creation, the patterns of nature, and the lived experience of building through both success and collapse. These reflections invite you to build in a way that is slower, deeper, and more deliberate; not as a retreat from ambition, but as a refinement of it.

If you are ready to build with intention rather than impulse, with rhythm rather than urgency, and with service rather than spectacle;

if you are ready to carry the candle rather than wield the sword; then turn the page. The work begins here.

Chapter 1

The Empty Vessel: Embracing Beginner's Mind

The Weight of Knowing

There is a point in every builder's journey where knowledge, once liberating, becomes a quiet burden. In the early stages, the absence of certainty is not a handicap; it is fuel. Beginners move with a kind of openness that invites learning. They question easily, absorb quickly, and adjust without the friction of ego. Their ignorance is not a void but a doorway; every step is a discovery, every mistake a data point, every experience an invitation to refine their understanding of the terrain. That early lightness is often what allows them to move with agility, to sense opportunities others overlook, to perceive signals without filtering them through old frameworks.

But as success accumulates, something subtle shifts. What was once instinctive curiosity begins to calcify into expectation. Experience, instead of sharpening perception, starts to shape conclusions before new information arrives. The builder who once listened before speaking now relies on pattern recognition, assuming that past solutions map seamlessly onto present complexity. Knowledge, if held too tightly, becomes less a compass and more a weight; an anchor to what used to be true rather than a guide to what is emerging now.

This is the danger that hides inside experience. Not incompetence. Not lack of intelligence. But the unexamined belief that learning is something that happens at the beginning rather than something that must be sustained throughout the entire arc of building. When the builder starts valuing certainty over inquiry, clarity over curiosity, strategy over perception, they quietly close the aperture through which real insight enters. What they know begins to overshadow what they need to see.

The burden of knowing is rarely felt all at once. It accumulates through small reflexes: dismissing a junior perspective because it contradicts a familiar pattern; relying on past victories as justification for present decisions; interpreting market shifts through yesterday's logic; assuming that mastery in one season guarantees relevance in the next. These habits do not announce themselves as arrogance, but they behave like it. They create a mental architecture that is sturdy, but not permeable; impressive in its structure, but stagnant in its evolution.

Entrepreneurship punishes this stagnation. The world does not pause to honor what you once understood. Markets move, technologies bend, customer psychology rewrites itself with each cultural shift. A builder who carries too much knowing; and too little openness; acts from a map that no longer resembles the terrain. Their expertise becomes a liability precisely when they need it to be an asset.

The danger, then, is not ignorance. It is the refusal to recognize the limits of knowledge accumulated under conditions that no longer exist. The world changes faster than the builder's certainty. And if that certainty is not regularly emptied, it becomes distortion rather than insight.

This is why the most experienced builders often find themselves returning, deliberately, to a posture they once occupied unintentionally: the posture of the beginner. Not because they have forgotten what they know, but because they understand the risk of knowing too much. They recognize that true expertise is not the accumulation of answers, but the discipline of remaining teachable. They understand that wisdom is light only when it is carried lightly.

To build with longevity is to treat knowledge not as identity, but as inventory; useful, but never sacred; relevant, but never complete. The entrepreneur who endures is the one who can set down the weight of knowing long enough to become available to what the moment requires. They recognize that the mind is most dangerous not when it is empty, but when it is full; and unaware of it.

The work, then, is not to abandon experience, but to prevent it from hardening into doctrine. To cultivate a mind capable of holding what it has learned without being confined by it. To return, again and again, to the beginner's clarity; not as regression, but as evolution.

Because the only thing heavier than ignorance is knowledge carried without humility.

The Empty Vessel

The idea of emptiness is widely misunderstood. In common language, to be empty implies deficiency; a lack of substance, conviction, or capacity. But in the discipline of serious building, emptiness carries a different meaning altogether. It is not an absence but a condition, not a void but a readiness. The empty vessel is not weak because it lacks content; it is strong because it can receive. It is the form that remains open to insight rather than crowded by assumption, able to adjust to new realities rather than imprisoned by the structures of its past.

A vessel's usefulness is determined not by its material, but by the space within it. A cup carved from the finest stone holds nothing if it is solid. What appears impressive from the outside becomes useless without capacity. The same dynamic governs the mind of the builder. Knowledge, experience, frameworks, strategies; all have value. But when they accumulate without being examined, when they fill every available space, they leave no room for new signals to enter. The builder becomes more informed but less perceptive. More prepared but less adaptable. More certain but less aligned.

Emptiness is the antidote to this narrowing. It is the discipline of creating internal space, of refusing to let prior learning occupy every inch of one's attention. It does not ask the builder to discard what they know, but to hold it lightly; to create enough openness that the present moment can be perceived on its own terms. Emptiness is not a passive state. It is a deliberate clearing. A refusal to allow noise, ego, or historical success to dictate what the builder sees.

This discipline becomes essential as a venture grows more complex. The early days of building are full of questions. But with time and achievement, questions are replaced by patterns, by systems, by established ways of thinking. Without intentional emptiness, those structures begin to dominate perception. The builder starts interpreting new challenges through old categories, reducing unfamiliar problems into recognizable shapes not because they fit, but because they are familiar. The mind becomes efficient but not wise.

Emptiness interrupts this reflex. It creates a pause; a mental clearing that allows the builder to observe without immediately concluding. It enlarges the capacity for nuance. It leaves room for contradiction. It honors the possibility that what is emerging may not resemble what has been. This openness is not naïveté. It is precision. It allows the builder to see the world without the distortion of their own expectations.

To be empty is also to be available. When the builder carries too much; too many conclusions, too many stories about how things "should" work, too many assumptions about what their role demands; they lose the ability to sense subtle shifts in the environment. Opportunities pass unnoticed. Weak signals go unexamined. The structure becomes reactive rather than responsive. Emptiness restores sensitivity. It sharpens perception. It widens the aperture through which insight arrives.

This is not to say emptiness is comfortable. It requires the builder to release the protective armor of certainty. It asks them to suspend the narrative that their past victories guarantee their future relevance. But this discomfort is what makes the practice transformative. Emptiness strips away the illusion of control and replaces it with presence. It teaches the builder to navigate by attention rather than by assumption.

In this way, the empty vessel becomes the foundation of enduring mastery; not the mastery of having all the answers, but the mastery of remaining open enough for new answers to emerge. The builder who cultivates emptiness does not regress into ignorance. They advance into awareness. They move through complexity without carrying unnecessary weight. And because they are not full, they are never finished. They remain teachable, perceptive, and aligned with the reality in front of them rather than the stories behind them.

The empty vessel is not the absence of knowledge. It is the architecture that makes learning possible.

Beginner's Mind in Practice

Beginner's mind is often reduced to a slogan; an appealing idea stripped of the rigor it actually requires. In practice, it is neither whimsical nor passive. It is a disciplined posture that demands the builder unsettle their own certainty long enough to see what is actually unfolding. The phrase is frequently misunderstood as an invitation to forget what one knows. But real beginner's mind does not erase experience; it repositions it. It moves knowledge out of the foreground so that perception can lead, rather than the reflexes that experience tends to produce. In this sense, beginner's mind is not naivety; it is maturity expressed through humility.

The builder who adopts this posture is not pretending to be inexperienced. They are choosing to suspend the authority of their experience long enough to perceive without distortion. They are resisting the instinct to categorize new information into familiar frameworks. They are refusing to impose old conclusions onto new circumstances. It is a conscious loosening; a softening of certainty that creates space for inquiry. Beginner's mind does not ask the builder to distrust what they know; it asks them to distrust the reflex that assumes what they know is sufficient.

This discipline becomes especially urgent as complexity increases. The early stages of building are filled with natural curiosity because everything is unfamiliar. But as the builder gains traction, as patterns emerge, as systems solidify, curiosity becomes optional; and eventually, inconvenient. The mind prioritizes efficiency over perception. Situations are interpreted through shortcuts. Conversations become filtered by expectation. The builder begins to see what they assume is there rather than what is actually present. Beginner's mind interrupts that drift. It slows interpretation long enough for the reality of the moment to reveal itself before being judged.

To practice beginner's mind is to make questioning habitual; not performatively, but privately, at the level of perception. It is asking: What if I am wrong? What if this situation is not what it resembles? What if the signals I'm receiving require a frame I have not used before? These questions are not evidence of insecurity. They are evidence of rigor. They keep the builder from collapsing the complexity of the present into the simplicity of the past.

Beginner's mind also shapes how the builder engages with others. A leader anchored in certainty tends to dominate conversation with conclusions. A leader anchored in beginner's mind listens differently. They listen not to confirm, but to understand. They invite perspectives that disrupt their assumptions. They create an environment where truth is more important than validation. This does not weaken authority; it strengthens discernment. People contribute more fully when they sense the builder is actually perceiving, not merely waiting to assert.

Crucially, beginner's mind does not mean slowing down decisions indefinitely. It means delaying distortion. It means allowing enough space for the right data; emotional, structural, interpersonal, market; to enter before the decision crystallizes. Builders often misinterpret speed as competence. But speed without clarity is recklessness disguised as momentum. Beginner's mind ensures that when action does come, it comes from alignment rather than habit.

Perhaps the most important aspect of this practice is its relationship to identity. Builders who define themselves by their expertise struggle to adopt beginner's mind because doing so feels like a threat to their status. But those who see themselves as students of reality rather than owners of it move with greater precision over time. They understand that the world is not asking them to be infallible. It is asking them to be attentive. They relinquish the pressure to always know and replace it with the discipline to always notice.

Beginner's mind is not a temporary mindset for early builders. It is a lifelong discipline that keeps perception sharp, ego light, and decisions grounded in what is rather than in what once was. It is the stance that allows the builder to grow without ossifying, to adapt without losing coherence, and to remain available to the truth even when the truth contradicts their expertise.

It is not innocence. It is clarity.
And clarity, not knowledge, is what allows the builder to endure.

The Architecture of Receptivity

Receptivity is often romanticized as openness; a vague willingness to hear new ideas or entertain alternative viewpoints. But for the builder committed to long-term creation, receptivity must be understood as an internal architecture, not a personality trait. It is a deliberate structure designed to keep perception unobstructed by ego, familiarity, or the momentum of one's own past. Without this architecture, even the most talented entrepreneur becomes deaf to meaningful signals, blind to emerging patterns, and insulated from the very feedback that would preserve their relevance.

The world rarely communicates in direct statements. It whispers. Markets shift in gradients, not declarations. People communicate through tone long before they articulate discontent. Cultural currents alter behavior months before they are noticeable on any dashboard. Builders who rely solely on explicit data miss the much earlier indicators embedded in the subtle, the peripheral, the informal. Receptivity is the discipline of tuning the mind to recognize these quiet signals before they become loud problems; or lost opportunities.

The first structural pillar of receptivity is listening without pretense. Most listening in organizational life is performative. People listen to appear collaborative, to gather ammunition for their response, or to confirm what they already believe. This is not listening; it is tactical waiting. Listening without pretense requires suspending the need to respond and relinquishing the subtle desire to maintain authority. The builder who practices this form of listening allows information to arrive unfiltered. They create a temporary neutrality within themselves so the signal is not distorted by defensiveness or expectation. This form of listening strengthens intuition not as a mystical attribute, but as a calibrated instrument sharpened by repeated exposure to undistorted reality.

The second pillar is noticing; the ability to detect the small deviations in behavior, sentiment, or pattern that precede major shifts. Noticing is quieter than analysis. It requires a mind capable of stillness even in motion. Builders who rush, who fill every space in their day, who seek constant stimulation, lose the ability to perceive nuance. Their attention becomes too coarse to detect subtlety. The architecture of receptivity is built, in part, by practices that slow the mind just enough for nuance to register. This is why stillness is not an aesthetic preference but a strategic necessity.

The third pillar is absorbing without distortion. Even when a builder listens and notices, the information they receive is often bent by their own desires; desires for a particular outcome, for validation, or for the preservation of an existing strategy. Absorbing without distortion requires the builder to develop an internal stillness that allows information to settle before it is interpreted. It is the discipline of resisting the urge to immediately classify, justify, or weaponize what is perceived. Instead, the builder holds the information long enough for its meaning; not their preference; to emerge. This distinguishes perception from projection.

When these pillars are practiced consistently, they form what can be called the inner chamber; a psychological space where noise is filtered out and reality can be examined without haste. The inner chamber is not removed from action; it precedes action. It becomes the builder's internal point of recalibration, the place they return to when complexity threatens to overwhelm clarity. A leader with such a chamber moves through volatility with less fragility; not because they are emotionless, but because their perception is not constantly hijacked by noise.

This architecture is exhausting to maintain without discipline, and it will decay quickly if left unattended. The builder must reinforce it through habits that promote silence, questioning, observation, and genuine humility. Without these reinforcements, receptivity collapses under the pressures of speed, ego, urgency, and the intoxicating familiarity of old solutions. When receptivity collapses, rigidity follows, and rigidity is fatal in environments defined by change.

Receptivity is not an indulgence. It is an operating system. It expands the builder's perceptual range, sharpens judgment, and strengthens the ability to act with precision rather than reactivity. It allows the builder to sense reality as it is, not as they hope or fear it to be. In the long arc of building, this architecture is not optional; it is the difference between relevance and obsolescence.

When Mastery Becomes Stagnation

Mastery has a peculiar trajectory. In the beginning, it is aspirational; a horizon the builder moves toward with hunger, curiosity, and relentless experimentation. Every challenge is an invitation to learn; every gap in understanding is a reason to stretch further. The early pursuit of mastery sharpens attention and keeps the builder intensely alive to the realities of their environment. But once mastery is achieved; or believed to be achieved; its psychological effects begin to shift. What once expanded the builder's range begins to narrow it. Mastery, left unattended, becomes a quiet threat to evolution.

The first danger emerges when skill turns into reflex. Reflex is efficient, but it is also unexamined. What once required deliberate thought becomes automatic, and automatic behavior is blind to context. Conditions change, but reflexes do not. A strategy that once worked brilliantly becomes a default response long after the environment has moved on. This is how mastery becomes rigid: not through arrogance alone, but through the seductive ease of patterns that once protected the builder from uncertainty. The problem is not the mastery itself; it is the lack of continual recalibration.

Another danger is the erosion of curiosity. Early in the journey, builders ask questions because they have no choice; their ignorance demands inquiry. But after years of competence, questions become optional, then inconvenient, then threatening. Expertise creates a gravitational pull toward confirmation; toward any information that affirms the builder's established worldview. This is where stagnation begins: not as a dramatic collapse, but as a subtle drift away from inquiry and toward assumption. The builder grows more confident but less perceptive, more prepared but less adaptable.

Success intensifies this drift. Each victory reinforces the illusion that the builder's methods are universally valid, that the conditions which enabled their rise were a product of wisdom rather than timing, context, or favorable circumstances. The narrative of mastery strengthens while the practice of learning weakens. The builder begins to trust their own conclusions more than the signals emerging around them. They defend what they know rather than investigate what they don't. It becomes easier to repeat what once worked than to question whether it still does.

The erosion that follows is almost always quiet. The company does not collapse overnight. Instead, novelty decreases. Innovation slows. Decisions become predictable. The team mirrors the leader's complacency. Early warning signs; changing customer behaviors, internal misalignments, subtle market shifts; are dismissed because they contradict the builder's established model. By the time the stagnation becomes visible, the root cause has already hardened: the builder's mind has become anchored to an outdated map.

This stagnation is not a failure of intelligence; it is a failure of humility. Mastery is dangerous not because it is wrong, but because it can become overly trusted. It offers the illusion that learning is a phase rather than a lifelong requirement. When mastery becomes identity, stagnation becomes inevitable. The builder who defines themselves by what they already know loses the flexibility required to perceive what they have not yet learned.

Avoiding this trap requires a reorientation of mastery itself. Instead of treating it as a destination, the builder must treat mastery as a tool; useful in the right context, irrelevant in the wrong one. Mastery must serve perception, not replace it. Experience must inform inquiry, not suppress it. When mastery is held lightly, it becomes a resource. When held tightly, it becomes an anchor.

The builders who endure understand this distinction intuitively. They resist the temptation to rely on reflex alone. They interrupt their own patterns. They revisit the assumptions that enabled their early success and treat them not as sacred truths but as hypotheses to be tested again and again. They understand that mastery must bend to reality, not the other way around.

In this way, mastery remains alive rather than ossified. It evolves with the builder. It adapts to new conditions. It supports innovation instead of obstructing it. When mastery is coupled with humility, it becomes a foundation rather than a cage. But when mastery stops evolving, it becomes indistinguishable from stagnation; and the builder who once led the change becomes the one most threatened by it.

The Builder's Discipline

The work of remaining open; of sustaining emptiness, of practicing beginner's mind; demands far more than intention. It requires discipline. Not the loud, performative discipline that chases productivity metrics or celebrates endurance for its own sake, but a quieter, internal discipline that governs how the builder relates to their own knowledge, their own reflexes, and their own identity. Without this discipline, even the most perceptive builder will drift back into the comfort of certainty, the ease of repetition, and the seduction of established patterns. The discipline is what preserves the flexibility that mastery threatens to erode.

At the center of this discipline is intentional unlearning. Unlearning is often misunderstood as discarding what one knows, but that is neither accurate nor useful. Unlearning is the refusal to let previous knowledge dominate perception. It is the practice of interrupting the automatic conclusions that arise from past experience. The builder does not abandon their history; they loosen its grip. Unlearning is a clearing mechanism: it creates space between stimulus and response so that new information can be evaluated without being immediately overshadowed by old narratives. In this way, unlearning becomes a form of intellectual hygiene; preventing the accumulation of assumptions that would otherwise harden into limitation.

The discipline also requires a commitment to inquiry over declaration. Declarations create clarity, but they also create inertia. Once a conclusion is spoken; especially by a leader; it gains authority. It becomes the premise upon which further decisions are built, often prematurely. Inquiry, by contrast, keeps the structure permeable. It prevents premature closure. A builder committed to inquiry does not rush to define what a situation means; they begin by asking what they might be missing. They do not default to explanation; they default to examination. The discipline lies not in doubting everything, but in refusing to grant certainty before the evidence has earned it.

In practice, this means the builder must cultivate habits that reinforce questioning as a foundational mode of thought. They revisit assumptions that have gone unchallenged for too long. They interrogate the hidden premises behind their own strategies. They invite perspectives that contradict their own conclusions not to perform collaboration, but to expose blind spots that would otherwise remain concealed. Inquiry is not a sign of weakness. It is a sign of seriousness; a recognition that the complexity of reality cannot be reduced to the simplicity of habitual thinking.

Discipline also manifests in the builder's willingness to replace momentum with stillness when necessary. Many builders fear slowing down because they equate motion with progress. But motion without clarity leads to misalignment, and misalignment compounds into avoidable crises. The disciplined builder creates moments of intentional pause to recalibrate their perception, to observe whether the direction still aligns with the conditions at hand. They resist the cultural pressure to act quickly for the sake of appearing decisive. They understand that precision often requires hesitation, and that hesitation; when grounded in perception; is not indecision but discernment.

Another dimension of the builder's discipline is the practice of releasing identity-based attachments. Builders often become overly invested in their own ideas, methods, or philosophies because these elements become intertwined with their sense of self. This is dangerous. A builder who cannot revise their own ideas cannot evolve. A builder who protects an outdated framework because it represents a previous victory is already behind the curve. The discipline here is internal detachment; the ability to evaluate one's own thinking without defensiveness. To let go of what no longer serves without interpreting the letting go as personal diminishment.

These practices are not dramatic, and they are rarely visible to anyone else. But they create the internal conditions that allow the builder to remain adaptive, perceptive, and grounded in reality rather than trapped in the inertia of their own expertise. The discipline is cumulative. It strengthens the builder's capacity to navigate uncertainty not by force, but by clarity. It ensures that their mastery stays fluid rather than fossilized, and that their leadership arises from alignment rather than impulse.

In the long run, the builders who endure are not the ones who know the most. They are the ones who can continuously unlearn, continuously inquire, continuously recalibrate. Their discipline is not loud, but it is unbreakable. It is the quiet engine that keeps them from becoming rigid, the internal structure that keeps them teachable, the steady force that keeps them alive to the truth of the moment rather than the comfort of the past.

Failure as Fertile Ground

Failure is typically framed as a disruption; an unwanted interruption to progress, a setback to be endured, a deviation from the expected trajectory of success. But for the builder committed to long-term creation, failure functions less as detour and more as foundation. It is one of the few forces capable of clearing accumulated rigidity, dissolving false narratives, and returning the builder to a state of perceptual openness. Success often inflates the mind; failure punctures it. And in the openness that follows, something essential becomes possible again: the ability to see without distortion.

The collapse of a venture, a product, or even a long-held assumption can feel like devastation because it destabilizes more than plans; it destabilizes identity. Builders often anchor their sense of competence, purpose, or legitimacy in their creations. When those creations falter, the builder interprets the failure not as an event but as a verdict. This misconception is what makes failure painful. But pain is not the same as meaning. What failure actually provides; if the builder is willing to face it without numbness or denial; is a profound clearing effect. It strips away the illusions that success tolerates. It reveals what was unnecessary, what was unexamined, what was fragile beneath the appearance of solidity.

This clearing is not gentle. It unseats narratives the builder has grown attached to. It disrupts the momentum they relied on. It exposes the gap between how they believed the world worked and how it actually works. Yet, in doing so, it restores the conditions under which real learning can occur. Failure returns the builder to a psychological terrain where they must observe again, inquire again, rebuild again; this time without the blinding weight of assumed knowing. It reconnects them to the humility that once fueled their earliest breakthroughs.

There is a kind of soil that only exists after collapse. It is darker, richer, more capable of supporting deep roots. Success often grows shallow systems that look impressive but fail under pressure. Failure, by contrast, disrupts the root structure entirely, giving the builder the opportunity to replant with far greater intentionality. In this soil, new seeds take hold: the humility to question what once felt unquestionable; the resilience forged not from confidence but from survival; the discernment to differentiate what is essential from what merely signals ambition. Builders who engage failure in this way emerge with a depth that success alone cannot produce.

Failure also performs a critical function: it restores beginner's mind. When success accumulates unchecked, it narrows perception. The builder begins to assume they understand their market, their team, themselves. But failure dismantles these assumptions. It forces the builder to re-enter the work with openness, to notice details they previously dismissed, to consider possibilities they once considered beneath them. Failure reintroduces uncertainty not as threat but as teacher. It forces the builder to question again, to listen again, to observe the world without the protective filter of past victories.

Not every builder rises from failure. Some cling to bitterness, interpreting collapse as a violation rather than an opportunity. Others attempt to rebuild the past rather than confront what the collapse revealed. But the builders who do rise; those who rebuild not out of desperation but out of renewed clarity; carry something rare. Their work becomes steadier, less entangled with ego, more aligned with truth. They act with fewer illusions. They are harder to seduce by momentum and less threatened by disruption. They know the terrain of collapse and do not fear it.

In the long arc of creation, failure is not an endpoint. It is a recalibration. It returns the builder to emptiness; not the emptiness of despair, but the emptiness of readiness. It clears the vessel of accumulated distortions and reopens the mind to the complexity of the world. It sharpens intuition and deepens judgment. It prepares the builder not simply to start again, but to build with greater integrity than before.

The builders who endure do so not because they avoid failure, but because they are transformed by it. They understand that collapse is not the enemy of creation; it is one of its most reliable architects.

The Paradox of the Empty Vessel

Emptiness is rarely seen as a desirable state. In most cultural narratives, fullness is equated with competence; full calendars, full pipelines, full certainty. Emptiness, by contrast, is mistaken for deficiency: an absence of knowledge, direction, or confidence. But for the builder committed to enduring creation, emptiness must be understood differently. It is not a void to be filled; it is a condition that enables precision. The empty vessel is not powerful because of what it contains, but because of what it can hold. Its strength lies not in accumulation, but in availability.

The paradox is simple: fullness restricts capacity; emptiness expands it. When the builder's mind is overfilled; with assumed knowledge, with recycled strategies, with the lingering debris of past successes and failures; they lose the ability to perceive the present accurately. Their mind becomes less a vessel and more a storage unit, cluttered with interpretations that distort incoming signals. The fuller the vessel becomes, the less flexible it is. It becomes rigid, defensive, and resistant to anything that threatens the internal arrangements it has grown attached to. In this sense, fullness masquerades as strength, but it is fundamentally brittle.

Emptiness, by contrast, is a form of structural flexibility. It allows the builder to receive new information without forcing it into predetermined categories. It creates space for nuance, for contradiction, for the complexity that modern environments demand. Emptiness is not passive; it is receptive. It is a disciplined openness that prevents the mind from ossifying around old patterns. When the vessel is empty, it can bend without breaking, absorb without shattering, respond without flinching. This is what gives emptiness its unusual strength.

Builders often fear emptiness because they associate it with indecision or lack of expertise. But emptiness does not diminish action; it purifies it. Action taken from fullness is often reactive, driven by habit or ego. It is tethered to the need to protect past conclusions or defend old strategies. Action taken from emptiness, however, is grounded in perception. It is responsive rather than reflexive. It does not rely on momentum for validation; it relies on alignment. The builder who acts from emptiness is not slower; they are more exact.

Part of the paradox lies in the relationship between emptiness and identity. Builders often tie their sense of self to what they know or have accomplished. This creates a reluctance to release outdated frameworks because doing so feels like eroding identity. But when identity is built on accumulated knowledge, it becomes fragile; threatened by change, destabilized by uncertainty, resistant to adaptation. The empty vessel, by contrast, bases identity not on content but on capacity. It allows the builder to revise, adapt, and evolve without interpreting that evolution as personal diminishment. Identity becomes expansive rather than defensive.

Another dimension of the paradox emerges in the cycle of building. Each season of creation brings new conditions, new constraints, new opportunities. The builder who approaches each season with a full vessel brings the past into the present without evaluating its relevance. They impose old maps onto new terrain. The builder who empties themselves before entering a new season approaches the work with clarity. They recognize that strategies, assumptions, and even internal narratives that once served them may no longer be appropriate. Emptiness becomes the reset that makes reinvention possible.

This is why the most resilient builders are those who repeatedly return to emptiness. They do not allow success to fossilize their thinking. They do not allow failure to fill the vessel with fear. They know that both triumph and collapse leave residue, and that residue must be cleared. Their emptiness is not a sign of lacking; it is a sign of preparedness. It is the internal structure that allows them to navigate complexity without being overwhelmed by it.

In the long arc of building, fullness exhausts. Emptiness renews. Fullness locks the builder into what has been. Emptiness opens them to what could be. The paradox is that emptiness, which appears to offer nothing, in fact offers the only condition in which everything meaningful can be received, perceived, and built.

The empty vessel is not the absence of strength. It is the architecture that makes strength sustainable.

Practical Applications

Principles are inert without practice. The disciplines of emptiness and beginner's mind cannot remain philosophical aspirations; they must be operationalized into habits that withstand the gravitational pull of urgency, ego, and accumulated knowing. The modern builder operates in an environment designed to erode spaciousness; every notification, meeting, metric, and expectation threatens to fill the vessel before the builder has consciously chosen what belongs inside. Without deliberate and recurring practices, emptiness collapses under the pressure of noise. What follows are not hacks or optimizations, but structural commitments that protect the internal clarity on which long-term building depends.

The first practice is the establishment of rituals of reflection. Reflection is often conflated with review; an assessment of progress against goals or outcomes. But true reflection serves a different function: it is a clearing mechanism. The builder creates consistent intervals; weekly, monthly, quarterly; dedicated not to planning the next move but to releasing what has accumulated. These intervals allow the builder to examine which assumptions have hardened without justification, which narratives are being carried out of habit rather than relevance, and which internal commitments no longer align with the present season. Reflection is not about polishing performance; it is about shedding residue. Without it, sediment accumulates until perception becomes opaque.

A second practice is the cultivation of beginner's questions. In a culture fixated on answers, questions perform a subversive function; they disrupt the inertia of expertise. The disciplined builder integrates questions into the architecture of decision-making: What would I see here if I knew nothing? What am I assuming without evidence? What has changed that I have not accounted for? These questions soften the rigidity that comes with experience. They prevent premature closure and keep the builder aligned with reality rather than personal preference. Over time, the presence of these questions becomes a safeguard against unconscious drift.

A third practice is scheduled withdrawal; intentional periods of stepping back from the operational machinery of building. Withdrawal is not rest in the conventional sense; it is strategic distancing that allows perception to reset. In these intervals, the builder detaches from the immediacy of execution to regain altitude and re-examine the structure of their thinking. Withdrawal may take the form of silent retreats, dedicated study weeks, or temporary removal from decision-making environments. Its purpose is to restore spaciousness so that the builder can return to the work with renewed clarity rather than accumulated noise.

A fourth practice is the adoption of an apprentice mindset. No matter how seasoned the builder becomes, they must continue to engage with the world as a student. This requires learning from unexpected sources; junior team members, adjacent industries, younger generations, or disciplines unrelated to their own. When the builder deliberately places themselves in roles where they are not the expert, they disrupt the internal hierarchy that privileges their own voice above all others. The apprentice mindset ensures that the builder does not confuse tenure with truth. It keeps the vessel permeable.

A fifth practice is the annual purge; the disciplined evaluation and elimination of commitments, projects, structures, or relationships that no longer serve the builder's direction. This is not minimalism for aesthetic purposes; it is strategic pruning. The builder examines what they are carrying and identifies which elements persist only because they feel familiar or flattering. The purge restores alignment by removing the inertia that slows adaptation. It prevents the year from becoming an extension of the last, ensuring that the builder does not move forward simply by repetition.

The final practice is non-attachment. This is perhaps the most challenging discipline because it confronts the builder's identity directly. Non-attachment does not mean indifference; it means full engagement without possession. The builder pours themselves into their work without allowing the work to define them. They hold their strategies, models, and structures lightly, knowing that each may need to be revised or discarded. Non-attachment preserves the builder's ability to adapt without injury to their sense of self. It allows them to release what is no longer true without interpreting that release as personal failure.

These practices, taken together, form the behavioral architecture that protects emptiness and sustains beginner's mind. They are not performed once, nor perfected. They must be lived cyclically;

repeated, adjusted, and renewed. They create the internal conditions that allow the builder to operate with clarity in a world that continually tests their capacity for distortion. In this way, practical discipline becomes more than a set of habits; it becomes the scaffolding that supports the builder's evolution.

Closing Meditation

Before moving on to the next chapter, pause; not to analyze or strategize, but to recalibrate. The work of building often pushes the mind toward accumulation: more ideas, more plans, more projections of what might come next. But understanding the empty vessel requires a different kind of moment, one in which the builder deliberately steps out of the momentum of doing and into the stillness of perceiving.

Imagine setting aside everything you believe you already know about your work. Not because it is wrong, but because it is heavy. Picture your mind as a surface cleared of tools, diagrams, metrics, and narratives; an uncluttered space free of the urgency that usually dominates your attention. In this quiet space, nothing demands interpretation. Nothing requires defense. The task is not to produce clarity, but to allow it.

Consider what remains when you release the need to be certain. Notice how quickly the body relaxes when it is no longer required to brace against the unknown. Notice how much more precisely the world reveals itself when you stop forcing it to match your expectations. This moment of emptiness is not a withdrawal from responsibility; it is preparation. It is the internal reset that enables the builder to return to the work with sharper perception and fewer distortions.

Let your attention rest on the possibility that emptiness is not a lack but a condition of readiness. It is the mental state in which you become capable of seeing what is actually present rather than what you assume should be there. It is the posture that frees you from the inertia of past strategies and the weight of accumulated conclusions.

In this state, you engage with the world not from habit, but from awareness.

Before you move forward, ask yourself quietly: What am I still carrying that no longer belongs? Where have certainty and familiarity narrowed my field of vision? What assumptions have I allowed to harden into truth? These questions are not meant to unsettle you, but to create space; space for revision, for reinvention, for the emergence of insight that rigid knowing would otherwise block.

Return to the work not with the pressure to have answers, but with the discipline to perceive. Let the next decision arise from clarity rather than reflex. Let your actions be guided not by the residue of past seasons, but by the reality in front of you now.

This is the function of the empty vessel. It is not an escape from creation. It is the internal preparation that makes creation clean. It is the clearing that allows precision. It is the state from which all enduring work begins.

Hold this emptiness for a moment longer than feels necessary. Then step back into your work; with a vessel ready to receive what the next season will require.

Chapter 2

The Inner Citadel: Building Character Before Empire

The Myth of External Success

Modern culture is constructed around the worship of what can be seen: towering buildings, global reputations, valuations, followers, the outward performance of significance. These visible symbols often masquerade as indicators of genuine strength, convincing builders and observers alike that scale implies stability and admiration implies permanence. But the structures celebrated in public rarely reveal the internal architecture required to sustain them. They offer the appearance of solidity without any guarantee of endurance. An empire can rise quickly on the momentum of market opportunity, aesthetic brilliance, or strategic dexterity, yet remain hollow at its core.

The illusion is seductive. When external success comes early; or arrives suddenly; it often convinces the builder that the foundation beneath them is stronger than it truly is. Growth, visibility, and acclaim are misinterpreted as indicators of wisdom. Demand is mistaken for validation. Profit is mistaken for permanence. A business can scale faster than the character of its founder. A reputation can expand beyond the emotional resilience it quietly depends on. And when the outer structure surpasses the inner one by too much, collapse is not merely possible; it is inevitable.

The early warning signs rarely appear in the metrics. They appear internally, in the builder's diminishing judgment, rising arrogance, narrowing curiosity, or in the slow erosion of personal relationships and physical well-being. What breaks a builder first is rarely the business; it is the widening gap between the empire they manage externally and the foundation they have neglected internally. Outer success creates the illusion that the collapse, when it comes, will be public. But collapse often begins in private, in subtle degradations of principle, clarity, and discipline long before the world ever notices.

This is the false equation the modern world teaches: if the outside looks strong, the inside must be strong. But the world rewards outcomes, not integrity. Markets reward efficiency, not character. Audiences reward spectacle, not substance. A builder may be celebrated, envied, and promoted as a model of achievement while quietly disintegrating behind the scenes. External success is never proof of internal strength. At best, it is a reflection. At worst, it is a distraction from the work that matters most.

The builder who seeks to endure must reverse the equation completely. Strength must emerge from the inside outward. Without a fortified interior; one rooted in restraint, clarity, humility, resilience; the empire is a precarious structure. It may impress temporarily, but it will not withstand pressure. Eventually, every builder confronts the truth: outward expansion cannot compensate for inward fragility.

The inner citadel is not ceremonial. It is the prerequisite for any structure that is meant to last.

What Is the Inner Citadel?

Before any tower can rise, before any strategy can take shape, the builder must construct an internal foundation; an architecture that stabilizes them through volatility and fortifies them against their own distortions. This is the inner citadel: not a philosophical metaphor, but a structural truth about endurance. It is the internal alignment of character, discipline, judgment, and clarity that enables the builder to survive the destabilizing forces inherent in creation.

The citadel is not built for admiration. It is not built for display. It is built for weight-bearing. Every level of external success increases the pressure on the builder. Markets fluctuate, partners betray, opportunities collapse, and public sentiment shifts without warning. No external structure; no matter how elegantly engineered; can compensate for a leader who lacks internal stability. The world teaches builders to focus on what can be scaled, sold, or showcased. But nothing can scale sustainably beyond the limits of the builder's internal resilience.

The inner citadel is the only asset that cannot be taken by competition or undermined by circumstance. It is not dependent on market conditions or cultural favor. It does not fluctuate with praise or criticism. It is constructed through private decisions, disciplined habits, and the slow, unglamorous work of self-governance. The stronger the citadel, the more weight the builder can carry; and success always brings weight.

Real strength is unglamorous. It is the quiet composure under pressure, the ability to maintain integrity in the midst of chaos, the capacity to endure loss without collapsing into despair or bitterness. Strength reveals itself in crisis, not in triumph. And every builder, regardless of ambition, will face moments where the citadel is tested: economic contraction, betrayal, public failure, personal hardship. The builder without an inner citadel will shatter when these moments arrive. The builder with one will not be spared the difficulty, but they will remain intact.

The citadel is architecture, not armor. Armor isolates and numbs; it creates rigidity that eventually fractures. Architecture supports, absorbs, and adapts. It provides stability without detachment, flexibility without fragility. A builder inhabits the citadel daily through small acts of discipline; truth-telling, restraint, reflection, humility; so that when the world shakes, the internal structure does not.

The inner citadel is the builder's true foundation. Every empire either rests upon it or collapses from the lack of it.

Character as Strategy

In the modern landscape, strategy is often reduced to frameworks: competitive positioning, growth loops, sales funnels, optimization models. These tools matter, but they are incomplete. Strategy is not merely a set of actions. It is an expression of the builder's internal posture. Character; integrity, discipline, humility; is not an accessory to strategy. It is the strategy that determines whether the others will hold under pressure.

Character is a long-term competitive advantage because it shapes how decisions are made, how crises are managed, how teams are led, and how trust is built. Integrity creates alignment; not only with values, but with reality. A builder who operates with integrity maintains coherence between what they know, what they say, and what they do. This coherence builds trust, and trust, over time, compounds more reliably than any financial instrument.

Discipline is the mechanism that channels ambition into meaningful action. An undisciplined builder dilutes their attention, exhausts their team, and destabilizes their vision. Discipline protects focus. It eliminates distractions. It curbs impulsivity. Without it, even the most brilliant strategy collapses under the weight of scattered execution.

Humility ensures adaptability. Markets change, technology evolves, and even the most experienced builder misjudges conditions. Humility allows the builder to revise rather than defend, to listen rather than dominate, to course-correct before damage becomes irreversible. In this way, humility is not meekness; it is strategic intelligence.

Character is tested most acutely in crisis. When revenue contracts, when partners falter, when public perception turns hostile, tactics lose their potency. What remains is the builder's internal architecture. Their response; panic or clarity, selfishness or stewardship, denial or discipline; determines whether the enterprise survives. Crisis reveals that strategy divorced from character is brittle. Character integrated with strategy is resilient.

Character also radiates into culture. A company's culture is not its written values; it is the lived behavior of its leadership. Employees emulate what they observe, not what they are told. A builder who embodies clarity, discipline, and humility creates an organization that mirrors those traits. Over time, culture becomes the invisible infrastructure that sustains the enterprise; hard to build, easy to lose, impossible to fake.

The most enduring builders understand this: strategy may shape the early trajectory, but character governs the long arc. It determines not how fast the empire grows, but whether it survives its own momentum.

The Fragility of the Unfortified Mind

To build outward without building inward is to construct a structure destined to fracture. Many of the most celebrated entrepreneurs fall not because of competitive pressure or market shifts, but because they lacked the internal foundation required to bear the psychological weight of creation. The mind, unfortified, becomes the primary point of failure.

Ego is the first internal destabilizer. Ego masquerades as drive but operates as insecurity. It demands recognition, expansion, and constant reinforcement. The ego-driven builder confuses visibility with value, overestimates their invulnerability, and resists correction. Ego amplifies risk while diminishing judgment. An unchecked ego cannot sustain a long-term enterprise; it drives the builder to expand prematurely, ignore warnings, and erode trust. Ego breaks the builder from the inside.

Fear is equally corrosive. Fear distorts perception, magnifies threats, and constrains action. A builder without an inner citadel becomes reactive, assigning catastrophic meaning to normal fluctuations. Fear leads to hasty decisions, unnecessary concessions, and the abandonment of principles under pressure. It turns leadership into a survival mechanism rather than a creative one.

Achievement, ironically, can be just as destabilizing. Each success whispers to the builder that they are exceptional, complete, exempt from the normal constraints of judgment. When achievement is not grounded in character, it breeds delusion. Builders begin believing their own mythology. They mistake being right before for being right now. They become brittle in the face of challenge because they have lost the humility to revise themselves.

Neglecting the inner citadel produces invisible deterioration long before any external sign of collapse appears. Patience erodes.

Gratitude shrinks. Impulsivity increases. Decisions are made for appearances rather than alignment. The collapse, when it eventually becomes visible, seems sudden. But it was years in the making.

Only by turning inward; by cultivating awareness, discipline, humility, and self-governance; can the builder prevent their own mind from becoming the greatest threat to their work.

Elements of the Inner Citadel

A citadel is not built from a single virtue or a single revelation. It is constructed from interlocking elements that together form an internal structure capable of bearing both pressure and uncertainty. These elements are not moral aspirations; they are functional components of endurance.

Resilience is the first element. It is the capacity to absorb impact without losing integrity. Resilience is not denial of pain; it is the ability to stay coherent through it. It emerges through repeated exposure to difficulty, not avoidance of it. A resilient builder survives failure not because they are indifferent, but because they are trained.

Temperance is restraint; in emotion, in appetite, in ambition. Temperance prevents excess, keeps impulses in check, and allows decisions to be made from clarity rather than compulsion. It disciplines the instinct to chase every opportunity or respond to every provocation. Temperance is strategic self-control.

Courage is the willingness to act in the presence of uncertainty and risk. It is not bravado but conviction; clarity about what matters enough to warrant loss. Courage ensures that fear does not dictate direction. Without courage, the builder avoids the necessary battles. Without temperance, courage becomes recklessness. Each element tempers the other.

Clarity is the rarest element. It is the disciplined perception of what is true; about the environment, about the work, about the self. Clarity enables revision, protects against delusion, and accelerates adaptation. It is not certainty; it is accuracy.

No single element is sufficient. Together, they form an internal architecture that remains stable even when conditions shift violently. The citadel is not a philosophy. It is a structure built through repetition, reflection, and disciplined correction.

Building the Citadel: Practice and Patience

The inner citadel is not constructed through inspiration or crisis alone. It is built slowly, through consistent practice. Modern culture trains builders to favor intensity over endurance; to celebrate dramatic bursts of effort rather than the invisible accumulation of disciplined habits. But character does not respond to intensity. It only submits to consistency.

There are no shortcuts. No book, mentor, or epiphany can replace the daily work required to cultivate integrity, clarity, courage, or restraint. These qualities are shaped through repetition: the daily decision to act with discipline when it would be easier to indulge; the quiet admission of error when ego resists; the deliberate pause before reacting; the intentional choice to align action with principle rather than impulse. Each act is a brick in the structure. Most go unnoticed. All matter.

Patience becomes a strategic asset in this process. Patience allows the builder to prioritize depth over speed, endurance over milestones, and clarity over performance. Impatience demands visible progress; patience builds invisible strength. When pressure comes, impatience collapses; patience endures.

Consistency; not intensity; is what fortifies the citadel. Intensity fluctuates with mood and circumstance. Consistency compounds. It transforms daily habits into structural resilience. Over time, the citadel becomes a quiet force within the builder; present, steady, reliable.

The reward for this slow construction is not perfection. It is the capacity to remain intact through volatility.

Defense Without Isolation

A citadel suggests protection, but protection is easily confused with withdrawal. Some builders, in their effort to fortify themselves, retreat from engagement; shielding themselves from criticism, relationship, discomfort, and vulnerability. But isolation is not fortification; it is decay.

Isolation diminishes creativity, weakens judgment, and shrinks perspective. It provides safety at the cost of growth. A builder who isolates may avoid immediate harm but loses the friction required for evolution. A sealed citadel becomes a prison.

Fortification requires permeability. The citadel must have gates; boundaries that allow the builder to engage fully with the world while maintaining internal stability. The fortified builder listens without absorbing every opinion, adapts without abandoning principles, collaborates without becoming dependent on approval. They remain open yet grounded, receptive yet discerning.

Strength is not the ability to resist all influence. It is the ability to engage deeply without losing coherence. Engagement without erosion is the posture of the fortified builder. They move toward the world, not away from it; capable of absorbing complexity, contradiction, and pressure without internal collapse.

The purpose of the citadel is not to keep life out. It is to enable the builder to move through life without being undone by it.

The Weight the Citadel Must Bear

Success introduces pressures far heavier than failure. Failure is acute; success is cumulative. With success comes visibility, expectation, responsibility, and the temptation to expand beyond what can be sustained.

Visibility magnifies every decision and misstep. It tempts the builder to perform rather than lead. Responsibility burdens the builder with the livelihoods and trust of others. Expansion tempts the builder to outpace their own capacity and abandon the discipline that made success possible.

Without an inner citadel, success distorts judgment. Builders become defensive under scrutiny, reckless under praise, or addicted to the momentum of growth. They begin to conflate their identity with their work, losing the separation necessary to remain grounded. The empire becomes a mirror of insecurity rather than strength.

The fortified builder withstands these pressures not by resisting them, but by carrying them differently. They remain anchored in principle, steady in judgment, and clear in purpose. They recognize that success is not relief from discipline but a deeper demand for it. The citadel must be strong enough to bear the weight of the empire, or the empire will crush the builder beneath it.

Enduring success requires deeper fortification than achieving it.

True Power: Mastery of the Self

There is a version of power that depends on external validation; followers, influence, wealth, visibility. It is loud, intoxicating, and precarious. It amplifies the builder's reach while shrinking their sovereignty. This power can be taken away by market shifts, public sentiment, or internal collapse.

Self-mastery is a different form of power altogether. It is quiet, internal, and durable. It emerges from mastery over one's impulses, desires, ego, and fear. It enables the builder to act from intention rather than compulsion, to remain steady in uncertainty, and to lead without relying on dominance or performance.

Self-mastery cannot be seized or revoked. It does not fluctuate with fortune. It produces a kind of authority that commands respect without demanding it. It allows the builder to operate from clarity even when conditions are chaotic.

The work of self-mastery is never complete. It requires daily examination, honest correction, and disciplined adjustment. It does not eliminate emotion or desire; it structures them. It does not suppress ambition; it refines it.

The builders who achieve self-mastery do not escape difficulty, but they navigate difficulty without losing themselves. Their power is not reactive but sovereign. It is the only power that endures after external influence fades.

Closing Meditation

Set aside, for a moment, the external architecture of your work; the plans, strategies, ambitions, and milestones. Imagine the empire you hope to build stripped of all ornamentation. What remains is not the product or the market but the builder.

The inner citadel is the structure that determines whether the work ahead can be carried without collapse. It is the quiet foundation beneath the visible towers, the structure that absorbs pressure, holds clarity, and keeps the builder aligned when the world becomes disorienting. It is shaped slowly, through disciplined choices no one sees, through the work of reflection, restraint, humility, courage, and truthfulness.

Before you construct what the world will witness, cultivate what only you will feel. Strengthen the interior until it is capable of bearing what success will demand. Build depth before height. Build steadiness before scale. Build clarity before visibility.

Empires rise and fall. The builder remains. And the builder either endures because the citadel is strong, or collapses because it was never built.

Return to the citadel. Tend it. Strengthen it. Live within it. Everything you build outward will depend on it.

Chapter 3

Tzimtzum: The Power of Sacred Withdrawal

The Myth of Constant Expansion

Modern leadership culture is built on the assumption that expansion is synonymous with progress. Growth is celebrated as the primary metric of success, and motion; any motion; is treated as evidence of vitality. Leaders are taught to believe that the only secure posture is acceleration, that momentum must be preserved at all costs, and that pausing, contracting, or slowing down signals weakness. This mindset does not emerge from strategy but from collective anxiety: the fear that stillness invites irrelevance, that reflection wastes time, and that any hesitation will allow competitors to overtake what has been built.

The pressure to expand relentlessly produces organizations that are constantly adding; new markets, new products, new initiatives, new obligations. At first, this abundance appears to signal strength. But expansion without discipline soon overwhelms the very capacity needed to sustain it. Complexity begins to increase faster than clarity. Systems stretch beyond their design. Teams operate under chronic overload. Leaders lose the ability to distinguish between what is essential and what is merely habitual. Growth, pursued uncritically, evolves from opportunity into burden.

The consequences of perpetual motion surface long before collapse is visible. Judgment begins to dull as the leader is forced into reactive decision-making. Focus, once sharp, becomes scattered across competing priorities. The mission becomes diluted as initiatives accumulate for reasons unrelated to purpose. The organization becomes fragile; not because it lacks potential, but because it refuses to rest. A structure that never pauses cannot deepen its roots; it remains tall but shallow, impressive from a distance yet vulnerable up close.

The most deceptive aspect of constant expansion is the illusion of safety. Activity feels reassuring. Motion feels protective. Leaders become addicted to the sensation of progress even when the trajectory is unclear. Growth becomes the idol that must be fed continuously, regardless of whether it serves the long-term integrity of the enterprise. But activity is not direction, and momentum is not stability. Without intentional pauses, even the most promising ventures drift into exhaustion, bloat, and misalignment.

Enduring builders eventually learn that the cultural narrative of relentless expansion is a myth. Progress requires rhythm, not acceleration; discernment, not volume. A system that cannot contract cannot endure. A leader who cannot pause cannot see. And an enterprise built on unexamined motion will one day exceed the limits of the foundation beneath it.

The alternative is not resistance to growth, but reverence for the structure required to sustain it. Expansion is powerful only when paired with the discipline to withdraw, reassess, and restore. Without this counterforce, growth becomes both the engine and the undoing of the work.

The Wisdom of Withdrawal

Withdrawal is often misunderstood in environments that equate constant visibility with relevance and nonstop activity with competence. To many builders, stepping back appears counterintuitive; almost dangerous. Yet withdrawal, when practiced consciously, is not a retreat from the work. It is the intentional creation of space in which clarity, resilience, and direction can be restored. It is not the collapse of momentum, but the governance of it. Withdrawal is what transforms raw effort into deliberate movement.

The modern builder operates under immense pressure to remain in perpetual motion. Markets shift quickly, competitors move aggressively, and attention spans shorten. In this climate, slowing down can feel irresponsible, even risky. But withdrawal is not the absence of movement; it is the shaping of it. It allows the builder to separate what is essential from what is merely urgent, to refine the direction rather than accelerate the drift, and to reassess whether the current trajectory still aligns with the deeper purpose of the work. Without withdrawal, every action becomes reactive, guided by noise rather than intention.

Creating space is fundamental to sustainable leadership. Space allows the builder to observe patterns that frantic motion obscures. It enables reflection before commitment, discernment before expansion, and recalibration before resources are exhausted. When space is absent, decisions are made impulsively, priorities compete chaotically, and the entire enterprise becomes vulnerable to minor disruptions. Withdrawal restores the capacity to think, to notice, and to adjust. It is the mechanism through which the builder regains access to the broader horizon beyond the day-to-day pressure.

Withdrawal also protects the builder from distortions that success and momentum quietly introduce. Achievements accumulate expectations. Growth breeds complexity. Visibility multiplies demands. Without creating intervals of distance, the builder becomes engulfed by the very structure they are trying to lead. Withdrawal reestablishes perspective. It allows the leader to step back from the narrative others impose, from the illusions that build around success, and from the ego that confuses activity with progress. In stepping back, the builder returns to the core of the work; not the performance of it.

One of the most powerful aspects of withdrawal is its ability to refine ambition. In the absence of noise, unnecessary pursuits fall away. Initiatives adopted out of fear or vanity reveal themselves as misaligned. Waste becomes visible. What remains is the essential structure; the mission stripped of distortion. Withdrawal sharpens ambition by eliminating its excess. It transforms effort into focus and restores the integrity of the work.

The rarity of withdrawal stems from its lack of immediate reward. It does not produce quick wins. It does not generate applause. It cannot be measured in quarterly reports. But its effects are foundational. Withdrawal preserves the builder's internal architecture, replenishes resilience, prevents reactive decision-making, and ensures that expansion is rooted rather than reckless.

It makes long-term creation possible in a world obsessed with short-term performance.

For the builder committed to endurance, withdrawal is not optional. It is a structural discipline, as essential to the rhythm of leadership as exertion itself. To build continuously without withdrawing is to build without breathing. But to withdraw consciously; to create space as part of the cycle of creation; is to ensure that when the builder moves again, they do so with clarity, strength, and purpose.

What Tzimtzum Teaches Us

The ancient principle of Tzimtzum offers one of the most powerful metaphors for modern leadership, though it is rarely invoked in discussions of building or strategy. At its core, Tzimtzum describes the idea that creation begins with contraction. Before anything new can take form, space must be made for it. This withdrawal is not abandonment, nor is it a disappearance of force. It is an intentional pulling back that allows something other than the self to emerge. The idea is both simple and profound: creation requires room, and room requires restraint.

In leadership, this principle challenges the instinct to occupy every corner of the work. Builders often believe they must be constantly present; directing, shaping, correcting; filling every gap with their vision and will. But this instinct can suffocate the very structures they hope to strengthen. Teams fail to mature because the leader occupies all available space. Strategies lose coherence because they are shaped by ego rather than mission. Processes become stagnant because the builder's constant involvement leaves no room for adaptation or innovation. Tzimtzum reframes this: effective leadership demands withdrawal so others; and the work itself; can develop their own integrity.

The practical implications of this principle are far-reaching. Withdrawal allows systems to become self-sustaining rather than dependent. It allows teams to develop judgment instead of waiting for instruction. It enables the enterprise to grow beyond the psychological boundaries of its founder. When the builder steps back, they create an environment where capability can form, where ideas can be tested without immediate correction, and where responsibility can be distributed rather than centralized. The leader's contraction becomes the team's expansion.

Tzimtzum also confronts the role of ego in creation. The ego seeks to occupy, to imprint, to dominate. It wants the enterprise to reflect its preferences, its anxieties, its need for control. But when the ego occupies too much space, the work becomes small; defined not by what it could become, but by the limits of the builder's own impulses. Withdrawal forces the ego to recede so the creation can take a shape that is not merely a mirror of the builder. What emerges is not ego-driven architecture but purpose-driven structure.

This principle reshapes how we understand authority. True authority is not exercised through constant involvement but through the creation of systems that function without perpetual intervention. Leadership matures when the builder learns to step aside at the right moments; not to disengage, but to allow others to step forward. Withdrawal becomes a form of trust, a signal that the enterprise is not a personal extension but a living structure capable of evolution.

Tzimtzum reveals that the most powerful builders are not those who fill every space, but those who know when to create it. Space is not emptiness; it is potential. It is the precondition for innovation, for independence, for resilience. Builders who withdraw intentionally do not diminish their impact; they magnify it. Their presence becomes more meaningful because it is no longer constant, and their influence becomes more durable because it does not depend on proximity.

In the logic of Tzimtzum, creation is not the assertion of self but the disciplined shaping of space. It is the recognition that strength lies not in perpetual presence but in the ability to withdraw enough for something new to emerge. For the builder, this becomes a foundational principle: withdraw to create, withdraw to empower, withdraw to build structures that can stand long after the builder steps out of view.

Creating by Contraction

Creation is often imagined as an outward motion; adding, expanding, building more. But the builders who endure understand that meaningful creation frequently begins with contraction. Contraction is the disciplined act of reducing what is unnecessary so that what is essential can be seen, strengthened, and developed. It is not the erasure of ambition; it is the refinement of it. In contraction, noise falls away, excess dissolves, and the core of the work comes into view.

When a leader pulls back, they create the conditions for clarity. Continuous expansion generates clutter: too many initiatives, too many priorities, too many signals competing for the same diminishing attention. Without contraction, the builder becomes overwhelmed by their own architecture. Contraction cuts through this accumulation. It clears the field so the builder can perceive the structure of their work without distortion. It forces a confrontation with what truly matters; the work that aligns with purpose rather than vanity, the commitments that produce value rather than distraction, the relationships that reinforce strength rather than drain it.

This process requires restraint, a trait that is often undervalued in high-velocity environments. Restraint protects the builder from the impulse to chase every opportunity or attach to every possibility. To create by contraction is to resist the cultural pressure to do more simply because doing more appears impressive. It is the willingness to accept temporary reduction so that long-term creation can take shape from a place of coherence.

Contraction also reveals latent potential within the system. When unnecessary elements are removed, teams regain focus. Processes strengthen. Strategy clarifies. Energy that was once diffused across too many projects becomes concentrated, and the enterprise begins to move with greater precision. This sharpening effect cannot be replicated through expansion alone. Addition multiplies complexity; subtraction restores alignment.

Importantly, contraction is not passive. It is an active form of creation. It shapes the environment in which new ideas can emerge without being overshadowed by outdated structures or obsolete commitments. It allows space for innovation to arise organically rather than being forced into an already overcrowded system. In the absence of contraction, creativity becomes incremental; tinkering around the edges of a bloated architecture rather than reimagining its fundamentals.

Contraction also strengthens the builder internally. It cultivates discipline, humility, and patience. It forces the leader to sit with the discomfort of reduction; a discomfort rooted in ego's attachment to expansion. By enduring this discomfort, the builder's relationship with creation changes. They no longer equate growth with worth. They begin to understand growth as a rhythm rather than a constant. They learn to trust the cycle: prune, strengthen, rebuild.

In the long arc of leadership, contraction is not a deviation from creation but a prerequisite for it. Without it, the work becomes unwieldy, the mission becomes obscured, and the builder becomes reactive rather than intentional. With it, the work regains coherence, the mission becomes focused, and the builder returns to creation with renewed force.

Creation through contraction is not smaller; it is sharper. It does not limit ambition; it purifies it. And it prepares both the builder and the enterprise for expansion that is grounded, sustainable, and aligned.

The Space Between Action and Outcome

One of the most overlooked elements in building is the space between action and outcome; the interval where results have not yet formed, where effort has been exerted but nothing visible has materialized. In a culture that prizes immediacy, this space is treated as an inconvenience, a gap to be eliminated through speed, optimization, or relentless iteration. But in reality, this space is structural. It is the quiet chamber in which ideas mature, systems stabilize, judgment develops, and resilience forms.

Every meaningful endeavor depends on this space. When actions produce instant outcomes, the builder is never forced to confront uncertainty or develop patience. They operate in a shallow cycle of stimulus and response, mistaking velocity for depth. But when work requires time; when the results unfold slowly; the builder must cultivate discipline. They must learn to discern whether adjustments are needed or whether they simply need to endure the discomfort of not knowing. The space teaches discernment through delayed clarity.

Margin; deliberate room for unpredictability; also resides in this space. Margin allows a system to absorb volatility without breaking. It creates breathing room for teams, buffers for unexpected challenges, and structural resilience for the enterprise. Without margin, every deviation becomes a crisis. Every misstep becomes catastrophic. Leaders who eliminate margin in pursuit of speed inadvertently construct systems that cannot withstand normal fluctuations. Their organizations appear efficient but are deeply fragile.

Innovation also depends on this interval. When builders rush from action to outcome, they eliminate the reflective distance necessary for new ideas to surface. Creativity rarely occurs under pressure to produce immediate results. It emerges when the mind has space to roam, when the builder steps back from execution long enough to see the broader pattern. Slowness; used deliberately; is not inefficiency. It is the condition that allows for unexpected insight and strategic evolution.

The space between action and outcome also strengthens the builder internally. It challenges the ego, which craves constant validation. It unsettles the impulse for immediate proof of competence. It forces the builder to anchor themselves in purpose rather than in performance metrics. This discomfort is not a flaw; it is the training ground for emotional durability. Builders who can withstand this interval without collapsing into anxiety or overcorrection develop a steadiness that cannot be acquired through speed alone.

This space becomes even more essential as enterprises grow. Larger structures move more slowly. Their outcomes take longer to manifest. Leaders who fail to adapt to this slower rhythm attempt to force action into artificial timelines, undermining the very systems they rely on. Mature builders understand that outcomes have their own pace. Pressuring them distorts the work; respecting them strengthens it.

Ultimately, the space between action and outcome is where endurance is cultivated. It is where clarity deepens, where patience becomes a strategic asset, and where the builder learns to navigate uncertainty without losing alignment. The work done in this space is not visible, but it is foundational. It is the difference between decisions made in haste and actions taken from wisdom.

The builders who learn to inhabit this space; without rushing it, without resenting it, without trying to collapse it; gain an advantage that cannot be copied. They operate from depth rather than urgency, from clarity rather than compulsion. And in the long arc of creation, this difference becomes decisive.

Ego and the Fear of Empty Space

Empty space; silence, pause, stillness; poses a particular threat to the ego. The ego depends on motion, noise, and constant reinforcement to sustain its sense of importance. It measures value by activity, visibility, and engagement. When space opens, these signals disappear, and the ego interprets the absence as danger. This is why many leaders avoid withdrawal: not because the work requires constant involvement, but because the ego demands it.

The ego fears space because space exposes fragility. When noise subsides, the leader is confronted with deeper questions: Who am I when I am not producing? What remains when I am not being watched? Does my work have meaning independent of my constant presence? These are questions the ego is unwilling to face because it is built on performance rather than truth. Empty space removes the performance, leaving only the builder.

This fear manifests in compulsive activity; projects added reflexively, meetings scheduled unnecessarily, decisions rushed without thought. Leaders fill the space to avoid confronting themselves. They mistake motion for relevance and busyness for worth. Yet this behavior quietly erodes clarity and resilience. Activity becomes a distraction from the work that actually matters, and the builder becomes trapped in cycles of urgency that they themselves created.

The ego also resists contraction because contraction feels like diminishment. To withdraw attention, influence, or involvement feels like handing over power. But this perception is illusion. A leader who cannot step back has no true authority; they are governed by their own insecurity. A leader who can withdraw intentionally demonstrates sovereignty over their impulses. They prove that their identity is not tied to perpetual activity.

Overcoming ego's resistance to empty space requires cultivating a different internal posture. First, the builder must recognize that space is not a threat; it is an asset. Space clarifies what noise conceals. It reveals inefficiencies, exposes unnecessary complexity, and allows intuition to strengthen. The leader becomes more capable, not less, when they operate from spaciousness rather than compression.

Second, the builder must practice tolerating the discomfort of non-action. This is not passivity; it is discipline. It is the ability to let a moment breathe without rushing to fill it. This discipline breaks the ego's dependency on activity and develops the leader's capacity to operate from intention rather than compulsion.

Third, the builder must decouple identity from output. When the ego no longer equates busyness with value, the leader becomes free to choose actions based on alignment rather than fear. They stop performing leadership and begin practicing it.

Ultimately, empty space becomes a proving ground. If the leader can remain steady in the pause, they have built genuine internal strength. If they cannot, the emptiness will reveal the instability that motion can temporarily disguise. The builders who learn to occupy space without collapsing into anxiety or self-doubt acquire a rare advantage: they become unhurried, undistracted, and internally grounded.

Empty space is not the enemy of progress. It is the condition that allows progress to mature. And the ego, once disciplined, becomes an ally rather than an obstacle; no longer threatened by stillness, but shaped by it into a foundation capable of bearing the weight of real leadership.

The Builder's Rhythm

Every enduring system, from the natural world to the human body, operates through rhythm; cycles of expansion and contraction, effort and restoration, movement and stillness. This oscillation is not a flaw in the system but the condition that keeps it alive. Yet builders, conditioned by cultural expectations of constant acceleration, often attempt to override this natural cadence. They push for perpetual expansion, interpreting any pause as regression, and any contraction as failure. This attempt to operate outside the laws of rhythm is one of the most common pathways to burnout, misalignment, and collapse.

Enduring leadership requires recognizing and embracing rhythm as a structural truth. Expansion is a vital phase, but it is only one half of the cycle. Expansion consumes resources, attention, energy, and emotional bandwidth. It increases complexity, adds weight, and stretches the system. Without periods of contraction, the enterprise becomes overstretched. Without recovery, the builder becomes depleted. Rhythm is not optional; it is the only sustainable pattern through which creation can occur.

Contraction is not a retreat from building but a recalibration of it. It provides the space for integration; where lessons from the previous cycle are absorbed, where systems are refined, where teams regain coherence, and where leaders re-anchor themselves in purpose. Without contraction, expansion becomes directionless. Projects proliferate without aligning to a central mission. The organization moves quickly but without depth. The builder loses the capacity to hear the subtle signals; the early signs of misalignment; that only become audible in quieter seasons.

This rhythm also shapes internal leadership. Builders experience cycles of high clarity, strong energy, and forward momentum, followed by periods where clarity softens and the need for reflection grows. The mature leader does not resist these cycles. They understand that forcing expansion in a season that requires contraction leads to misjudgment and unnecessary strain. Likewise, withdrawing during a season that demands action leads to stagnation. Rhythm teaches discernment: knowing when to press and when to pause.

The most effective leaders design their organizations to reflect this natural pattern. They integrate cycles of planning and execution, innovation and stabilization, growth and consolidation. Teams that operate in endless sprint mode erode their own capacity. Teams that are given structured intervals for recalibration develop depth, resilience, and creativity. Rhythm becomes a cultural asset.

There is also a psychological rhythm to leadership. As the enterprise grows, the demands placed on the builder increase, not decrease. Their decisions carry more weight, their visibility expands, and the consequences of misalignment intensify. Without a personal rhythm; periods of rest, reflection, solitude, and re-centering; the builder becomes reactive, overwhelmed, or unanchored. This internal dissonance inevitably reverberates through the entire organization.

Embracing rhythm requires rejecting the myth that progress is linear. True progress is cyclical. It loops, deepens, resets, and advances in waves. Builders who understand this avoid the traps of panic during contraction and complacency during expansion. They remain steady across the cycle because they trust its necessity. They do not mistake contraction for collapse; they see it as the preparation for the next arc of creation.

In the long trajectory of meaningful work, rhythm is not a luxury. It is the architecture of endurance. Leaders who build with rhythm create enterprises that can breathe, adapt, and evolve. They create cultures capable of sustaining excellence rather than sprinting toward exhaustion. And they build within themselves the internal cadence required to navigate the volatility, pressure, and responsibility that accompany serious creation.

The builder who honors rhythm does not merely survive the long arc. They travel it with strength, clarity, and coherence.

Withdrawal in Practice

Withdrawal becomes meaningful only when it is translated from concept into structure; when it is no longer an emergency response to exhaustion but a built-in discipline that shapes how the builder leads, decides, and sustains themselves. Without deliberate practice, the demands of work will always expand to fill every available space. Urgency will override intention. Noise will drown out clarity. The builder must therefore design withdrawal as a recurring element of their life and enterprise, not a luxury reserved for moments of collapse.

At the smallest scale, withdrawal begins with daily practices that create micro-intervals of spaciousness. These may take the form of moments of silence before entering a meeting, short walks without devices, deliberate pauses before responding to difficult messages, or designated periods where no decisions are made. These practices are not symbolic; they recalibrate attention. They prevent the builder's mind from being hijacked by immediacy. Over time, these micro-withdrawals develop into a mental habit: the ability to create space even in high-pressure environments.

Weekly rhythms deepen the practice. The builder sets aside protected time that is not assigned to operational tasks; no meetings, no execution, no reactive work. Instead, this time is dedicated to thinking, reviewing, noticing what has drifted, and reconnecting with the deeper logic of the work. These intervals prevent the leader from being swallowed by the machinery of the enterprise. They restore perspective and offer early correction before misalignment becomes costly.

Seasonal withdrawal is where the practice becomes transformative. Every few months, the builder steps back in a more substantial way; reducing noise, pausing expansion, or physically removing themselves from the environment to regain clarity. These periods allow the leader to assess whether the trajectory still aligns with the mission, whether the organization's design supports resilience, and whether their own internal state is fit to lead the next cycle. Seasonal withdrawal is not a vacation; it is the structural maintenance required to sustain serious creation.

Withdrawal must also be embedded into the design of the enterprise itself. Systems need intervals for stabilization. Teams need periods of reduced intensity to integrate learning and restore energy. Projects require moments of reassessment. Organizations that operate in unbroken cycles of urgency exhaust their talent and erode their strategic judgment. When withdrawal is built into the structure; through rest cycles, iteration pauses, or strategic retreats; teams develop greater clarity, creativity, and long-term commitment.

Leadership withdrawal has another critical dimension: stepping back to allow others to step forward. Withdrawal creates opportunity for team members to make decisions, solve problems, and take ownership in ways that strengthen the organization's long-term resilience. Leaders who fail to withdraw become bottlenecks. Leaders who withdraw intentionally create scalability; not merely operationally, but culturally.

These practices are not static; they must evolve with the builder and the enterprise. What is restorative in the early stages may be insufficient at scale. As pressure increases, withdrawal must become more intentional, more frequent, and more protected. The demands of leadership will not lessen; the discipline of withdrawal must therefore strengthen.

Ultimately, withdrawal in practice is about sovereignty. It restores the builder's ability to choose rather than react, to think rather than scramble, to lead from clarity rather than exhaustion. It ensures that expansion is grounded, not frantic. And it protects the long arc of creation from the erosion that relentless activity inevitably produces.

Withdrawal, practiced consistently, becomes part of the architecture of the work itself; a rhythm that sustains ambition rather than restricts it.

The Power in the Pause

The pause is the distilled form of withdrawal; the smallest container that holds the same transformative power as a full season of contraction. A pause is not the absence of action; it is the intentional interruption of momentum. It is a moment in which the builder steps out of the current of urgency and returns to a position of authorship. In a world that equates speed with competence, the pause becomes a radical act of leadership. It challenges the assumption that movement is inherently valuable and asserts that clarity is more important than pace.

Stillness is often mistaken for idleness, but the pause is neither passive nor empty. It is the interval where perception recalibrates, where impulses lose their grip, and where intuition becomes audible again. When the builder pauses, they create the conditions for their mind to shift from reaction to discernment. Patterns become visible. Options that seemed unavailable under pressure suddenly reveal themselves. The pause restores cognitive and emotional range; the ability to perceive nuance rather than default to habit.

The strategic value of the pause becomes clear in moments of heightened pressure. Urgency compresses judgment, narrows perspective, and accelerates decisions beyond the speed at which they can be made wisely. Inserting a pause into these moments breaks the spell of immediacy. It forces the builder to step back from the illusion that everything must be decided now. This simple interruption prevents decisions driven by fear, ego, or fatigue; decisions that often create far more damage than the original tension ever posed.

The pause also strengthens the builder's internal architecture. It teaches them to tolerate discomfort without escaping into action. It cultivates patience, composure, and the ability to remain grounded while others react. Leaders who master the pause cannot be rushed, manipulated, or destabilized by external pressure. Their steadiness becomes a source of stability for the entire organization. In their presence, teams learn that thoughtful action is not slow action; it is action taken from alignment rather than panic.

The pause influences the culture of the enterprise as well. When leaders model stillness, teams learn to value quality over haste and clarity over constant output. Meetings become more intentional. Communication becomes more precise. Execution becomes more thoughtful. A culture that respects the pause does not burn itself out chasing superficial momentum. It concentrates its efforts on what actually moves the work forward.

What makes the pause powerful is not its duration but its discipline. Even a brief moment; one breath, one deliberate count, one silent reflection; can disrupt the momentum of reactivity and bring the builder back to a state of intentional action. Over time, these accumulated pauses reshape the builder's internal rhythm. They move through complexity with more clarity, endure uncertainty with more stability, and make decisions with far greater precision.

Ultimately, the pause is a training ground for sovereignty. It is where the builder learns to govern themselves before governing their enterprise. It is where the next arc of creation begins; not in the frenzy of motion but in the quiet of recollection. The pause prepares the builder to act with conviction rather than compulsion, to lead from clarity rather than obligation, and to build with endurance rather than exhaustion.

In the long arc of creation, the pause is not a deviation from progress. It is the mechanism that ensures progress remains aligned, sustainable, and true.

Closing Meditation

Before moving forward, allow yourself to step out of the momentum of the work and into a moment of deliberate stillness. Set aside the instinct to produce, analyze, or strategize. Let the noise of the day settle, not because the tasks ahead are unimportant, but because clarity requires space. Withdrawal is not what happens when you are too tired to continue; it is what happens when you choose to lead from intention rather than inertia.

Consider, for a moment, how much of your effort has been shaped by urgency rather than alignment. How often have you moved simply because movement felt safer than stillness? How often has activity crowded out discernment? In this quiet pause, notice what becomes visible when the compulsion to act softens. Notice the ideas that feel truer than the rest, the responsibilities that feel essential rather than habitual, the paths that still resonate when urgency is removed from the equation.

Let the mind unclench. Let the breath deepen. Let the pace of your thoughts slow until you can feel the ground beneath them. Withdrawal is not a retreat from your work but a return to yourself;

the part of you capable of discerning what matters in the long arc rather than the short cycle. What emerges in this space is not passivity but coherence. From coherence comes strength.

The invitation here is simple: build from the inside out. Do not wait for exhaustion to force you into stillness. Do not rely on crisis to break the momentum of habits that no longer serve you. Practice withdrawal as a form of stewardship, an active choosing of rhythm over frenzy, of clarity over noise, of depth over speed. Allow yourself to contract when needed so that your next expansion can be grounded rather than frantic.

Carry this stillness with you as you re-enter the work. Let it inform your next decision, your next conversation, your next act of creation. Return to withdrawal not as an escape, but as the place where your leadership finds its shape. In honoring this rhythm, you preserve your capacity to build with endurance; and to build something worthy of enduring.

Chapter 4

Breathwork for Builders: Rhythm, Expansion, Contraction

The Misuse of Energy in Modern Building

Modern building often treats energy as an expendable commodity; something to be poured into work without limit, measured only by visible output and external progress. The prevailing culture encourages builders to equate constant exertion with commitment, long hours with discipline, and relentless expansion with strategic intelligence. The message is clear: those who slow down risk irrelevance, and those who rest signal weakness. Under these assumptions, energy becomes something to be spent aggressively rather than stewarded deliberately.

But energy is not infinite, and it is not neutral. When used without rhythm, it degrades the very capacities that meaningful creation depends on. Endless output dulls judgment and narrows perception. The builder begins responding to pressure rather than shaping direction. Decisions become reactive, not because the leader lacks skill, but because exhaustion has overtaken discernment. The quality of work declines even as the quantity appears to increase. From the outside, the enterprise may seem active and ambitious; internally, it is degrading; too strained to adapt and too depleted to endure.

The erosion caused by misused energy does not announce itself immediately. It begins subtly: a decline in curiosity, a shortening of patience, a growing dependence on urgency as a motivator. The builder's internal landscape becomes compressed. They lose the spaciousness required to notice weak signals, to interpret complexity, or to sense the early indicators of misalignment. Their leadership shifts from intentional to mechanical. Momentum continues, but coherence fades.

This misuse of energy also imposes structural consequences. Teams emulate the builder's pace, adopting urgency as culture rather than as an occasional requirement. Processes accelerate beyond their capacity, producing instability rather than progress. Systems become brittle because they were scaled under strain rather than built under clarity. In the pursuit of more; more output, more growth, more visibility; the organization gradually forfeits resilience. It becomes capable of moving quickly but incapable of absorbing disruption.

What makes this pattern particularly dangerous is how easily it masquerades as success. A builder who exhausts themselves can still appear productive. A company operating at unsustainable intensity can still post impressive metrics. But these achievements are temporary. Without rhythm, energy becomes misallocated and mismanaged, leading to burnout, turnover, strategic drift, and a long-term decline in creative capacity. The cost of this model is not paid immediately, which is why so many builders adopt it unknowingly. But the debt always comes due.

Energy must be viewed not as fuel to burn, but as breath to regulate. Without cycles of renewal, the builder's strength deteriorates. Without periods of contraction, the enterprise's structure weakens. The pursuit of constant output is not ambition; it is imbalance disguised as drive. Builders who abandon natural rhythm ultimately compromise their ability to build at all.

The work ahead requires a different philosophy; one grounded in the understanding that energy is not renewed through willpower, but through rhythm. Those who master that rhythm endure. Those who ignore it collapse under the weight of their own momentum.

Breath as the Blueprint

Before any builder takes action; before the first decision, the first strategy, the first exertion; there is breath. It is the most fundamental rhythm a human body knows: inhale and exhale, expansion and contraction. This rhythm predates every form of work, yet it provides the clearest blueprint for how sustainable work must unfold. Breath is the original architecture of endurance, a cycle that functions not through force but through balance. It is a living reminder that strength arises not from constant intake or constant release, but from the disciplined alternation between the two.

Breath is often ignored because it is quiet. It does not demand attention, and it continues regardless of how the builder conducts their day. Yet this very constancy offers a lesson that modern building consistently violates: anything sustained must move rhythmically. The inhale strengthens; the exhale stabilizes. The inhale gathers capacity; the exhale prevents overload. Breath is not frantic, not hurried, and not continuous expansion. It is measured, restorative, and inherently self-regulating. The builder who overlooks this model inevitably drifts into patterns of work that the body; and the enterprise; cannot sustain.

When breath is shallow or rushed, the body weakens. Endurance diminishes, clarity fades, and the system becomes vulnerable to stress. The same occurs when a builder disregards the rhythms of their own work. Expansion without pause drains resilience. Contraction avoided out of fear leads to rigidity and fragility. A leader who moves only in one direction; forward, outward, aggressively; eventually consumes the internal resources required for creativity and judgment. Breath shows us that sustainability is not an accident; it is a rhythm that must be honored.

Breath also models the difference between force and capacity. A deep inhale draws in what the body can actually use; not more, not less. A shallow inhale creates the illusion of movement but starves the system of what it needs to perform. Builders often fall into the same trap. They mistake busyness for depth, activity for capacity, motion for progress. Work executed without rhythm becomes shallow, no matter how impressive it appears. Breath teaches that depth comes from pacing, from allowing room for the full cycle to occur.

Most importantly, breath introduces the idea that every period of expansion must be supported by an equal commitment to contraction. Growth is not self-sustaining; it must be balanced with periods of stabilization, reflection, and consolidation. Breath is an embodied demonstration of this truth. It asks no permission to pause. It slows when needed. It deepens when required. It expands only as far as the system can safely support. If breath were governed by the logic of modern building; always inhale, never exhale; the body would collapse within minutes.

To treat breath as the blueprint is to understand building not as a race but as a rhythm. It is to recognize that expansion must be deliberate and contraction must be embraced. It is to accept that stillness is not a failure of momentum but a necessary phase of creation. Breath reveals an ancient pattern that builders must reclaim: effort followed by renewal, growth followed by grounding, motion balanced by stillness. This rhythm is not optional. It is the architecture upon which endurance is built.

Expansion: The Power of the Inhale

Expansion is often misinterpreted as relentless accumulation; more markets, more output, more visibility, more everything. The modern builder is conditioned to believe that growth should be aggressive, continuous, and celebrated simply for its size. But true expansion, like a deliberate inhale, is not a frantic grasping for more. It is a measured intake, purposeful and calibrated, shaped by capacity rather than by ambition's appetite.

A deep inhale does not rush. It draws in only what the body can use, filling the system with strength rather than strain. Expansion guided by this principle is not about conquering ground but about gathering resources intelligently; people, systems, opportunities, and capabilities that the enterprise can actually support. Expansion that outpaces capacity creates instability; expansion aligned with internal readiness creates endurance. The power of the inhale lies in its intentionality, not in its volume.

Builders often confuse expansion with momentum. When growth accelerates, it can feel exhilarating; proof of competence, market validation, a signal of upward trajectory. But momentum alone is not strength. Without a solid foundation, rapid expansion becomes a form of self-sabotage. It stretches the organization faster than culture can adapt, strains systems before they mature, and burdens the builder with responsibilities they are not prepared to manage. Like a breath taken too quickly, expansion pursued too aggressively destabilizes the entire structure.

The wise builder expands the way the body inhales: steadily, deeply, without panic. They resist the urge to react to every opportunity or to chase growth purely for external validation. Instead, they select opportunities that strengthen the core rather than dilute it. They scale only at the speed resilience allows. They maintain awareness of the organizational "lungs"; the systems, culture, leadership, and judgment that must expand proportionally if the enterprise is to sustain its growth.

This kind of expansion is not flashy. It is quiet, disciplined, and often invisible in its early stages. It may lack the drama of explosive scaling, but it produces a foundation capable of supporting the weight of future cycles. Expansion becomes preparation, not performance. It fortifies the enterprise for the inevitable contractions, challenges, and resets that all long-term ventures face. It ensures that when pressure increases, the structure does not tear under strain.

Another essential dimension of the inhale is restraint. The body does not hoard breath; it takes what is necessary and stops. Expansion governed by restraint prevents overreach. It acknowledges that the goal is not to absorb every opportunity but to absorb the right ones. Greed in expansion; taking on more than the enterprise can metabolize; creates bloat, confusion, and vulnerability. Deliberate expansion creates alignment, capacity, and strength.

In this way, the inhale becomes a model for sustainable growth. It teaches that expansion is not inherently virtuous; it is virtuous only when paced, purposeful, and grounded in structural readiness. Just as the body inhales to prepare for movement, the builder expands to prepare for the next season of creation; not to impress, not to dominate, but to ensure the work can endure.

The true power of the inhale lies not in how much is taken in, but in how wisely it is gathered. Expansion done with this awareness forms the bedrock of stability, enabling the builder to move forward not with frenzy, but with force anchored in resilience.

Contraction: The Strength of the Exhale

If expansion is the deliberate gathering of strength, contraction is the equally deliberate release and stabilization of it. The exhale is not the opposite of power; it is its regulator. In the body, the exhale restores balance, prevents overload, and prepares the system for the next inhale. In leadership and building, contraction plays the same role. It is the disciplined release of what no longer serves, the shedding of excess, and the recalibration required for endurance. Without contraction, expansion becomes distortion.

Contraction is often misinterpreted as loss; a retreat, a reduction of ambition, or an admission of failure. But the exhale disproves this fear. The body does not weaken when it exhales; it resets. It releases carbon dioxide, tension, and pressure so that capacity can be renewed. Builders must approach contraction with the same perspective. Letting go is not diminishing; it is clearing the path for the next cycle of strength. A leader who refuses to exhale becomes overextended, rigid, and brittle, burdened by outdated structures and unnecessary commitments.

The power of contraction lies in its ability to restore coherence. Over time, every enterprise accumulates excess; projects once valuable that now dilute focus, systems that were necessary early on but have since become cumbersome, relationships that once contributed but now drain energy. Contraction allows the builder to remove this weight intentionally. It requires the courage to differentiate the essential from the merely familiar and the discipline to act on that distinction. What remains after contraction is not less; it is truer, stronger, and more aligned with the long-term mission.

Contraction also stabilizes the organization. Expansion increases complexity; contraction consolidates it. Expansion stretches systems; contraction strengthens them. Expansion accelerates movement; contraction ensures that movement does not exceed what the foundation can support. Without contraction, organizations fracture. They grow faster than their culture can mature, take on more than their systems can bear, and create obligations that suffocate creativity and judgment. Contraction prevents this by preserving structural integrity.

On the personal level, contraction forces the builder to examine their own attachments. It reveals where ego has accumulated unnecessary responsibilities, where insecurity has driven overreach, and where momentum has replaced discernment. Contraction requires humility; the willingness to release ideas, roles, or strategies that once elevated the builder but now limit them. It demands that the leader prioritize clarity over pride, alignment over appearance, and endurance over immediate gratification.

What makes contraction powerful rather than punitive is its intentionality. It is not collapse; it is choice. It is the decision to shed what is heavy so that what is essential can move forward with greater force. The builder who masters contraction learns to travel lighter without sacrificing ambition. They develop a rhythm of release that keeps the enterprise agile, the culture aligned, and their own leadership grounded.

In the long arc of creation, contraction is not a detour. It is the strengthening phase of the cycle. It preserves capacity, protects clarity, and ensures that the next expansion rests on a stable foundation. Just as the exhale prepares the body for the next inhale, contraction prepares the enterprise for its next arc of growth. Builders who embrace this rhythm do not fear letting go; they recognize that endurance depends on it.

Contraction is strength; quiet, disciplined, and essential. Without it, nothing built in the inhale can survive the weight of its own expansion.

The Danger of Holding the Breath

In the body, breath must flow. The inhale gathers strength, the exhale releases it, and the steady alternation between the two maintains balance and vitality. When this rhythm is interrupted; when the breath is held; pressure accumulates, clarity diminishes, and the body enters a state of strain it cannot sustain. The same principle applies to leadership and building. When a builder refuses to move through the natural cycle of expansion and contraction, when they cling to momentum out of fear or ego, they recreate the physiological effects of holding their breath: rigidity, fragility, and ultimately collapse.

Holding the breath feels, at first, like control. The builder assumes that continuous expansion signals dominance, that constant output protects against vulnerability, and that pausing will jeopardize everything they have built. They interpret stillness as risk and withdrawal as weakness. This mindset convinces the builder that releasing pressure will cause the entire structure to fall apart. But the opposite is true. Refusing to exhale only amplifies the internal strain until the system fails under forces it was never designed to bear.

The illusion of invincibility is one of the most dangerous byproducts of holding the breath. Builders begin to believe that they can outrun exhaustion indefinitely, that their teams can stretch without consequence, and that their systems can absorb endless expansion. They dismiss early warning signs; fatigue, declining morale, rising friction, diminishing creativity; because they mistake these symptoms for temporary turbulence rather than structural distress. By the time the damage becomes visible, the foundation has already been compromised.

When breath is held, flexibility disappears. In the body, rigid muscles are prone to injury; in the enterprise, rigid systems are prone to failure. A company that expands without releasing pressure cannot pivot when the market shifts. A culture that operates under chronic strain loses adaptability and trust. A leader who refuses to pause becomes reactive, irritable, and emotionally depleted. Rigidity is not resilience. It is the precursor to breakdown.

On an individual level, holding the breath manifests as burnout disguised as productivity. The builder continues to move quickly, but their pace is fueled by adrenaline rather than clarity. Their decision-making becomes impulsive, their creativity dries up, and their sense of purpose erodes. Outwardly, they may still appear successful; busy, in demand, constantly active. Inwardly, they are collapsing. They are surviving by force rather than leading from strength.

What prevents builders from exhaling is rarely lack of understanding; it is fear. Fear of losing relevance. Fear of disappointing others. Fear of slowing down enough to confront the inner dissonance they have been avoiding. Fear that if they stop, even briefly, everything will fall apart. But the truth is that everything falls apart precisely because they refuse to stop. Recovery denied becomes collapse enforced.

Restoring rhythm requires willingness to relinquish this illusion of control. It requires accepting that sustainable leadership depends not on the absence of pause, but on the regulation of it. The exhale; letting go, stepping back, releasing pressure; is not a threat to progress. It is the only mechanism that preserves the builder's capacity to continue. It is what allows the next inhale, the next cycle of growth, to occur with integrity rather than force.

The builder who learns to stop holding the breath does not lose momentum; they gain resilience. They abandon the fantasy of invincibility and replace it with the strength of adaptability. They no longer operate as if success depends on constant exertion because they have experienced the stability that rhythm provides. They inhale with purpose, exhale with discipline, and lead from a posture that can endure the long road ahead.

Holding the breath is the beginning of collapse. Breathing; fully, rhythmically, without fear; is the beginning of mastery.

Finding the Natural Cadence of the Enterprise

Every enterprise carries its own rhythm; an underlying cadence that determines the pace at which it can grow, adapt, and sustain itself. Just as the body has an optimal tempo for breath and movement, an organization has a speed at which it thrives and a speed at which it begins to fracture. The mistake many builders make is imposing an artificial tempo on the business, driven by ambition, fear, or external pressure, without listening to the natural rhythm already present within the system. When cadence is forced, strain replaces strength, and the enterprise loses its capacity to endure.

The natural cadence of an enterprise cannot be dictated. It must be discovered. A leader who pays careful attention will observe patterns in how the organization responds to pressure, how quickly teams can absorb new initiatives, how fast systems can scale without compromising quality, and how much complexity the culture can tolerate before clarity begins to erode. These observations reveal a pulse; sometimes steady, sometimes variable, but always instructive. To lead effectively is to attune to this pulse rather than overpower it.

When cadence is ignored or overridden, the consequences accumulate quickly. Growth accelerates beyond what the internal culture can metabolize. Innovation is pursued at a speed that surpasses the organization's ability to maintain coherence. Decisions are made faster than information can be processed. The enterprise begins to show symptoms of forced rhythm: rising turnover, declining morale, increased errors, loss of strategic focus, and a sense of constant internal pressure. What looks like productivity is often the early stage of collapse.

Listening for cadence requires humility. It demands that the builder set aside the belief that their will alone determines the organization's trajectory. Instead, they must recognize that the enterprise is not merely an extension of their ambition; it is a living structure with its own limits, capacities, and timing. A wise builder observes not only what the business *can* do, but what it can do *sustainably*. They understand that endurance is found not in matching the speed of competitors, but in matching the rhythm of the organization itself.

Once this cadence is understood, the builder can design systems that breathe. This means structuring periods of expansion followed by periods of consolidation; initiating ambitious pushes only when the foundation is strong; allowing time for cultural integration after major shifts; and avoiding continuous escalation as a default mode. These rhythms keep the enterprise agile rather than brittle. They create a pattern of movement that supports both innovation and stability.

Financial and operational systems must also reflect this cadence. Budget cycles should anticipate seasons of investment and seasons of harvesting. Hiring should follow the organization's actual capacity for onboarding and cultural absorption. Product development should alternate between rapid iteration and slower refinement. Teams should experience periods of intense focus followed by deliberate reduction of load. When systems breathe this way, the enterprise becomes resilient; capable of stretching without tearing and contracting without collapsing.

Cadence is not only a structural principle; it is a cultural one. When leaders honor rhythm, they cultivate environments where rest, reflection, and recalibration are normalized rather than treated as disruptions. Teams feel permission to speak honestly about strain. Decision-making becomes calmer and clearer. The enterprise grows not through frantic expansion, but through consistent, well-timed movement. In such cultures, trust deepens and creativity flourishes because pressure is managed, not ignored.

Ultimately, finding the natural cadence of the enterprise is an act of stewardship. It respects the limits of the system, protects the people within it, and ensures that growth aligns with capacity rather than with ego. Builders who lead this way do not sacrifice long-term resilience for immediate gains. They recognize that the enterprise, like breath, thrives through rhythm; expansion supported by contraction, motion balanced by stillness, progress paced according to what the structure can truly sustain.

The leader who honors this cadence builds not only a successful organization, but a durable one; an enterprise capable of breathing through change, absorbing uncertainty, and enduring far beyond the initial burst of ambition.

The Builder's Internal Rhythm

Just as every enterprise has a natural cadence, every builder possesses an internal rhythm; cycles of energy, clarity, creativity, and execution that rise and fall over time. This rhythm is not a flaw or a limitation. It is a biological and psychological truth, as intrinsic as breath itself. Yet many leaders ignore it. They push through depletion, override fatigue, dismiss the need for reflection, and demand from themselves a level of constant intensity that no human system can sustain. In doing so, they sever themselves from the very source of their strength.

A builder's internal rhythm is composed of seasons, not moments. There are seasons of expansive clarity; periods when ideas flow, decisions feel natural, and ambition aligns with capacity. There are seasons of disciplined execution; times when the work requires consistency more than inspiration. And there are seasons of contraction; periods that call for reflection, recalibration, and reduced output so the next stage of growth can be grounded. Leadership falters when these seasons are treated as interruptions rather than essential phases of long-term creation.

Ignoring internal rhythm leads to a form of self-induced distortion. Builders begin to believe that any dip in energy is a personal failure rather than a normal part of the cycle. They compensate by pushing harder, often relying on adrenaline to replace clarity. They take on commitments that outpace their actual capacity, and their decision-making becomes increasingly reactive. This creates a feedback loop of strain: the more they push, the more their rhythm deteriorates; the more it deteriorates, the more they feel compelled to push. Over time, the internal architecture that supports good judgment erodes.

Honoring internal rhythm begins with observation. Builders must learn to notice the signals that indicate a shift in season. Rising restlessness may signal the need for new creative input. Increasing irritability may reveal fatigue rather than external pressure. A sudden drop in clarity may indicate depletion, not incompetence. When these signals are acknowledged rather than overridden, the builder becomes better equipped to adapt their pace, reallocate their energy, and prevent burnout before it takes root.

Working with internal rhythm does not mean reducing ambition. It means aligning effort with the conditions that make ambition sustainable. During high-clarity seasons, the builder can move decisively and make significant progress. During reflective seasons, they refine strategy, prune unnecessary commitments, and strengthen their foundation. During lower-energy periods, they protect their capacity rather than squandering it. This approach does not slow progress; it creates progress that endures.

Leaders who respect their rhythm also model a healthier cadence for their teams. When a builder operates with awareness and discipline, the culture absorbs that steadiness. It learns that rest is not indulgence, that reflection is not delay, and that strategic pauses are part of excellence, not a deviation from it. Teams become more resilient because they are not constantly pushed into unsustainable modes of operation. The organization inherits the builder's steadiness rather than their strain.

This internal rhythm is ultimately a form of intelligence. It teaches the builder when to accelerate, when to maintain pace, and when to withdraw. It prevents the kind of overexertion that leads to collapse and the kind of hesitation that leads to stagnation. It aligns the leader's internal world with the demands of the external one. Most importantly, it grounds leadership in coherence; an internal consistency that cannot be shaken by urgency or instability.

The builder who learns to honor their rhythm becomes not only more effective but more enduring. They do not burn out prematurely or oscillate between extremes of intensity and exhaustion. They move through the long arc of creation with steadiness, clarity, and the quiet authority of someone who knows how to govern themselves before attempting to govern anything else.

Breathwork as Strategic Practice

To treat breathwork merely as a wellness exercise is to overlook its deeper relevance to leadership. Breathwork is strategy; not metaphor, not symbolism, but a practical method for regulating pace, attention, emotional stability, and decision quality. Just as breath anchors the body, rhythmic practices anchor the builder. They create deliberate interruptions in the momentum that otherwise pushes leaders into reactivity and misalignment. Breathwork becomes a tool for preserving clarity in environments designed to erode it.

Daily rhythm is the first layer of strategic breathwork. Short, intentional pauses act as the micro-exhales of leadership. These may take the form of brief moments before entering a meeting, a slow breath before responding to conflict, or a short walk taken without a device. These intervals recalibrate the nervous system and prevent urgency from hijacking the day. They also train the mind to step back from automatic reactions, creating space for deliberate choice. When practiced consistently, these pauses accumulate into a habit of presence that strengthens decision-making.

Weekly rhythm deepens this practice. Leaders must create protected time that is reserved not for execution but for alignment. This may involve reviewing commitments, revisiting priorities, or assessing whether the week's actions matched the week's intentions. This structured withdrawal allows the leader to course-correct before misalignment becomes entrenched. It is the equivalent of a deep breath; a larger pattern of contraction that restores coherence to the builder's internal and external systems.

Seasonal rhythm is where breathwork becomes strategic architecture. Every few months, the builder needs a deliberate reset; a period marked by reduced demands, increased reflection, and more spacious thinking. During these resets, leaders can step out of operational intensity long enough to examine whether their vision remains intact, whether their energy is being allocated wisely, and whether the business is following the cadence it was designed to follow. These larger inhales and exhales guide the organization through cycles of expansion, stabilization, and renewal.

Breathwork as strategic practice also involves calibrating pace with intention. Builders are often seduced by speed, confusing acceleration with progress. Breathwork returns them to a more truthful metric: alignment. A leader who moves quickly while misaligned only magnifies their drift. A leader who moves slowly with precision advances the work more effectively. Breathwork teaches the discipline of pace; moving neither too fast for the enterprise nor too slowly for the moment. It equips leaders to sense when to press forward, when to pause, and when to release.

Another dimension of breathwork is emotional governance. Stress compresses breath. Fear shortens it. Ego inflates it. Breathwork reverses this cycle by returning the builder to a state of internal spaciousness. A regulated breath produces a regulated mind; a regulated mind produces coherent leadership. This is not abstraction. Decisions made from a grounded physiological state are consistently clearer, less reactive, and more strategically sound. Breath becomes a form of risk management.

Finally, breathwork trains the builder to tolerate stillness. Most leaders are more comfortable with action than with pause. They rush to fill silence, accelerate through ambiguity, or make premature decisions to alleviate internal tension. Breathwork strengthens the capacity to remain present without fleeing into action. It develops endurance not through exertion but through composure.

In this way, breathwork becomes the scaffolding of long-term leadership. It shapes how the builder enters the day, manages conflict, sets rhythm, and navigates seasons of pressure. It creates structure where urgency would otherwise dictate pace. And it ensures that the builder's energy is not spent reactively but invested intentionally; inhale by inhale, exhale by exhale; across the long arc of creation.

Working Without Straining

Most builders equate effort with strain. They assume that meaningful work must feel heavy, that leadership must operate at the edge of exhaustion, and that pushing themselves beyond their natural limits is evidence of commitment. But strain is not a measure of excellence. It is a sign of misalignment. True endurance; and true mastery; comes not from working harder, but from working in a way that preserves stability, clarity, and internal coherence. Strain is what happens when the builder's rhythm is violated. Sustainable exertion is what happens when it is honored.

Working without straining does not mean working less or avoiding difficulty. It means channeling effort through a structure that supports it. In physical training, strain comes from poor form, not from intensity. The same is true in leadership. The wrong posture; disorganized priorities, reactive decision-making, fear-driven urgency; creates unnecessary friction. Energy leaks. Tension builds. Tasks that should feel straightforward become burdensome. When the builder operates from a grounded posture, even demanding work becomes manageable because it flows through alignment rather than resistance.

Strain also arises when the builder attempts to sustain peak intensity without rhythm. Continuous output depletes emotional and cognitive reserves. It reduces the quality of attention. It erodes patience, creativity, and strategic vision. Leaders often discover too late that they have been moving not from strength but from compulsion. Working without straining requires recognizing that intensity is a tool; not a permanent state. It must be applied selectively, followed by recovery, so that pressure strengthens rather than fractures the system.

Another source of strain is the builder's internal narrative. Many leaders carry an unspoken belief that they must justify their role by constantly proving their value. This belief manifests as unnecessary overwork, personally taking on tasks that should be delegated, or intervening in situations that require trust rather than control. These behaviors create strain not because the work is inherently difficult, but because the builder's identity becomes entangled with the performance of effort. When leaders decouple their worth from their workload, strain diminishes. They begin to apply their energy with precision rather than desperation.

Working without straining is also an environmental skill. Builders must design systems that support sustainable performance; structures that reduce friction, clarify expectations, simplify workflows, and allow teams to operate without chronic overload. Many organizations produce strain not because their goals are too ambitious, but because their systems are too incoherent. When leaders remove unnecessary complexity, they unlock capacity without increasing pressure. Sustainable exertion becomes a cultural norm rather than an individual exception.

At its core, the ability to work without strain is a form of emotional discipline. It requires the builder to remain steady in the presence of urgency, grounded in the face of uncertainty, and calm while navigating complexity. This discipline does not eliminate stress; it prevents stress from dictating behavior. It teaches the builder to access strength from stability rather than from adrenaline. Leaders who master this internal posture are not easily rattled. Their presence becomes a stabilizing force, and their work becomes more effective because it is not clouded by tension.

Endurance is built quietly. Not through spectacle, not through heroic sprints, but through the consistent application of aligned effort over time. Builders who work without straining move more intelligently, recover more quickly, and make decisions from clarity rather than fatigue. Their energy lasts because it is not spent fighting themselves. It is directed solely toward the work that matters.

Ultimately, working without straining is not a luxury; it is a prerequisite for long-term creation. Strain fractures; alignment fortifies. And only those who learn to operate from alignment can carry the weight of serious work without being crushed by it.

Closing Meditation

Before you move forward, take a moment to return to the simplest rhythm available to you; the inhale, the exhale, the quiet cadence beneath every action you take. Set down the pace of the day and listen for a slower one. Notice how the breath expands without force, contracts without hesitation, and sustains you without demanding attention. This is the rhythm that precedes all creation. It is the blueprint that the builder must learn to honor if they expect their work to endure.

Let your attention settle on the spaces between breaths. In those small intervals, clarity sharpens. Pressure softens. The mind becomes less entangled with urgency and more attuned to what is actually present. These spaces mirror the pauses required in leadership; the moments when stepping back reveals what constant motion conceals. Breath reminds you that rest is not the opposite of exertion; it is what allows exertion to be meaningful.

Reflect for a moment on where your work has drifted out of rhythm. Where have you inhaled too aggressively; taking on more than your structure can hold? Where have you resisted the exhale; delaying necessary release out of fear, ego, or momentum? Where have you held the breath entirely; pushing through strain rather than returning to alignment? Notice these places without judgment. Awareness is the beginning of rhythm.

When you breathe deeply, the body softens into strength rather than bracing against pressure. Leadership works the same way. When you operate from rhythm instead of strain, clarity returns. Decisions become less reactive. Creativity re-emerges. You regain access to the internal stability that constant acceleration quietly erodes.

This meditation is not an escape from the work. It is a return to the foundation that makes the work possible. As you step back into your responsibilities, carry with you the understanding that breath is not merely a biological function; it is a disciplined reminder that nothing sustainable is built through continuous force. Creation that lasts is created in rhythm: expansion supported by contraction, motion balanced by stillness, effort held together by pauses long enough to recalibrate direction.

Breathe as you build. Let the rhythm guide you. And allow your work to emerge from the same quiet intelligence that governs every inhale and every exhale.

Chapter 5

The Economy of Attention: Focus as Sacred Capital

The Attention Crisis in Modern Building

Modern building is defined not by a lack of resources but by a lack of focus. Leaders operate in an environment engineered to fracture concentration, dilute intention, and scatter the mind across a constant stream of competing signals. Markets move quickly, communication never stops, and every device in the builder's pocket is designed to siphon attention in increments so small they are almost invisible. The result is a culture where distraction becomes normal, fragmentation becomes habitual, and depth becomes rare. This erosion of attention occurs quietly, yet it undermines the very foundations on which serious work depends.

Distraction is not a dramatic failure; it is a slow corrosion. It steals in moments; an unnecessary meeting here, a reflexive notification check there. None of these interruptions appear consequential on their own. But over time, they accumulate into cognitive clutter that weakens judgment and fractures presence. The builder loses the ability to settle deeply into thought, to perceive nuance, or to sustain effort long enough for meaningful insights to emerge. Work that once required seriousness is reduced to surface engagement. Leadership becomes reactive rather than intentional, and the enterprise begins to drift; not because anyone made a catastrophic error, but because attention was never fully held.

This crisis is amplified by the mistaken belief that productivity depends primarily on time. Time is measurable, schedulable, and visible. Attention is none of these. Yet attention is the true engine of meaningful output. A single hour of focused concentration accomplishes what scattered effort cannot achieve in days. A single decision made with full presence shapes direction more effectively than dozens made hastily. Builders often pride themselves on their ability to multitask, to manage complexity, to stay constantly connected. But these habits degrade the very capability that distinguishes serious leaders from frantic ones: the ability to direct attention deliberately.

Enterprises also suffer when attention collapses. Organizations mirror the internal state of their leaders. When leadership operates in a fragmented manner, teams begin to emulate the same patterns; jumping between priorities, losing depth, mistaking noise for progress. Strategy becomes a sequence of reactions rather than a coherent arc. Culture becomes defined by urgency rather than clarity. Over time, the enterprise loses its ability to build anything that requires sustained focus, because its people have been conditioned to operate in fragments.

The silent threat of scattered attention is its plausibility. Distraction feels harmless in the moment. Multitasking feels efficient. Constant engagement feels responsible. But each of these erodes the builder's capacity to do deep work, make disciplined decisions, and maintain the clarity required for endurance. Attention is not simply a cognitive function; it is the builder's first discipline. When it weakens, everything built upon it weakens with it.

The modern builder must confront this reality directly. Before they refine strategy, before they optimize operations, and before they expand their enterprise, they must reclaim the ability to focus; to inhabit their work fully, to direct their mind with intention, and to protect their attention as if it were the rarest resource in their possession. Because it is.

Attention as the True Scarcity

Time has long been treated as the primary constraint in leadership, but time is not what determines the quality or endurance of a builder's work. Attention is. Time can be allocated, stretched, reorganized, and even wasted without immediate consequence. Attention cannot. It is finite, exhaustible, and deeply sensitive to how it is used. While time measures hours, attention measures presence;

the degree to which the builder's mind is fully engaged with what they claim to value. In modern building, this is the rarest resource, and the one most carelessly spent.

Attention is not distributed evenly across days. It fluctuates with energy, clarity, emotional state, and environmental conditions. When attention is divided, judgment deteriorates. The builder misses signals, overlooks patterns, and misinterprets information. Decisions made without full attention often appear reasonable in the moment but produce misalignment downstream. The cost is rarely immediate, which is why leaders underestimate it. But over months and years, divided attention compounds into a form of intellectual debt; one that eventually demands repayment through crisis, rework, or collapse.

Scattered attention also erodes resilience. A mind pulled in multiple directions loses the ability to recover. It becomes overstimulated, fatigued, and easily overwhelmed. Builders who confuse hyperactivity with engagement slow-drain their capacity to think deeply, to strategize effectively, and to regulate their own emotional state. As attention fractures, so does the builder's internal stability. What begins as minor distraction evolves into chronic agitation, diminished creativity, and a growing inability to sustain focus long enough for meaningful insights to form.

The scarcity of attention becomes most visible in moments requiring depth. Strategic thinking, creative problem-solving, and thoughtful leadership cannot occur in a fractured mind. These domains require immersion; uninterrupted concentration that allows the builder to perceive complexity without distortion. When attention is compromised, the builder gravitates toward shallow tasks, quick wins, and reactive behavior. They lose access to the very qualities that their role demands. The enterprise feels this loss long before the builder notices it: drift replaces direction, chaos replaces cohesion, and the organization begins to scatter in the same pattern as its leader.

Attention becomes even more scarce as enterprises grow. Complexity increases. Demands multiply. Stakeholders compete for mental bandwidth. Without deliberate management, the builder becomes a custodian of everyone else's priorities rather than a steward of their own. Their attention is consumed by the urgent, the loud, and the externally imposed, leaving little available for the work that actually determines the future. This is how vision erodes; not from lack of skill, but from lack of cognitive space.

To treat attention as the true scarcity is to elevate it above time, money, opportunity, and even talent. It is to recognize that the quality of the builder's attention determines the quality of the enterprise. It shapes judgment, culture, strategy, and resilience. When attention is misallocated, everything built upon it becomes unstable. When attention is directed with discipline, everything it touches strengthens.

Attention is sacred capital. The builder who understands this stops scattering it across noise and begins investing it where it yields endurance, insight, and transformation.

The Architecture of Focus

Focus is often treated as a matter of willpower; as though concentration is simply a choice, a mindset, or a momentary act of effort. But sustained focus is not an act; it is an architecture. It must be built, structured, protected, and reinforced through systems that remove friction and reduce cognitive noise. Without this architecture, even the most disciplined builder will find their attention continually hijacked by the demands of modern work. Focus fails not because the builder lacks strength, but because their environment lacks design.

The architecture of focus begins with intentional constraint. A builder cannot attend to everything, and anything that tries to accommodate all inputs becomes structurally unsound. Constraints; clear priorities, defined scope, deliberate boundaries; filter out noise so that the essential can emerge. Leaders who create too many pathways for distraction inadvertently sabotage their own capacity for depth. Focused work is possible only when the field of attention is narrowed and aligned with the mission.

Structure is the second pillar. Focus thrives when the builder's day, week, and operating environment are designed to channel attention rather than fracture it. This means creating predictable periods for deep work, establishing communication windows that prevent constant interruption, and setting up systems that minimize decision fatigue. Builders often underestimate the cognitive cost of an unstructured environment. Every unplanned request, every moment of ambiguity, every poorly defined workflow consumes attention that could have been directed toward meaningful creation.

A third element of the architecture is environment; both physical and digital. Physical spaces saturated with noise, movement, or clutter make focus difficult. Digital ecosystems filled with alerts, notifications, and constant connectivity degrade attention even more severely. The builder must take responsibility for shaping environments that support concentration. Silence is not indulgent; it is infrastructure. Disconnection is not avoidance; it is protection. A builder who structures their environment well gains a competitive advantage over those who operate in ambient chaos.

Rituals form the fourth component. Focus is reinforced through repeated patterns that cue the mind for depth. Rituals; beginning-of-day grounding, pre-work pauses, reflective closing cycles; signal to the brain that it is entering a state of sustained attention. These rituals are not ornamental. They form the psychological scaffolding that transitions the builder out of scattered cognition and into intentional presence.

Finally, the architecture of focus requires subtraction. Too many leaders attempt to build focus by adding tools, systems, and time-management strategies. But focus is rarely strengthened through addition. It is strengthened through removal: fewer commitments, fewer meetings, fewer points of decision, fewer demands on the builder's cognitive bandwidth. Each subtraction restores a portion of attention that has been lost to clutter. Over time, this reclaimed attention accumulates into a reservoir of clarity that fuels deep, meaningful work.

Focus is not something the builder must fight for. It is something they must build. When the architecture is sound; when constraints are clear, structure is intentional, environments are supportive, rituals are in place, and noise is removed; focus becomes natural rather than forced. It emerges as the default state rather than an elusive ideal.

The builders who master this architecture possess a distinct advantage: they can sustain depth in a world that fragments it. They can think clearly when others are overwhelmed. They can build enduring systems in an environment addicted to distraction. Their work reflects a quality that cannot be replicated through speed or effort; only through disciplined attention shaped by deliberate design.

What Demands Attention Must Earn It

Attention is often treated as an obligation; something the builder must give to anyone who asks, any issue that arises, any possibility that appears. But attention is not charity. It is an investment. And like all investments, it must be allocated with discernment. Most leaders do not suffer from a shortage of opportunities; they suffer from a shortage of clarity about which ones deserve their focus. When everything feels important, nothing is prioritized. When nothing is prioritized, the builder's attention fractures, and the enterprise follows.

To reclaim attention, the builder must adopt a more demanding standard: nothing receives focus simply because it asks for it. Requests, ideas, crises, and opportunities must earn the right to occupy the builder's mind. This requires evaluating each claim on attention through a simple but rigorous question: *Does this serve the mission, or does it merely generate noise?* The distinction is not always obvious in the moment, especially when urgency or ego attempts to disguise itself as importance. But disciplined evaluation reveals the truth quickly. Most demands do not deserve attention. They are distractions masquerading as obligations.

Ruthless clarity is the cornerstone of this discernment. The builder must learn to differentiate between what is essential, what is supportive, and what is irrelevant. Essential work moves the mission forward. Supportive work maintains the infrastructure that makes essential work possible. Irrelevant work drains energy without contributing to anything meaningful. Many leaders collapse these categories into one, treating all tasks as equally deserving of mental effort. In doing so, they dilute their attention across areas that do not warrant it, weakening their capacity to lead.

Another dimension of earning attention involves understanding the long-term cost of divided focus. Every moment spent on tasks that do not matter steals cognitive bandwidth from those that do. Depth requires sustained focus; sustained focus requires the removal of shallow commitments. Builders must therefore cultivate the discipline to decline opportunities; even tempting ones; when they do not align with the strategic arc of the work. Declining is not a sign of limitation. It is a sign of stewardship.

This clarity must also apply to relationships and communication. Not all conversations deserve equal access to the builder's attention. Not all feedback is relevant. Not all conflicts require involvement. Leaders frequently entangle themselves in issues that teams should handle, not because the leader is needed but because they have not established boundaries. When attention is consumed by the wrong problems, the right ones remain unresolved. A leader's presence must be reserved for the moments where it creates real leverage, not for the moments where it provides temporary relief to others.

The discipline of attention allocation extends to the builder's internal world as well. Thoughts, worries, and emotional distractions attempt to hijack focus just as insistently as external demands. Discernment requires separating legitimate concerns from habitual anxiety, strategic thinking from rumination, intuition from impulsivity. The builder who cannot apply discipline internally will struggle to apply it externally. Attention must be earned not only by tasks and people but by the builder's own thoughts.

What emerges through this discipline is a new form of clarity; one that sharpens judgment, strengthens boundaries, and elevates the quality of every decision the builder makes. Attention becomes concentrated rather than scattered, intentional rather than reactive. The enterprise feels this shift in the form of cleaner priorities, stronger execution, and a culture that respects focus rather than sacrificing it.

When attention becomes something that must be earned rather than something that is freely given, the builder regains control over their most valuable resource. They stop responding to noise and begin directing the signal. They learn to invest attention where it produces endurance, depth, and meaningful progress.

Attention is not owed. It is allocated. And only the work that deserves to endure should receive it.

Focus as Capital, Not Charity

Attention is not something to be handed out freely, nor is it a courtesy the builder owes to every demand placed upon them. Attention is capital; scarce, powerful, and capable of generating extraordinary returns when allocated wisely. Treating attention as charity leads to depletion; treating it as capital leads to creation. The difference lies in discipline: charity responds to whatever asks for attention, while capital is invested only in what has earned the right to shape the future.

When attention is viewed as capital, it gains weight. The builder begins to see each moment of focus as a form of investment that will compound, stagnate, or deteriorate depending on where it is placed. A day spent firefighting trivial issues is not simply a tiring day; it is a misallocation of capital that weakens tomorrow's progress. A week consumed by shallow tasks is not simply inefficient; it is structurally expensive. Conversely, even a small period of deep, undistracted work can generate insight, alignment, and strategic clarity that echo across the enterprise. The return on attention is often far greater than the return on time.

Capital allocation requires a hierarchy. Some initiatives deserve major investment because they move the mission forward. Others deserve limited attention because they maintain infrastructure. Many deserve nothing at all. Builders who struggle with focus often lack this internal hierarchy; they treat all tasks as equal shareholders of attention. But capital invested without discernment is capital wasted. The builder must learn to apply the same rigor to attention that investors apply to financial decisions: evaluate risk, assess potential return, and ignore anything that cannot justify its cost.

This perspective also transforms how the builder relates to people. Not every relationship warrants priority. Not every voice warrants influence. Not every request warrants interruption. Leaders often dilute their attention across countless interactions; responding immediately to every message, attending meetings where their presence adds no value, engaging with stakeholders whose motives are unclear. When attention is treated as capital, these patterns begin to shift. Presence becomes intentional. Influence becomes precise. The builder begins to understand that where they place their attention signals what the enterprise should value.

Focusing attention as capital also requires emotional discipline. Many leaders invest attention reactively; into anxieties, unresolved grievances, imagined futures, or internal narratives that drain energy without producing insight. This internal leakage is as costly as external distraction. Capital must be directed toward clarity, not rumination; toward strategic insight, not emotional churn. A builder who learns to interrupt unproductive thought patterns preserves an enormous amount of cognitive capacity that would otherwise be lost to mental noise.

Finally, capital allocation demands patience. Investments take time to mature. One cannot expect the benefits of deep work if the mind is constantly interrupted. One cannot expect a coherent strategy if attention is fragmented. One cannot expect culture to strengthen if leadership attention is spent on theatrics rather than substance. Treating attention as capital forces the builder to slow down long enough for depth to emerge. It creates the conditions for compounding; where each focused effort builds on the last rather than cancelling it out.

When the builder commits to treating attention as capital, not charity, their entire approach to work changes. They stop scattering focus across noise and begin directing it toward leverage. They stop responding to every demand and begin selecting the few that merit investment. They stop operating from depletion and begin operating from strength. The enterprise becomes sharper because its leader has become sharper.

Attention invested wisely builds empires. Attention given away thoughtlessly destroys them.

Attention and Enterprise Culture

An enterprise becomes what its leaders consistently pay attention to. Culture is not shaped primarily by slogans, values statements, or onboarding documents. It is shaped by focus; what leadership notices, what it ignores, what it reinforces, and what it allows to drift. Attention is the silent architect of culture. It organizes behavior, sets priorities, and teaches teams what the organization actually values. When a leader's attention is scattered, the culture becomes scattered. When their attention is disciplined, the culture becomes disciplined.

Teams naturally mirror the internal posture of their leaders. If leadership constantly pivots between priorities, teams learn that depth is optional. If leadership reacts impulsively to every new crisis, teams learn that reactivity is the norm. If leadership treats every issue with equal urgency, teams learn that strategic clarity does not matter. Conversely, when leaders demonstrate focus; by protecting time for deep work, by being present in conversations, by directing energy toward the essential; teams begin to internalize that focus as a cultural expectation. It becomes part of how the organization functions.

Attention also determines morale. A leader who is perpetually distracted signals to their team that their presence is divided and their engagement is shallow. Over time, this erodes trust. People feel unseen, unheard, and undervalued. But when a leader gives full attention; even briefly; the effect is profound. Focused presence communicates respect, seriousness, and stability. It tells the team that their contributions matter and that the work is worth doing well. Cultures built on presence create environments where people bring their best thinking, because they know their effort is entering a space of seriousness rather than noise.

The allocation of leadership attention also shapes how organizations handle conflict and complexity. When leaders invest attention only in fires, the culture becomes crisis-driven. When they attend only to metrics, the culture becomes transactional. When they prioritize optics, the culture becomes performative. But when leaders focus on clarity, alignment, and long-term resilience, the culture becomes strategic. People stop operating for short-term approval and begin working with a sense of purpose.

Another dimension is how organizations treat distractions. Many enterprises operate in a state of constant interruption; meetings layered on meetings, notifications always active, communication channels open at all hours. These norms quietly erode the capacity for depth. Leaders must design cultures where attention is protected, not pillaged. This means establishing policies that limit unnecessary meetings, creating systems that respect uninterrupted work time, and modeling the expectation that deep work is not only permitted but required.

Importantly, leaders must demonstrate their own adherence to these boundaries. A leader who demands focus but emails at midnight teaches the opposite of what they intend. A leader who calls urgent meetings for non-urgent issues signals that noise outranks clarity. Culture is shaped by consistency, not by instruction. When leaders show that they value attention, the organization learns to value it as well.

Over time, a culture that protects attention becomes a strategic advantage. It produces teams that think deeply, solve problems with nuance, and execute with precision. It reduces burnout, preserves cognitive capacity, and enables innovation because people are not operating in a state of constant depletion. It fosters resilience because clarity remains accessible even under pressure.

In the long arc of building, culture is one of the few assets that cannot be copied. Competitors can imitate strategy, replicate features, and match pricing. They cannot replicate a culture built around disciplined attention. It is a unique signature; an internal advantage that strengthens everything the enterprise attempts to build.

Attention is not only a personal discipline. It is a cultural one. And the leader who honors it creates an organization capable of depth, coherence, and endurance in a world that rewards the opposite.

The Discipline of Deep Work

Deep work is the builder's most powerful advantage, yet it is the discipline most frequently abandoned in modern leadership. The world incentivizes surface engagement; rapid responses, constant availability, fragmented attention. These habits create the illusion of productivity while hollowing out the builder's capacity to think deeply, solve complex problems, and create work of enduring value. Deep work demands concentration, presence, and uninterrupted time. It requires structure, not willpower. And it is nearly impossible to achieve in an environment that has not been deliberately shaped to protect it.

The discipline of deep work begins with commitment. Builders must decide that depth is not optional; that meaningful creation cannot occur in fragments, and that serious thinking cannot be done between notifications. This commitment requires a clear boundary: deep work must have a defined place in the builder's schedule, and the rest of the world must accommodate that boundary rather than dictate it. Without this clarity, deep work becomes something the builder hopes to do "when time allows," which is another way of saying it will not happen at all.

Rituals strengthen this discipline. Deep work begins not with the first keystroke or the first sentence, but with the transition into a deeper cognitive state. This transition can be supported through small, consistent rituals; a moment of silence before beginning, a clearing of physical space, a brief breathwork practice, or a dedicated environment used only for serious thinking. These rituals function as cues to the mind, signaling that it is entering a different mode of operation. Over time, the mind learns to associate these cues with depth, making the transition smoother and the work more potent.

Eliminating interruptions is essential. Even a brief distraction; an email, a knock on the door, a stray notification; can fracture attention and cost far more time than the interruption itself. Builders must construct systems that protect their cognitive environment: turning off notifications, setting communication boundaries, creating physical separation, and ensuring their team understands when and how they can be reached. This is not isolation. It is stewardship.

Deep work cannot survive in an environment designed for interruption.

The discipline also requires emotional tolerance. Many leaders abandon deep work not because they lack focus, but because depth brings discomfort. Stillness reveals uncertainty. Serious thinking exposes gaps in understanding. Complex problems do not yield quick answers. The mind resists this discomfort by seeking easier tasks; emails, calls, meetings that provide the illusion of progress. The builder must learn to stay through this resistance, to remain with the difficulty long enough for clarity to emerge. This tolerance is a form of leadership maturity.

Protecting depth is equally important for teams. An organization cannot expect serious output from people who are never allowed uninterrupted time. Builders must model deep work themselves and then institutionalize it; creating protected hours or days, designing workflows that reduce unnecessary communication, and structuring meetings so that they do not cannibalize the most cognitively valuable parts of the day. Teams that are permitted to think deeply create higher-quality work, make fewer mistakes, and innovate more effectively.

Deep work is not fast. It is not flashy. It rarely produces immediate gratification. But it generates breakthroughs that reactive work cannot reach. It builds intellectual infrastructure. It deepens judgment. It strengthens the internal muscles required for endurance. Builders who cultivate this discipline consistently outperform those who rely on speed, multitasking, or charisma alone. Their work carries a weight and clarity that cannot be faked.

In a world designed to scatter attention, deep work becomes an act of defiance; and a strategic necessity. The builder who learns to protect depth creates an internal engine capable of carrying them through complexity with stability and insight. And the enterprise shaped by such a leader gains access to a rare form of intelligence: work done without fragmentation, focus applied without dilution, and creation grounded in true presence.

Attention as Leadership Power

A leader's power does not come from authority, position, or expertise alone. It comes from their ability to direct attention; first their own, then the attention of others. Leadership is, at its core, the intelligent allocation of focus across people, priorities, and time. When a leader's attention is disciplined, the organization aligns. When it is scattered, the organization fragments. This dynamic is subtle but decisive: the quality of leadership is inseparable from the quality of the leader's attention.

Presence is the first expression of this power. When a leader is fully present, even briefly, it anchors the environment. People feel seen, heard, and taken seriously. Presence communicates that what is happening in the moment matters enough to receive undivided focus. The opposite is equally true: divided attention communicates indifference, instability, or disrespect. A distracted leader creates a distracted culture. A present leader elevates the entire room.

Leadership attention also functions as a spotlight. Wherever the leader looks, the culture looks. If leadership pays attention to urgency, the culture becomes chaotic. If they fixate on optics, the culture becomes performative. If they prioritize clarity, the culture pursues truth. If they reward depth, the culture values depth. The builder's focus signals the organization's priorities far more effectively than any written value statement. People do not follow instructions; they follow attention.

Directing collective focus is one of the most strategic acts a leader can perform. Meetings, messaging, rituals, and decisions all signal where energy should concentrate. When attention is directed well, teams coordinate effortlessly. Effort compounds. People move in the same direction. When attention is directed poorly, teams disperse, misalign, or work on parallel but conflicting priorities. Leadership power lies in defining; not through force, but through clarity; what deserves the collective mind of the organization.

Another dimension of attention as power is the emotional signal it sends. A leader's attention tells people whether the situation requires urgency or patience, whether the moment demands innovation or restraint, whether the enterprise should expand or consolidate. Leaders who panic scatter attention, creating confusion and amplifying instability. Leaders who remain calm create coherence. Their steadiness acts as a counterweight to external volatility. People look to leadership not simply for direction, but for cues on how to interpret the moment. Attention becomes a stabilizing force.

This power also carries responsibility. Leaders must remain conscious of what they choose to amplify. Attention given to trivial matters inadvertently legitimizes them. Attention poured into drama or internal conflict strengthens dysfunction. Attention directed at high performers signals excellence; attention directed at chronic issues signals tolerance for mediocrity. The leader's attention is always teaching, always shaping, always redistributing energy throughout the organization.

There is also a quieter dimension to this power: the attention the leader withholds. When a leader refuses to engage in distractions, refuses to legitimize noise, refuses to participate in cycles of urgency or reactivity, the culture learns to differentiate between what merely demands attention and what actually deserves it. Absence can be as instructive as presence. What leadership does *not* look at is often as important as what it does.

Ultimately, leadership attention is not loud. It is not about dominating the room or becoming the center of every decision. It is about choosing with precision where the collective mind should go; and holding that direction long enough for alignment to take shape. This is why focused leaders build stronger enterprises: their attention becomes a north star, providing orientation and coherence in environments that would otherwise drift.

When attention is used with this level of discipline, leadership becomes potent. Not because the leader exerts more effort, but because the effort they do exert moves the right things. Their presence influences not by force, but by gravity. And the enterprise, attuned to that gravity, becomes capable of depth, clarity, and long-term endurance in a way that scattered cultures never can.

Guarding Attention in Seasons of Crisis

Crisis has a way of scattering attention more violently than any ordinary distraction. It accelerates time, narrows vision, and amplifies the sense of urgency until everything appears critical. Leaders often respond by directing their attention everywhere at once; trying to solve every problem, address every emotion, and predict every outcome. But this instinct, while understandable, is dangerous. In seasons of crisis, attention becomes even more valuable, and even more vulnerable. The leader who cannot guard their focus will lose not only clarity, but the authority needed to guide others through the storm.

Crisis compresses the mind. It tempts the builder into reactive thinking, where short-term pressure eclipses long-term judgment. Signals become harder to interpret. Noise becomes louder. In this state, attention gravitates toward whatever demands the most emotional energy rather than what deserves the most strategic weight. If left unchecked, the leader begins resolving symptoms instead of causes, solving peripheral issues while the core problem deepens. Crisis does not merely test leadership; it exposes the leader's relationship with their own attention.

Guarding attention in crisis begins with slowing down internally, even when the external world accelerates. This slowing is not denial; it is discipline. The leader must create an internal buffer between stimulus and response; a pause long enough for discernment to override instinct. In these moments of quiet, the mind regains altitude. Patterns that were blurred become visible again. The leader can differentiate what is urgent from what is important, what is noise from what is signal. This internal stillness becomes the strategic vantage point from which effective action emerges.

The second discipline is prioritization under pressure. In crisis, the list of possible actions expands dramatically, but the list of effective actions shrinks. The leader must identify the few interventions that will stabilize the system and protect them from dilution. Attention must be allocated to the highest-leverage decisions, not diffused across the emotional volatility of the moment. This requires the courage to ignore certain problems temporarily; not because they do not matter, but because they do not matter *first*.

Communication also becomes an arena for disciplined attention. Teams in crisis look to leadership not just for answers, but for cues on how to think and feel. A leader who communicates from panic spreads panic. A leader who communicates from clarity concentrates the team's focus. Tone becomes as important as content. Timing becomes as important as decisions. Attention in communication must be intentional, measured, and anchored in the long-term context, not the short-term intensity.

Crisis also requires boundaries. The leader's attention cannot be accessible to everyone at all times, or it will be consumed entirely by urgency. Boundaries; clear roles, protected thinking time, designated decision windows; create the structure necessary for resilience. Without them, crisis becomes a vacuum that devours every hour and every mental resource. Boundaries preserve not only attention but judgment.

There is also the internal dimension: guarding attention from fear. Fear amplifies catastrophe narratives, narrows focus to worst-case scenarios, and pulls attention toward imagined futures rather than present realities. A leader must learn to separate data from fear, signal from projection. This does not require optimism; it requires precision. Fear is a poor strategist. Attention grounded in reality is a powerful one.

Finally, the leader must remember that crisis magnifies the importance of rhythm. Even in turbulent seasons, small moments of withdrawal; brief pauses, deep breaths, structured silence; restore coherence. These micro-resets prevent the leader's mind from fracturing under pressure. They allow the builder to return to the crisis with intention rather than compulsion.

Guarded attention is leadership under fire. It is what allows the builder to remain a stabilizing force rather than a participant in the chaos. It ensures that decisions made in crisis reflect the long arc of the work rather than the panic of the moment. And it teaches the organization that clarity is possible even in difficulty, because the leader has demonstrated it.

In seasons of crisis, attention is not merely a resource; it is the anchor that keeps the enterprise from drifting into catastrophe. When the leader protects it, the organization survives. When they lose it, the organization fractures.

Closing Meditation

Let the noise of the day settle for a moment. Set aside the open loops, the unfinished tasks, the mental clutter that pulls your attention in directions that do not serve you. Allow yourself to step into a quieter internal space; one where your mind is not yet occupied, one where focus can gather without being pulled apart. Attention, when reclaimed, feels like returning to yourself after having been dispersed.

Consider how much of your energy has been spent not on what matters, but on what is merely loud. Reflect on how often your attention has been captured rather than chosen. Notice the degree to which distraction has shaped your days, not through dramatic interruption, but through small, persistent claims on your time and mind. In this still moment, acknowledge that attention is not simply a tool; it is the structure that determines the quality of everything you build.

As you breathe, imagine your attention drawing inward; away from the scattered fragments of demand, toward the center of what actually deserves your focus. Feel how your mind sharpens when you stop giving yourself away in small, unconscious increments. Feel how your internal weight shifts when you place your awareness deliberately, rather than allowing it to be carried by momentum. This is the beginning of disciplined focus: the choice to direct your attention rather than surrender it.

Ask yourself: What in my life has not earned the attention I have given it? What needs to be released? What deserves far more of my presence than I have offered? These questions clarify the landscape of your mind. They illuminate commitments that have drifted out of alignment and reveal the few pursuits worthy of your full capacity. Attention becomes sacred when it is given consciously.

Hold the understanding that your attention is the most valuable resource you possess. It is the source of your clarity, the driver of your judgment, and the foundation of your leadership power. Everything you create; every structure, every decision, every relationship; emerges from the quality of the attention you bring to it. Protecting it is not selfishness; it is stewardship.

As you return to your work, carry this centered awareness with you. Let your attention move with intention, not urgency. Let it rest where the work is meaningful, not merely demanding. Let it shape your days the way breath shapes your body; steady, rhythmic, selective, deliberate.

Attention is sacred capital. Treat it accordingly. And let your work be shaped by the clarity that only protected attention can produce.

Chapter 6

The Tree of Life: Mapping Service onto Structure

Why Structure Without Service Fails

An enterprise can become large, efficient, and outwardly impressive, yet remain fundamentally fragile if it is not anchored in service. Structure alone does not create endurance. It can organize people, scale operations, and generate visibility, but without a deeper purpose guiding its growth, it becomes hollow. Hollow structures collapse not because they lack sophistication, but because they lack soul. The builder who equates structure with permanence misunderstands the nature of resilience. What is unrooted will not survive pressure; what is unanchored will not withstand change.

Growth that is not anchored in service often reveals its emptiness only in retrospect. It produces metrics that look strong but relationships that weaken. It creates systems optimized for efficiency but disconnected from meaning. Over time, the organization begins to drift. Decisions are made for momentum rather than mission. Strategies prioritize optics over value. People become interchangeable resources rather than individuals whose lives the enterprise exists to improve. The larger the structure grows under these conditions, the more dramatic its eventual collapse. Scale amplifies fragility; it does not conceal it.

The collapse of such enterprises appears sudden to the outside world, but internally it has been unfolding for years. Cultures erode. Loyalty weakens. The original mission becomes diluted by expansion for expansion's sake. What was built without a stable root system becomes vulnerable to even minor disruptions. Market turbulence, leadership turnover, or competitive pressure becomes enough to expose the hollowness beneath the surface. The failure seems circumstantial, but it is structural; the predictable outcome of growth unmoored from purpose.

Enduring enterprises are built differently. They begin with a commitment to service that runs deeper than profit and broader than reputation. This commitment becomes the reference point for strategy, culture, and operational design. It acts as the stabilizing force that holds the structure together when external conditions change. Service gives structure its resilience, its direction, and its capacity to withstand time. Without it, the most elaborate architecture is nothing more than scaffolding; visible, impressive, and destined to fall.

Service is not an accessory. It is the foundation. Without it, scale becomes emptiness, efficiency becomes brittle, and growth becomes unsustainable. The builder who fails to understand this builds not for endurance but for collapse.

Service as the Root System

Every enduring structure rests on something unseen. Trees draw their strength not from the height of their branches but from the depth of their roots; an underground system that anchors, nourishes, and stabilizes the entire organism. Service functions in the same way for enterprises. It is the quiet, invisible force that gives weight to ambition, coherence to structure, and resilience to growth. While the world may measure a company by its revenues or reach, its true durability depends on how deeply it is rooted in service.

Service is not a slogan or a marketing posture. It is an orientation; a commitment to improving the lives of the people the enterprise touches. This orientation shapes decisions long before they become visible. It influences how products are designed, how teams are led, how conflicts are resolved, and how success is defined. Organizations rooted in service make choices that strengthen long-term trust rather than chase short-term rewards. They think generationally rather than transactionally. Their growth emerges not from exploitation, but from contribution.

Roots do more than hold a tree in place; they feed it. They draw nutrients that cannot be accessed any other way. Similarly, service nourishes the enterprise with meaning; an internal resource that cannot be manufactured through incentives, branding, or external validation. Meaning sustains teams through difficulty. It attracts people who want to build something real. It fuels creativity, perseverance, and integrity. Without this deeper nourishment, even well-designed enterprises eventually exhaust themselves.

Service also provides orientation. Just as roots determine whether a tree grows straight or begins to twist under environmental pressures, service determines whether an organization remains aligned with its core or drifts into misalignment. The pressures of scale, profit, competition, and complexity can pull a company in countless directions. Without a root system strong enough to anchor it, the enterprise begins to shape-shift in pursuit of opportunity rather than purpose. This drift may feel like adaptation, but it is erosion; the slow weakening of the organization's identity.

Importantly, service does its work quietly. It rarely appears in headlines or reports. It does not announce itself in quarterly updates. Its influence can be felt only in the stability of culture, the clarity of decisions, and the coherence of the enterprise's actions over time. Like roots, it is not glamorous, but it is indispensable. The builder who overlooks this foundational role mistakes visibility for vitality and shapes an organization that looks strong but is internally vulnerable.

To root an enterprise in service is to begin with the right question: *Whom do we exist to serve?* Every subsequent decision; strategy, structure, hiring, design; must reinforce the answer. When this alignment is maintained, the organization grows in a manner that strengthens rather than strains it. The branches extend only as far as the roots support.

Service is the root system. It shapes the invisible, nourishes the visible, and grounds the entire structure. Without it, nothing the builder intends to create will stand for long.

Mapping Service into the Architecture

Service cannot remain an abstract intention. It must be engineered into the structure of the enterprise; expressed in processes, embedded in systems, and reflected in every layer of design. Many organizations claim service as a value, but only a fraction build their architecture around it. When service is treated as sentiment rather than structure, it becomes optional. And anything optional erodes under pressure. For service to shape the enterprise meaningfully, it must be mapped directly into how the organization functions.

This mapping begins with clarity: identifying exactly whom the enterprise serves and what form that service must take. Without this clarity, structure becomes generic; optimized for efficiency rather than purpose, capable of producing output but incapable of producing value. True architectural alignment requires the builder to design systems that channel service, not replace it. Systems become conduits, not barriers. Processes become expressions of purpose, not obstacles to it.

When service is mapped into architecture, design choices shift. Hiring prioritizes character and alignment rather than mere competence. Workflows emphasize responsiveness and dignity rather than speed for its own sake. Policies are crafted to reinforce respect, responsibility, and long-term trust. Feedback loops are built not just to measure performance, but to listen; to understand whether the enterprise is fulfilling its responsibility to the people it claims to serve. The structure becomes a living representation of purpose, not a neutral container for activity.

This mapping also influences how power is distributed. In a service-oriented architecture, authority flows toward those closest to the people or communities being served. Decision-making prioritizes frontline insight over hierarchical distance. Structures become flatter not for cultural trendiness, but because service demands immediacy, listening, and adaptability. Bureaucracy shrinks because its weight suffocates service. The architecture becomes lean enough to move, but grounded enough to hold.

Most importantly, mapping service into structure prevents drift. As organizations grow, pressures multiply; efficiency demands, revenue targets, investor expectations, competitive threats. Without a structural anchor, these pressures distort purpose. Service becomes something referenced nostalgically, not something actively practiced. But when service is woven into the architecture, the enterprise cannot betray its purpose without breaking its own systems. Misalignment becomes immediately noticeable because the structure resists it.

Efficiency alone cannot create loyalty. Complexity alone cannot create trust. Scale alone cannot create meaning. These arise only when the architecture reinforces the deeper intent behind the work. Design that reflects purpose creates an organization capable of acting with coherence; where every part, from strategy to execution, points in the same direction.

When builders treat service as the blueprint rather than the decoration, structure becomes more than a way to manage activity. It becomes a mechanism for expressing the mission in every interaction, decision, and outcome. The enterprise grows not by accident but by alignment. And the people it serves feel that alignment because it is not merely spoken; it is engineered.

Branches and Boundaries

Growth is often imagined as an endless outward stretch; more branches, more reach, more visibility. But healthy growth requires limits. In nature, a tree that grows faster than its root system can support becomes vulnerable to wind, drought, and its own weight. The same is true for enterprises. Expansion without boundaries is not strength; it is imbalance. Purpose, not hunger, must determine how far and how fast an organization grows.

Branches represent the outward expression of the enterprise; its offerings, markets, partnerships, and reach. Boundaries represent its discipline; what it will not pursue, whom it will not serve, and the lines it will not cross even for opportunity. When branches outpace boundaries, the organization becomes overextended. Resources stretch thin. Culture cracks. Priorities blur. What initially looks like success begins to feel like strain. Without boundaries, growth becomes indistinguishable from drift.

Boundaries are not restrictions; they are stabilizers. They protect the organization from pursuing opportunities that dilute focus, weaken service, or compromise integrity. Effective boundaries clarify identity. They force the enterprise to choose depth over breadth, quality over expansion, and alignment over allure. Boundaries ensure that growth nourishes rather than cannibalizes the mission. In this way, boundaries strengthen the branches by ensuring they grow in the right direction.

Purpose must act as the compass. When growth is guided by hunger; ambition unmoored from service; it becomes reckless. The organization begins to chase markets simply because they are available, not because they are aligned. It says yes to opportunities that generate revenue but erode capability. It diverges from its center under the belief that more is always better. But "more" pursued blindly becomes fragmentation. It leads to complexity the team cannot support and commitments the culture cannot uphold.

In contrast, growth guided by purpose is measured, coherent, and sustainable. The enterprise expands only where its root system can support it; where service can be delivered authentically and where the organization's internal capacity can grow alongside its external reach. These expansions feel natural, not forced. They reinforce identity rather than dilute it. They extend the organization's impact without compromising its integrity.

Boundaries also protect people. Teams operating in undefined territory quickly become overwhelmed. They struggle to prioritize. They lose sight of the mission. Burnout, confusion, and resentment take root. When boundaries are clear, teams understand the scope of their responsibility and the direction of their efforts. They can focus deeply because they are not stretched across competing agendas. Boundaries simplify complexity and clarify expectations.

Importantly, boundaries must evolve. As the enterprise grows, new opportunities emerge, new threats appear, and new capabilities form. Boundaries that once protected the organization may become outdated; others may need to be strengthened. A living enterprise requires living boundaries; structures that adapt without abandoning their purpose.

Branches and boundaries form a symbiotic relationship. The branches reveal what the organization aspires to become. The boundaries ensure it does not lose itself in the process. Together, they create a growth pattern that is both ambitious and stable; a structure that can rise high because it knows where it stands.

Resilience Through Rootedness

Resilience is often mistaken for flexibility or endurance alone, but true resilience comes from rootedness; the deep structural anchoring that allows an enterprise to withstand shocks without losing its identity. A tree survives storms not because its trunk resists wind, but because its roots hold firm beneath the surface. Likewise, organizations rooted in service and purpose can absorb pressure, adapt to change, and endure disruption without fracturing. Rootedness is not rigidity. It is stability.

Enterprises without roots respond to volatility with panic. Their identity shifts with market conditions. Their strategies oscillate in response to external pressure. Their culture destabilizes the moment circumstances challenge their assumptions. Without a deep anchoring force, these organizations drift; not because they lack intelligence or effort, but because they lack orientation. They try to adapt by bending in every direction at once, losing coherence in the process. What appears as flexibility is often simply uncontrolled movement.

In contrast, enterprises with strong roots are able to pivot without collapsing. Their purpose provides an internal compass when external conditions become uncertain. They do not need to reinvent themselves in every storm; they simply need to adjust their branches. Rootedness preserves clarity. It allows leaders to differentiate between what must change and what must not. It produces a steadiness that teams can rely on; a psychological and strategic ground that remains firm even when circumstances are not.

Rootedness also strengthens decision-making. When pressure rises, leaders without clear roots tend to overreact. They make short-term decisions that contradict long-term vision. They sacrifice principle for convenience or survival. But rooted organizations evaluate crises through a stable lens: *What choice aligns with who we are and whom we serve?* This question filters out panic-driven responses and reveals the path that sustains both integrity and endurance.

Importantly, rootedness is not the opposite of adaptability. It is what makes adaptability possible. A deeply rooted tree can flex with wind precisely because its foundation holds. A deeply rooted enterprise can innovate, experiment, and transform because its identity is not at risk. Flexibility without rootedness is drift. Rootedness without flexibility is stagnation. Resilience requires both: a stable core that allows for dynamic expression.

Rooted cultures also recover more quickly. When teams understand the mission at a deep level; beyond slogans, beyond directives; they know how to act even when guidance is scarce. They do not collapse into confusion. They do not wait helplessly for direction. Rootedness gives them internal reference points, a shared understanding that guides behavior when conditions are uncertain. This collective clarity becomes one of the strongest protective forces an organization can possess.

Finally, rootedness shapes reputation. Enterprises grounded in service tend to earn trust that outlives crisis. Customers return not because the organization avoided difficulty, but because it acted from principle within it. Partners stay because they sense stability beneath the turbulence. Reputation becomes the external reflection of internal roots, strengthening resilience through loyalty that cannot be bought or forced.

In the long arc of building, storms are inevitable. Shocks will come. Markets will shift. Leaders will change. Structures will evolve. The only enterprises that endure are those grounded deeply enough to hold while still flexible enough to adapt. Rootedness is the source of that endurance. It is the quiet strength beneath the visible structure; the stability that survives long after the winds of circumstance have passed.

The Dangers of Hollow Growth

Growth is often celebrated uncritically; chart lines rising, headcount expanding, markets multiplying. These surface indicators create the impression of success, but growth without substance is one of the greatest risks an enterprise can face. Hollow growth occurs when expansion outpaces purpose, when structure outpaces service, and when visibility outpaces integrity. It is the growth of branches without roots, scale without soul. It may look impressive for a time, but it is structurally unsound.

Hollow growth is seductive because it produces early rewards. Revenue increases. Opportunities multiply. Attention rises. The organization feels alive with momentum. Yet beneath this activity, weakness begins to take shape: teams become overstretched, culture becomes diluted, and decision-making becomes reactive. Expanding too quickly forces the enterprise to substitute coordination for cohesion, control for clarity, and speed for depth. The internal architecture strains under the weight of unexamined ambition.

The danger intensifies as the organization begins to mistake acceleration for alignment. Leaders may see growth as validation, assuming that if the enterprise is expanding, it must be doing so for the right reasons. This is a dangerous illusion. Growth for its own sake is indifferent to purpose. It rewards appetite, not intention. It pulls the organization toward opportunities that dilute identity and erode service. Over time, the mission becomes secondary to the mechanics of scaling. The enterprise becomes a machine consuming its own energy with little regard for direction.

Hollow growth also produces brittleness. A structure that expands without strengthening its foundation becomes vulnerable to shocks. A downturn becomes catastrophic. A shift in the market becomes destabilizing. A moment of misalignment becomes existential. Because the enterprise has built outward rather than downward, it lacks the depth required to absorb disruption. What looked like strength is revealed as fragility.

Culturally, hollow growth corrodes commitment. People begin to feel that the organization is moving too quickly for them to stay connected to its purpose. Their work becomes transactional. Their decisions become mechanical. The emotional and moral coherence of the team weakens. In this environment, burnout rises; not because the workload is inherently impossible, but because the work no longer feels anchored in meaning. Growth has replaced service as the organizing principle, and teams feel the difference immediately, even if leadership does not.

The organizational reputation suffers as well. Enterprises that chase expansion without substance eventually break promises, overextend capacity, or fail to deliver on commitments. Trust erodes quietly at first, then rapidly. Stakeholders begin to sense that the structure is wider than it is stable, impressive but unreliable. Trust, once lost, becomes one of the most difficult assets to rebuild.

Hollow growth collapses not from a single failure but from accumulated neglect of the root system. The collapse appears sudden, but the cause is slow erosion: purpose diluted, boundaries ignored, service forgotten. Hollow growth does not nourish the enterprise; it consumes it. It produces height without depth, movement without direction, and scale without endurance.

The cure for hollow growth is not slower expansion; it is anchored expansion. Growth must be rooted in service, aligned with purpose, and supported by systems capable of sustaining it. When the root system is strong, growth becomes strength. When it is weak, growth becomes threat.

In the long arc of building, hollow growth is the most dangerous illusion because it looks like success right up until the moment it fails.

Building Systems that Nourish, Not Deplete

Systems exist to sustain the enterprise; to strengthen, support, and stabilize its ability to serve. But many organizations build systems that do the opposite: systems that drain energy, distort priorities, and create friction that slowly exhausts the people within them. These systems may appear efficient on paper, yet they deplete the root system rather than nourish it. The most enduring enterprises understand that systems must feed the mission, not starve it. Structure must amplify service, not obstruct it.

A nourishing system is one that aligns its inner mechanics with its outer purpose. It simplifies rather than complicates. It clarifies rather than confuses. It removes friction instead of generating it. Every process, workflow, and policy should reinforce the organization's core intent. When systems drift from purpose; becoming bureaucratic, bloated, or self-referential; they transform into burdens rather than supports. The organization begins to serve the system instead of the system serving the organization.

Systems that deplete share predictable characteristics. They create unnecessary steps that obscure ownership. They reward compliance over contribution. They prioritize efficiency at the expense of humanity, or speed at the expense of discernment. Over time, these patterns crush initiative, erode morale, and silence the very insight the enterprise needs to evolve. When people spend more time navigating systems than doing meaningful work, the structure has begun to consume its own vitality.

Nourishing systems operate differently. They are designed to channel energy; not trap it. They allow information to flow clearly, authority to be distributed intelligently, and feedback to move without obstruction. They give teams the tools and clarity they need to do their best work. These systems increase capacity because they reduce cognitive load. People think better because the structure supports clarity rather than undermining it.

Feedback loops are essential to nourishing systems. Trees thrive when soil provides nutrients and when the environment communicates what must be strengthened or shed. Organizations are the same. Systems must provide accurate and unfiltered insight from the front lines; what customers experience, what teams struggle with, what patterns are emerging. Without these feedback loops, leadership begins operating at a distance from reality. Decisions lose precision. Strategy becomes theoretical. Drift accelerates.

For systems to nourish, they must be adaptable. Conditions change, markets shift, and internal needs evolve. Systems built rigidly; even with noble intent; eventually suffocate growth. Flexibility does not mean chaos; it means responsiveness. Nourishing systems evolve with the enterprise, strengthening what works and pruning what no longer supports the mission. They breathe with the organization's rhythm rather than resisting it.

Leaders play a central role in shaping systems that nourish. Their responsibility is not only to build processes but to continuously evaluate whether those processes are enhancing or diminishing strength. This requires humility, curiosity, and a willingness to dismantle what no longer serves; even if those systems were once necessary. Systems should reflect the enterprise as it is becoming, not as it once was.

Ultimately, systems are expressions of values. When an organization prioritizes service, its systems elevate dignity, clarity, and contribution. When it prioritizes optics or speed alone, its systems produce exhaustion and drift. Systems either reinforce the root system or erode it. There is no neutral.

A nourishing system makes the work feel purposeful and possible. A depleting system makes the work feel heavy and endless. Builders who understand this design systems with the same care they give to strategy; because they know the structure beneath the work determines the strength of the work itself.

The Builder as Gardener

Leadership is often imagined as command; directing effort, enforcing standards, and shaping outcomes through force of will. But enduring enterprises are not built this way. They are grown. And the builder who understands this begins to see themselves not as an architect imposing control, but as a gardener tending an ecosystem. Gardens cannot be coerced into flourishing; they must be cultivated. Structure must be supported, not dominated. People must be nourished, not driven. Growth must be guided, not forced.

The gardener's role is defined by attentiveness. They observe the soil, the roots, the leaves, the surrounding conditions. They notice small signs of stress long before they become crises. They understand that every organism within the garden responds to different needs; light, shade, water, pruning, space. Leadership works the same way. A wise leader listens for what the enterprise requires rather than imposing a single formula. They recognize that service does not flow from control; it flows from the ability to see clearly and respond with care.

The gardener also understands limits. They know that plants grow according to season, not desire; that overwatering can kill as quickly as neglect; that forcing growth produces fragility rather than strength. Builders often forget this. They pressure the organization to expand beyond its capacity, push teams past sustainable limits, and demand results on a timeline that violates the natural rhythm of development. The result is burnout, brittleness, and drift. The gardener-builder rejects these impulses. They pace growth with intention, trusting that what is nurtured steadily will endure longer than what is forced prematurely.

Tending also involves creating conditions rather than dictating outcomes. Gardeners enrich soil, manage shade, and regulate water; but they do not pry open buds or stretch branches by hand. They focus on the environment because they know that healthy conditions produce healthy expression. Leaders must do the same. Their job is not to extract performance, but to design systems, cultures, and structures that allow people to grow into their fullest capability. When conditions are right, excellence emerges naturally.

Service-minded leadership also requires patience. Growth often happens quietly, underground, unseen. In organizations, foundational work; cultural alignment, skill development, structural refinement; rarely produces immediate results. Yet these invisible layers determine whether the visible layers will survive. The gardener trusts the process. The builder must learn to do the same. They resist the pressure to chase optics or speed. They prioritize strength over spectacle.

Finally, the gardener-principle reframes authority. A gardener does not dominate the garden; they serve it. Their authority comes not from control but from responsibility; responsibility to protect, nourish, prune, and preserve. When leaders adopt this posture, they create enterprises that feel alive rather than mechanized, purposeful rather than performative. People respond differently to a leader who tends rather than commands. They become more engaged, more committed, and more aligned with the mission because they sense they are part of something being grown, not exploited.

The builder who leads as a gardener cultivates an enterprise capable of weathering seasons, adapting to change, and growing with integrity. They understand that power lies not in forcing outcomes but in tending the conditions that allow excellence to take root. They build structures that live, not merely operate.

Pruning as Preservation

Pruning is often misunderstood as reduction; a loss of potential, a cutting back, a step away from growth. In reality, pruning is preservation. It is the disciplined removal of what weakens the whole so that the structure can survive, strengthen, and expand with integrity. Trees that are never pruned grow in chaotic patterns: branches cross, resources are misallocated, and the organism becomes vulnerable to disease and collapse. Enterprises are no different. Without pruning, they grow in ways that look impressive but lack coherence. Their expansion becomes their undoing.

Pruning requires clarity about what the enterprise is becoming. The builder must decide which branches align with the mission and which distract from it. Not every opportunity deserves pursuit. Not every idea deserves lifespan. Not every initiative supports the core. The discipline lies in recognizing that eliminating a misaligned effort often strengthens the organization far more than adding a new one. Subtraction clarifies direction. It concentrates energy. It restores health.

Pruning also protects against drift. As enterprises expand, they accumulate complexity; projects launched for the wrong reasons, roles created to solve temporary problems, systems built around outdated assumptions. These elements consume resources long after their usefulness has expired. They divide attention. They slowly distort the structure. Pruning returns the enterprise to alignment by removing what no longer serves. It is a structural reset that preserves coherence.

Emotionally, pruning demands courage. Builders often form attachments to what they have created; ideas, teams, products, markets, processes. But attachment is not justification. A branch may hold sentimental value and still weaken the whole. Leaders who avoid pruning delay the inevitable, allowing small misalignments to grow into significant fractures. The longer pruning is postponed, the more costly and disruptive it becomes. The gardener understands that early pruning prevents major structural failure later.

Done correctly, pruning increases vitality. In nature, removing congested branches increases airflow, sunlight, and nutrient distribution. In organizations, pruning improves communication, simplifies workflows, and frees teams to focus on what matters most. It creates spaciousness; both cognitive and structural; that allows creativity to flourish. When unnecessary burdens are removed, the enterprise can move with greater clarity and strength.

Pruning is not punishment. It is stewardship. It preserves the integrity of the mission and the health of the system. It ensures that growth does not compromise the structure and that ambition does not overshadow purpose. Leaders who practice regular pruning build organizations that remain agile, purposeful, and resilient. They protect the enterprise from becoming bloated, confused, or misaligned.

Ultimately, pruning is an act of devotion. It reflects the builder's commitment to sustaining the life of the enterprise rather than indulging the ego's attachment to expansion. It is a recognition that to build something enduring, one must continuously remove what threatens its coherence. Preservation is not passive. It is a series of deliberate choices that keep the structure aligned with the root system that feeds it.

Pruning is not a reduction of possibility. It is the protection of potential.

Closing Meditation

Pause for a moment and imagine the enterprise you are building not as a machine, but as a living structure; a tree shaped by intention, grounded by service, strengthened by boundaries, and sustained by the quiet work of its roots. Let the noise of metrics and momentum fade long enough for you to sense the deeper architecture beneath your work. Growth is visible, but life is not. What endures is always anchored in what cannot be seen.

Consider where your structure has grown without nourishment. Where have branches extended beyond what the roots can support? Where has ambition outpaced alignment? Where has expansion overshadowed service? Let these questions settle without defensiveness. They are not accusations. They are invitations; to return to the root system, to deepen rather than widen, to strengthen rather than accelerate.

Bring your attention to the places within your enterprise that feel congested or depleted. These are signals of misalignment. Ask yourself what needs pruning; not as an act of reduction, but as an act of protection. Pruning preserves the integrity of the whole. It restores clarity to the mission and vitality to the structure. It is a devotion to what must endure rather than what merely impresses.

Now shift your focus to the roots; the service that grounds everything you build. Service does not shout. It does not announce itself. It works quietly, invisibly, deep beneath the surface. Yet it is the source of all resilience. Without it, growth becomes hollow. With it, growth becomes meaningful. Let yourself feel the steadiness that comes from remembering why the work exists at all; who it serves, how it uplifts, what it contributes beyond profit or scale.

As you breathe, recognize that your role is not to force the structure into existence but to tend it. To listen. To guide. To prune. To protect. To nourish. Leadership becomes lighter when it shifts from domination to stewardship. You are the builder, yes; but you are also the gardener, responsible for cultivating conditions under which the enterprise can grow with integrity.

When you return to your work, carry this image with you: roots deep, branches intentional, systems nourishing, growth aligned. Let this frame shape your next decisions. Let it clarify what deserves your attention and what does not. Let it remind you that the strength of the enterprise is found not in how tall it stands, but in how deeply it is grounded.

Build what lives. Build what serves. And let everything else fall away.

Chapter 7

Blueprint for Brotherhood: Business as Communion, Not Conquest

The Failure of the Conquest Model

For generations, the dominant metaphor in business has been war. Leaders are told to conquer markets, crush competitors, dominate territory. This conquest model is seductive because it offers a simple narrative: success equals victory, and victory is achieved through force, speed, and the unrelenting pursuit of dominance. Yet this worldview destroys more than it builds. Conquest may deliver quick wins, but it corrodes the internal architecture required for endurance. It encourages leaders to prioritize escalation over coherence, extraction over contribution, and visibility over vitality. The pursuit of dominance demands constant expansion, constant vigilance, constant defense. It exhausts the builder long before it strengthens the enterprise.

Enterprises built on conquest share predictable weaknesses. They move fast but without depth, accumulate scale without stability, and pursue growth without grounding. Their strategies are driven by fear; fear of losing relevance, fear of appearing weak, fear of falling behind. Such organizations burn through resources, relationships, and people because conquest frames every interaction as a zero-sum contest. Customers become territory. Employees become expendable assets. Partners become threats. This mindset erodes trust both inside and outside the enterprise, undermining the very forces that create true resilience.

The conquest model also produces brittleness disguised as strength. Leaders armor themselves in postures of confidence and superiority, but beneath that armor lies fragility; cultures held together by pressure rather than purpose, teams motivated by fear rather than commitment, and strategies designed for short-term supremacy rather than long-term service. Conquest forces the organization into a perpetual state of motion, where rest is weakness and reflection is dangerous. The builder becomes trapped in escalation cycles that consume energy without producing clarity. Burnout becomes normalized, and exhaustion becomes mistaken for dedication.

Perhaps most dangerously, conquest blinds the enterprise to its own internal decay. Early victories reinforce the illusion that aggression is working, even as the organization becomes more dependent on force and less capable of adaptation. Markets shift, technologies evolve, customer expectations change; but conquest-driven enterprises cannot adjust without perceiving adaptation as defeat. They double down on aggression when the situation calls for humility, doubling their exposure to structural collapse.

Conquest wins quickly, but it cannot hold what it captures. It creates organizations optimized for battle, not for service; for velocity, not for longevity. The builder who anchors their enterprise in conquest may achieve notoriety, but they will not achieve endurance. In the long arc of building, conquest is not a strategy. It is a destabilizer; an intoxicating philosophy that delivers short-term reward at the expense of long-term resilience. What is taken by force must be defended by force. What is built in communion can endure without siege.

Business as Communion

Business is often framed as a competitive arena; individuals and enterprises jockeying for advantage, each seeking to outmaneuver the other. But the most enduring form of enterprise is not built on competition; it is built on communion. Communion does not mean softness or naivety. It means recognizing that building is fundamentally a collective act, one that gains strength from shared purpose, mutual respect, and the alignment of many hands working toward a common good. When an enterprise understands itself as a system of interdependence rather than a battlefield of opponents, it gains access to a deeper form of resilience and depth.

Communion reframes enterprise as service; not merely to customers, but to colleagues, partners, and the larger ecosystem in which the organization operates. It positions the business not as a conqueror of markets but as a contributor to them. This shift fundamentally alters how decisions are made. Instead of maximizing extraction, the enterprise seeks to magnify value. Instead of pursuing dominance, it pursues coherence. Instead of treating others as obstacles, it recognizes them as participants in a shared landscape of possibility.

In this model, collaboration becomes a strength rather than a compromise. Collaboration is not the dilution of standards; it is the expansion of capability. When people feel a sense of communion within an enterprise, they contribute more freely, share insight more openly, and invest emotionally in outcomes because they are not merely executing tasks; they are participating in something they believe matters. The emotional architecture of communion is sturdier than the fear-based architecture of conquest. It produces cultures where people stay not because they must, but because they choose to.

Communion also deepens strategic intelligence. When enterprises interact with their environment from a posture of connection rather than domination, they gain access to more information, more trust, and more opportunity. Partners become allies rather than competitors. Customers become co-creators rather than transactions. Industry shifts become signals to interpret rather than threats to suppress. This openness enhances adaptability, because the organization is not isolated in its own aggression; it is in relationship with the world it serves.

Importantly, communion is not passive. It requires discipline, clarity, and strength. It demands that the enterprise hold its standards while honoring its interdependence with others. Communion rejects exploitation and demands integrity. It requires leaders to act with intention, to communicate with honesty, and to remain oriented toward the collective benefit even when short-term incentives suggest otherwise. This is not weakness; it is stewardship. It is leadership that recognizes the long arc of consequence.

When business is treated as communion, growth becomes a shared achievement rather than an individual conquest. Success is measured not only by scale or profit, but by the extent to which the enterprise strengthens the lives it touches. This orientation creates organizations capable of weathering storms and changing eras because their foundation is not built on dominance; which must constantly be defended; but on contribution, which naturally attracts loyalty, trust, and opportunity.

In the end, enterprises that operate as communion endure because they do not fight against the world; they participate in it. They build with, not against. They serve, and therefore they last.

Brotherhood as Structural Principle

Brotherhood is often spoken of as sentiment; camaraderie, warmth, a sense of interpersonal closeness. But in the architecture of enduring enterprises, brotherhood is not emotional; it is structural. It is a design principle that determines how people relate, how systems function, and how leadership distributes power. Brotherhood, in this context, refers to a disciplined commitment to operating from mutual respect rather than internal competition, from collective strength rather than individual supremacy. It is the recognition that an enterprise is at its strongest when its members are aligned in purpose and dignity.

In organizations built on competition, trust erodes. People withhold information, protect their turf, and prioritize personal advancement over collective progress. Hierarchies become steep and brittle. Decisions concentrate at the top because leaders do not trust their teams, and teams do not trust their leaders. The entire structure becomes rigid and defensive. Brotherhood offers an alternative; a system in which respect is the connective tissue, and contribution is distributed rather than hoarded.

When brotherhood becomes a structural principle, hierarchies remain, but their function shifts. The purpose of hierarchy is no longer control; it is support. Leaders exist to elevate the work of those they oversee, not to dominate them. Authority becomes stewardship. Accountability becomes shared. Information flows more freely because people are not strategizing against one another internally. The structure becomes less about power and more about coherence.

Mutual respect forms the backbone of brotherhood. Respect is not politeness; it is discipline. It demands that individuals honor the dignity, perspective, and role of others, even when they disagree. It requires listening without defensiveness and speaking without aggression. In a structural sense, respect becomes the standard that governs communication, conflict resolution, and decision-making. It creates conditions where people can challenge each other without hostility, collaborate without fear, and contribute without self-protection.

Brotherhood also reshapes the psychology of teams. When competition is replaced with respect-based collaboration, people stop operating from scarcity. They no longer believe that someone else's success threatens their own. They understand that the enterprise's strength increases when each individual is supported, not when they are pitted against one another. This shift reduces anxiety, increases innovation, and encourages honest dialogue; ingredients essential for long-term resilience.

Importantly, brotherhood does not eliminate standards. It does not ask the enterprise to lower expectations or dilute performance demands. In fact, brotherhood often raises standards, because individuals feel safer to stretch, to grow, and to be held accountable without humiliation. Brotherhood creates an environment where excellence is pursued collectively rather than competitively. Strength is shared. Responsibility is distributed. The culture becomes both firmer and kinder; firm in its commitment to the mission, kind in its treatment of people.

As a structural principle, brotherhood creates organizations that do not fracture under pressure. When storms arise, people do not scatter into defensive postures; they anchor to each other. Trust becomes infrastructure, not aspiration. Communication remains open rather than collapsing into fear. Teams respond with unity rather than fragmentation. This cohesion is not created in moments of crisis; it is built in the daily reinforcement of respect and shared purpose.

Brotherhood is not a feeling. It is a framework for building enterprises capable of enduring complexity, change, and time.

When respect is engineered into the system, the organization becomes stronger than any one individual within it.

The Power of Shared Stewardship

Stewardship is one of the most misunderstood dimensions of leadership. Many builders assume that authority rests in ownership; that the person who holds the title, the equity, or the decision-making power is the one who carries the enterprise. But enduring organizations reveal a different truth: the strongest enterprises are built not on centralized ownership, but on shared stewardship. In these environments, responsibility is distributed, contribution is valued over control, and the enterprise is treated as something to be protected rather than possessed.

Stewardship shifts the leader's posture from dominion to guardianship. A guardian recognizes that the enterprise is larger than any individual and that their role is to tend, guide, and protect rather than dominate. This mindset creates a different quality of leadership; less performative, more grounded; less about command, more about clarity; less about personal victory, more about collective progress. When stewardship is shared across the organization, leadership becomes an ecosystem rather than a hierarchy.

The power of shared stewardship lies in its ability to activate ownership at every level. When individuals feel they are guardians of something meaningful, they act with greater intention. They make decisions with more care. They hold themselves and others to higher standards. They contribute not because they are being supervised, but because they feel responsible for the integrity of the whole. This responsibility is not imposed; it is invited by the culture. It is the natural result of being treated with trust and respect.

Cultures built on shared stewardship outperform those built on rigid control because they harness a broader intelligence. No single leader, no matter how capable, can perceive everything or anticipate every challenge. When stewardship is distributed, insight comes from all directions; frontline employees, cross-disciplinary teams, long-standing partners. Decisions become wiser because they reflect collective intelligence rather than the perspective of a single authority. The enterprise becomes more adaptive because more people are attuned to its needs.

Shared stewardship also dissolves the fragility created by dependency on a few central figures. In control-driven organizations, the departure or failure of key individuals destabilizes the entire structure. But in stewardship-driven organizations, leadership is a shared practice embedded across roles and departments. The enterprise can withstand turnover, transition, and unexpected disruption because responsibility does not sit precariously in one place; it is held in many hands.

Critically, stewardship does not eliminate hierarchy; it redefines its purpose. Hierarchy exists to support clarity and coordination, not to concentrate power. Leaders still make decisions, set direction, and carry the highest level of responsibility. But they do so while empowering others to act intelligently within their own sphere. Control contracts; capability expands. Influence flows not from title, but from contribution.

Shared stewardship also strengthens psychological safety. When people know they will not be punished for taking responsible initiative, they become more willing to innovate, to voice concerns, and to challenge assumptions. They stop guarding their territory and start guarding the enterprise. The result is a culture where people feel both accountable and supported; a rare combination that fuels long-term excellence.

In the long arc of building, enterprises rooted in shared stewardship become stronger because they are held collectively. They are cared for, protected, and improved by many minds and many hands. Their resilience does not depend on the brilliance of one leader but on the commitment of an entire community.

Stewardship makes the enterprise something sacred. Shared stewardship makes it something that endures.

Collaboration Without Fragility

Collaboration is often romanticized as harmony; people working together seamlessly, agreeing naturally, moving as one. But real collaboration is not effortless. It requires clarity, strength, and structure. Without these, collaboration becomes fragile. Teams fall into indecision, standards blur, accountability dissolves, and the work loses definition. Brotherhood does not mean softness. It means the ability to collaborate without collapsing into ambiguity.

Many organizations misunderstand collaboration as the absence of conflict. They adopt a posture of perpetual agreement, believing that unity depends on avoiding tension. But tension is not a sign of weakness; it is evidence that people are thinking deeply and contributing honestly. Fragile collaboration silences tension. Strong collaboration channels it. It allows disagreement to refine the work rather than destabilize the relationships within it.

A key component of collaboration without fragility is clarity of purpose. People cannot collaborate effectively if they are not aligned on what they are trying to achieve. Purpose sharpens decision-making, defines boundaries, and eliminates unnecessary debate. When everyone understands the mission, collaboration becomes an act of alignment rather than negotiation. Fragility emerges when teams do not know what they are collaborating *toward*.

Another component is clarity of roles. Brotherhood does not erase hierarchy; it strengthens it by grounding it in respect rather than dominance. When roles are well-defined, people understand where their authority begins and ends. They know when to lead, when to contribute, and when to follow. Collaboration becomes coherent because decision-making flows naturally from the structure. Fragility arises when people are unsure whose responsibility something is, leading to confusion, duplicated effort, or paralysis.

Standards also protect collaboration from fragility. When teams hold themselves to high expectations, the quality of the work becomes the shared metric; not ego, not politics, not comfort. Standards provide a non-personal reference point that people can return to during conflict. This ensures that disagreements are directed toward improving the work rather than undermining each other. Fragile collaboration collapses under pressure; disciplined collaboration sharpens under it.

Trust is the final stabilizer. In low-trust environments, collaboration becomes guarded. People hold back ideas, protect their territory, and engage halfheartedly. In high-trust environments, people contribute fully because they know they will not be punished for showing initiative or challenging assumptions. Trust does not eliminate the need for accountability; it makes accountability possible without fear. It allows people to disagree without jeopardizing their standing in the group.

Collaboration without fragility is a practice, not a mood. It requires leaders to create an environment where respect is constant, clarity is enforced, and contribution is valued more than position. It also requires individuals to show up with strength; to speak directly, listen openly, and prioritize the mission over their personal comfort. When these conditions exist, collaboration becomes a powerful engine of innovation and endurance. It produces outcomes no individual could have created alone, without sacrificing the integrity of the work or the coherence of the team.

In the long arc of building, enterprises that master collaboration without fragility become unbeatable. They think together, adapt together, and move together; with clarity, with respect, and with the collective strength that comes from true brotherhood.

Trust as Infrastructure

Trust is often spoken of as an emotional quality; something people feel toward one another, something fragile, something that emerges gradually and dissolves easily. But in an enduring enterprise, trust is not an emotion; it is infrastructure. It is a structural element as critical as strategy, capital, or talent. Without trust, an organization becomes mechanically functional but spiritually inert. With trust, it becomes capable of coherence, adaptability, and speed without chaos.

In low-trust environments, every action becomes expensive. Meetings multiply because people fear being misunderstood. Emails elongate because individuals feel compelled to justify every decision. Projects stall as teams wait for permission or reassurance. Innovation slows because risk becomes synonymous with danger rather than progress. Distrust is a tax; paid daily, repeatedly, and at great cost to morale and momentum. It drains the enterprise even when the work appears to be moving.

High-trust environments operate differently. Because people believe in the competence and intentions of those around them, communication becomes streamlined. Delegation becomes natural. Alignment emerges without coercion. Teams respond to complexity with unity rather than fragmentation. Trust becomes the invisible highway that carries information, responsibility, and initiative across the organization without friction. It is not softness; it is structural efficiency.

Building trust as infrastructure requires design, not hope. It must be engineered through systems, expectations, and behaviors that reinforce reliability and integrity. Leaders demonstrate consistency in their decisions, transparency in their communication, and fairness in their treatment of people. Teams practice accountability not as punishment but as commitment to the whole. When individuals see that standards apply equally and that the enterprise honors its commitments, trust becomes self-reinforcing. It becomes a cultural constant.

Trust also depends on clarity. People cannot trust what they do not understand. When roles are ambiguous, goals are vague, or communication is inconsistent, even talented teams struggle to operate with confidence. Clarity reduces anxiety. It gives people the information they need to act intelligently and independently. It reduces the cognitive load of guessing and interpreting. An enterprise committed to trust invests heavily in clarity; of purpose, of strategy, of responsibilities, of boundaries.

Importantly, trust is not the absence of conflict. It is what allows conflict to serve its purpose. In high-trust environments, disagreements sharpen ideas rather than fracture relationships. People challenge each other because they believe the intent behind the challenge is constructive. They risk being honest because they know the relationship can withstand the weight of truth. Trust turns conflict from a threat into a tool; a means of refining thought and strengthening alignment.

The presence of trust also accelerates adaptation. When shocks occur; market shifts, strategic pivots, crises; organizations without trust crumble into blame, hesitation, or territorial thinking. In contrast, organizations with trust adjust quickly because people rely on shared intention rather than personal protection. They move as a coordinated organism, not as isolated individuals. Trust grants the enterprise the ability to respond fluidly without losing coherence.

Trust, when constructed intentionally, becomes a strategic asset. It allows the organization to move with speed, consistency, and depth. It transforms leadership from oversight to empowerment. It turns teams from collections of individuals into communities of contribution. And it ensures that the enterprise remains strong not because people are controlled, but because they are aligned.

Trust is not a feeling. It is the framework that holds the structure together.

The Discipline of Mutual Respect

Respect is often misunderstood as a feeling; something that arises naturally when we admire someone or appreciate their qualities. But in an enduring enterprise, respect is not a mood. It is a discipline. It is a standard of behavior that must be upheld regardless of circumstance, emotion, or personal preference. Mutual respect becomes the stabilizing force that allows the organization to operate with coherence, even under strain. Without it, systems fragment, communication deteriorates, and brotherhood collapses into hierarchy or hostility.

Respect begins with the recognition of dignity; the understanding that every person in the enterprise, regardless of role or rank, contributes to the integrity of the whole. This recognition is not sentimental; it is structural. When people feel respected, they communicate honestly, take responsibility willingly, and engage with the work more deeply. When respect falters, so does the organization's capacity for collaboration, innovation, and resilience. Disrespect; whether subtle or overt; introduces fractures that eventually compromise the entire structure.

The discipline of respect requires consistent practice, especially in difficult moments. It demands that leaders speak without derision, correct without humiliation, and make decisions without diminishing those affected. It requires that team members challenge ideas without attacking people and voice concerns without contempt. Respect governs *how* disagreements occur, not whether they occur. In this way, it becomes the foundation for productive conflict rather than fragile harmony. When respect is present, conflict refines. When respect is absent, conflict destroys.

Mutual respect also shapes the quality of accountability within an enterprise. In low-respect cultures, accountability is weaponized; used to shame, punish, or reinforce hierarchy. This creates fear and compliance but not commitment. In high-respect cultures, accountability strengthens the individual and the group. It is a form of honoring the mission rather than enforcing obedience. People feel safe enough to own their mistakes and confident enough to correct others when necessary. Respect transforms accountability from a threat into a practice of stewardship.

Clarity further strengthens respect. Ambiguity creates unnecessary tension, often interpreted as negligence or disregard. When responsibilities, expectations, and decisions are communicated clearly, respect becomes easier to maintain because people understand the context for one another's actions. Clarity reduces the need for interpretation, which is where disrespect often enters. Clear structures prevent confusion from becoming resentment.

Importantly, the discipline of respect is not dependent on harmony. Brotherhood does not require sameness of perspective or constant agreement. It requires the willingness to uphold dignity even in disagreement, to maintain steadiness even in frustration, and to value the relationship even when the moment is difficult. Respect is not an emotion that fluctuates with mood; it is a commitment to the health of the enterprise and the people within it.

In the long arc of building, respect becomes a core mechanism of resilience. It prevents emotional volatility from fracturing teams. It allows communication to remain open in times of stress. It builds psychological safety, which fuels creativity and innovation. And it sustains trust, which allows the organization to move together rather than splinter under pressure.

Respect must be practiced daily, reinforced deliberately, and modeled consistently by leadership. It is not the soft edge of brotherhood; it is its spine. Without respect, brotherhood is sentiment. With respect, brotherhood becomes structure.

Brotherhood and Strategic Resilience

Resilience is often described as endurance; the ability to withstand pressure, recover from setbacks, and continue forward despite difficulty. But endurance alone is insufficient. True strategic resilience emerges not from individual strength but from collective cohesion. Brotherhood; understood as a disciplined system of trust, respect, and shared responsibility; creates an internal structure that absorbs shocks, adapts intelligently, and sustains integrity under strain. Enterprises built on brotherhood survive what others cannot because they do not face adversity alone.

When pressure rises, organizations without brotherhood fragment. Individuals retreat into self-protection, departments become territorial, and communication collapses. Fear overrides clarity. People stop contributing honestly because they no longer believe the environment can hold their truth. Leadership becomes isolated, making decisions in a vacuum. This fragmentation weakens the enterprise long before external conditions do. The failure appears to come from the crisis, but it originates in the absence of brotherhood.

In contrast, enterprises rooted in brotherhood respond to adversity with unity. Trust allows information to move quickly and without distortion. Respect ensures that conflict remains productive rather than destructive. Shared stewardship distributes responsibility so that no single point of failure endangers the whole. People lean into the mission rather than withdrawing from it. They bring their intelligence, not their defensiveness; their commitment, not their fear.

The organization becomes more coordinated under pressure, not less.

Brotherhood strengthens resilience by reducing internal friction. In environments built on conquest or competition, much of the organization's energy is wasted internally; navigating politics, managing egos, mitigating mistrust. These hidden costs drain capacity. In brotherhood-driven enterprises, that energy is redirected outward toward solving real problems. Internal alignment becomes a force multiplier. The organization moves with greater clarity and speed because nothing essential is being lost to internal struggle.

Another dimension of resilience emerges from the psychological safety brotherhood creates. People take risks when they trust that failure will not be weaponized against them. They innovate when they believe their contributions matter. They communicate openly when they know they will be met with respect. This environment accelerates learning and adaptation; two of the most critical components of resilience. An enterprise does not survive disruption through rigidity, but through its capacity to learn in real time.

Brotherhood also protects the organization's identity during turmoil. When external conditions shift rapidly, enterprises often lose themselves; abandoning their values, compromising their service, or diluting their mission in pursuit of survival. Brotherhood acts as a stabilizing force. Shared values and mutual respect anchor decision-making. Even under pressure, the enterprise remains recognizable to itself. This identity coherence strengthens trust among employees, customers, and partners, making recovery faster and more sustainable.

Finally, brotherhood creates endurance by reducing isolation at the leadership level. Leaders who operate alone become brittle. The weight of decision-making, responsibility, and expectation eventually overwhelms them. But when leadership is shared; when stewardship is distributed and brotherhood is practiced; leaders have support structures that enable long-term strength. They do not carry the burden of the enterprise in solitude. The organization itself becomes a source of resilience.

In the long arc of building, enterprises fail not from lack of opportunity but from lack of internal coherence. Brotherhood provides that coherence. It is the quiet architecture that keeps the structure intact when the world outside becomes unstable. It transforms resilience from an individual virtue into a collective capability.

Brotherhood is not a sentimental ideal. It is a strategic advantage.

Reimagining Leadership as Brotherhood

Leadership is often portrayed as elevation; standing above, guiding from a distance, making decisions on behalf of others. But in an enduring enterprise, leadership is not separation; it is participation. To lead through brotherhood is to understand that the leader is not positioned above the structure but within it, bearing responsibility as a member of the community rather than as its ruler. This reframing does not diminish authority; it strengthens it by grounding leadership in contribution rather than domination.

When leadership is imagined as elevation, it breeds distortion. Leaders become insulated from reality. Teams feel regulated rather than supported. Communication becomes filtered. And authority becomes defensive; more concerned with maintaining status than serving the mission. This isolation weakens judgment and erodes trust. A leader detached from the lived experience of the enterprise cannot steward it effectively.

Brotherhood offers an alternate model: leadership as shared participation in the work, shared responsibility for the mission, and shared accountability for the health of the whole. This does not dilute the leader's authority; it clarifies its purpose. Authority exists not for control but for coordination, not for superiority but for stewardship. The leader is responsible for setting direction, making final decisions, and protecting the integrity of the enterprise; but they perform these tasks as part of the collective, not above it.

This model reshapes how leaders interact with their teams. Instead of commanding from a distance, leaders listen deeply. Instead of issuing directives in isolation, they engage with the intelligence of the group. Instead of treating leadership as a performance, they treat it as a practice; consistent, grounded, and oriented toward the good of the whole. Their presence becomes a stabilizing force because it is rooted not in status but in service.

Brotherhood also redefines leadership identity. Many leaders feel pressured to appear invulnerable, believing their authority depends on never showing uncertainty or asking for help. But invulnerability is brittle. It creates distance and fear. Brotherhood allows leaders to acknowledge limits without losing authority. By participating as human beings rather than distant figures, they build trust that strengthens leadership rather than weakening it. Vulnerability becomes a source of coherence rather than a threat to power.

This approach also expands leadership capacity across the organization. In a brotherhood-driven enterprise, leadership is not confined to titles. It emerges wherever stewardship is practiced; on the frontlines, in collaborative teams, in moments of crisis, in acts of initiative. The enterprise becomes a network of leaders rather than a pyramid of followers. This distributed leadership strengthens resilience, accelerates adaptation, and deepens cultural alignment.

Finally, reimagining leadership as brotherhood preserves the integrity of the mission across generations. Leaders who participate rather than dominate create conditions where successors can step into stewardship without dismantling what came before. The enterprise becomes something handed from leader to leader, each contributing to a lineage rather than asserting personal ownership. This continuity is one of the strongest indicators of organizational maturity.

The leader who embraces brotherhood understands that their role is not to elevate themselves above others, but to elevate the work with others. Their authority is not diminished by proximity; it is amplified by trust. And the enterprise grows not through conquest but through communion; through many hands working with shared purpose, guided by leaders who see themselves not as conquerors but as brothers among brothers.

Closing Meditation

Take a moment to release the idea of business as a battlefield. Let the imagery of conquest; opponents, victories, territory; fall away. Set down the posture of defense, the internal armoring, the reflex to dominate or outperform. Permit your mind to shift into a quieter frame, where enterprise is not a contest but a communion. Where building is not an act of force, but an act of participation.

Let your attention settle on the people who stand beside you; the colleagues, partners, collaborators, and contributors who shape the work with you. Consider how different the enterprise becomes when you view these individuals not as tools to be managed or competitors to outperform, but as companions in the creation of something larger than any one person. Brotherhood is not sentiment; it is recognition. Recognition that no enduring structure is built alone.

Feel into the possibility that leadership may be lighter than you have been taught. That authority does not require distance. That responsibility is not a burden meant to be carried in isolation. That strength grows deeper when shared. Imagine what it would mean to lead without posturing, to contribute without domination, to build without conquest. Imagine a leadership model where dignity, respect, and trust are not aspirational soft edges but operational infrastructure.

Reflect on where you have built from fear; fear of losing ground, fear of being overshadowed, fear of appearing weak. Notice how these fears constrict your imagination and harden your posture. Then imagine what becomes possible when these fears loosen. When you no longer guard your position, but guard the mission. When you no longer compete internally, but collaborate with clarity. When you relate not from scarcity, but from shared stewardship.

Pause and breathe into the understanding that brotherhood is not the opposite of strength; it is a form of it. It is the strength that endures storms because it is distributed, not concentrated. It is the strength that adapts because it listens. It is the strength that does not fracture because its foundation is mutual respect rather than fear.

As you return to your work, carry this image with you: an enterprise as a community, not a conquest. Leadership as participation, not elevation. Teams as brothers, not rivals. Structures held together by trust, not tension.

Build in communion. Build with others, not above them. Let brotherhood be the quiet scaffolding that allows your enterprise to stand with integrity through every season.

Chapter 8

Building for Others: The Entrepreneur as Host

The Fallacy of Building for the Self

Enterprises built for the self always contain the seeds of their own collapse. When the builder becomes the center of gravity, the organization narrows around the limitations of a single person; their stamina, their insecurities, their ego, their need for validation. What may appear as ambition is often a structure designed to reinforce the builder's identity rather than serve a meaningful purpose. These self-referential enterprises may grow quickly, but they do not grow deeply. They shine brightly for a moment, then erode under the weight of their own fragility.

The core weakness is structural. A self-centered enterprise relies on the builder's constant presence, approval, and direction. Decisions become filtered not through truth or mission but through the builder's pride. Feedback is softened or suppressed. Teams calibrate their behavior to protect the builder's image rather than the organization's integrity. This creates a brittle system; one that lacks the distributed intelligence required for endurance. When the builder tires, so does the enterprise. When the builder falters, the organization loses coherence. Growth becomes a mirror held up to the founder, not a service offered to the world.

Over time, the consequences multiply. Teams disengage because they sense that their contributions are ornamental rather than essential. Customers drift because they recognize that the enterprise ultimately serves the builder's narrative, not their needs. Culture deteriorates as people begin operating for survival rather than alignment. The builder, trapped at the center of every decision, becomes the bottleneck to progress. What started as empowerment turns into exhaustion as the builder attempts to carry a structure that was never designed to stand without their constant reinforcement.

The illusion of legacy further distorts the enterprise. Builders who construct organizations to immortalize themselves often mistake visibility for vitality. They chase recognition rather than resilience, crafting monuments rather than systems. But legacy cannot be secured through ego; it can only be secured through service. A structure built for the self dies with the self because it was never built to serve anyone else. The enterprise has no reason to endure beyond the builder's relevance, and it lacks the internal architecture to evolve once the founder steps aside.

Self-centered building is not morally wrong; it is strategically unsound. It creates organizations that cannot outgrow their origin story. It replaces mission with identity, resilience with strain, and service with spectacle. The serious builder must confront this fallacy early: an enterprise built primarily to elevate the self cannot last. Enduring structures are built for others. They outlive the ego that shaped them because they were never designed to orbit it.

The Entrepreneur as Host, Not Hero

The traditional image of the entrepreneur is the hero; an extraordinary individual who fights against odds, commands attention, and bends the world to their will. This myth endures because it flatters the ego and dramatizes the journey. Yet it distorts the true nature of sustainable building. Heroic leadership is performative; it demands visibility, constant exertion, and an inflated sense of individual centrality. It also breeds fragility. When the enterprise depends on the hero's charisma, energy, or approval, it becomes structurally weak. The moment the hero falters, the entire system trembles.

A more enduring model is the entrepreneur as host. A host does not seek the spotlight. A host creates the conditions under which others can thrive. Their focus is not on spectacle but on service; crafting an environment where customers feel cared for, where employees feel respected, where collaborators feel valued. This shift from heroism to hosting fundamentally reorients the enterprise. The builder stops performing for the world and begins preparing a space within it. They stop demanding attention and start directing it. They stop centering themselves and begin centering the mission and the people it touches.

Hosting requires a different internal posture. Heroes dominate the room; hosts elevate the room. Heroes seek admiration; hosts offer presence. Heroes pull the enterprise toward themselves; hosts build an enterprise that stands independent of them. This shift does not diminish the builder's authority; it matures it. The host-leader does not abandon strength or standards; they simply express them through stewardship rather than spectacle. Their power comes not from being the most important person in the room, but from creating a room where everyone else can contribute meaningfully.

This posture also clarifies the builder's responsibility. A hero asks, *How do I win?* A host asks, *How do I make this space worthy of the people who enter it?* This question reshapes decisions at every level; from product design to hiring, from customer engagement to culture formation. The enterprise becomes less about the builder's self-expression and more about the experience of those it serves. This orientation produces resilience because the structure no longer depends on the builder's identity to function; it depends on the quality of the environment they create.

Hosting also eliminates the insecurity that fuels heroic leadership. Heroes must constantly prove themselves; through expansion, through success, through visibility. Hosts do not carry this burden. Their worth is not tied to applause but to the integrity of the space they steward. This frees them to lead with steadiness, to make decisions without posturing, and to admit uncertainty without losing authority. Presence replaces performance.

Most importantly, the host-leader builds organizations that endure. Hero-driven enterprises burn out because they rely on the hero's constant presence. Host-driven enterprises grow because they empower the presence of others. They develop talent, distribute responsibility, and cultivate belonging. They build cultures that do not collapse when the founder steps away because the center of the organization was never the founder; it was the mission, and the mission was always oriented toward serving others.

The entrepreneur as host is not a softer version of leadership. It is a more disciplined one. It demands clarity, humility, restraint, and an unwavering commitment to the people the enterprise exists to serve.

In the long arc of building, heroes fade. Hosts endure; because they build structures that do not depend on them but are strengthened by the care they bring.

Creating Spaces, Not Monuments

Many entrepreneurs secretly hope to build monuments; structures that immortalize their names, validate their ambitions, and cement their legacy. Monuments, however, are static. They exist to be admired, not inhabited. They do not evolve, they do not respond, and they do not serve. An enterprise built as a monument becomes rigid, ceremonial, and inward-facing. It may display the builder's achievements, but it offers little to those who enter it. Over time, monuments lose relevance because they were never designed to meet the needs of others; they were designed to praise the builder.

Spaces, by contrast, are alive. They are designed to be used, not admired. They are shaped by the needs, behaviors, and aspirations of the people they serve. A space evolves with its community. It adapts to new contexts, expands to meet new demands, and transforms as purpose requires. When an entrepreneur builds a space rather than a monument, the enterprise becomes a living environment; one that supports contribution, fosters belonging, and invites continuous participation.

Building a space requires discipline. It demands that the builder resist the temptation to center themselves in the architecture. Instead, they must focus on the people who will inhabit the structure; customers, employees, collaborators, partners. What do they need? What allows them to flourish? What makes their experience dignified, seamless, meaningful? These questions anchor the enterprise in service rather than spectacle. They create organizations that remain relevant because they remain useful.

Monuments are designed to preserve the past. Spaces are designed to host the present and prepare for the future. This difference is not aesthetic; it is strategic. A monument is built around identity; the founder's story, the founder's ambition, the founder's desire for permanence. A space is built around purpose; an ongoing commitment to solving real problems, meeting real needs, and creating real value. Monuments resist change; spaces anticipate it. Monuments demand admiration; spaces invite participation.

Building a space also protects against the emotional pitfalls of entrepreneurship. When builders pursue monuments, they become overly attached to their own ideas. They fear critique because it threatens their identity. They resist adaptation because it threatens the monument's form. But when they build a space, they become stewards rather than performers. They welcome feedback because it refines the environment. They adapt willingly because the space must serve evolving needs. They maintain momentum because the structure is never complete; it is always becoming.

A space-centered enterprise is more resilient. It can be reconfigured when markets shift. It can be expanded when opportunities arise. It can be renewed when culture grows stale. Because it is built for others, not for admiration, it thrives through relevance rather than legacy.

The builder who chooses to create spaces instead of monuments discovers a quieter form of significance. Their work becomes useful rather than symbolic, impactful rather than ornamental. And their legacy, ironically, becomes stronger; not because they built a monument to themselves but because they built a space where others could grow, contribute, and endure.

Hospitality as a Strategic Discipline

Hospitality is often mistaken for warmth; an emotional gesture, a pleasant atmosphere, an optional layer of generosity. But in an enduring enterprise, hospitality is not an accessory; it is a strategic discipline. It is the deliberate practice of designing every interaction, system, and environment with the guest in mind. The "guest" may be a customer, an employee, a partner, or anyone who enters the orbit of the enterprise. Hospitality asks a simple but transformative question: *What must this experience feel like for them to thrive here?* This question reshapes architecture.

At its core, hospitality is the art of anticipating needs before they are expressed. It is the discipline of removing friction, eliminating confusion, and creating clarity. It is the practice of honoring the dignity of others through design and execution. This attention creates resilience because people return to environments where they feel seen. Customers stay loyal not because the product is perfect, but because the experience respects them. Employees stay committed not because the work is effortless, but because the culture honors their humanity. Partners remain engaged because they know the relationship is built on care, not convenience.

Strategic hospitality begins with design. Processes are crafted not for internal convenience, but for external ease. Communication is structured to be clear, timely, and considerate. Workflows are built to reduce unnecessary burden. The physical and digital spaces of the enterprise are shaped around the comfort, clarity, and safety of those who enter them. Hospitality is not sentiment; it is architecture. A well-hosted environment creates trust effortlessly because it communicates that the builder has taken responsibility for the guest's experience.

Hospitality then extends into culture. A culture committed to hosting treats every interaction as an opportunity to affirm dignity: how meetings are run, how feedback is given, how conflict is navigated, how newcomers are welcomed, how veterans are honored. These practices become the emotional infrastructure of the enterprise. They create an atmosphere where people feel supported rather than scrutinized, valued rather than used. This internal hospitality becomes a competitive advantage. Teams perform better when they are not simultaneously bracing for impact.

Finally, hospitality shapes resilience. Enterprises that practice strategic hospitality can weather disruption because they have built reservoirs of goodwill. People forgive missteps in environments where they have been consistently treated with care. Customers stay through imperfect product cycles. Employees rise to the occasion during difficult seasons. Partners remain loyal even when conditions tighten. Hospitality creates a relational margin; a buffer of trust that sustains the enterprise when external pressure mounts.

To practice hospitality is to accept a higher standard. It requires discipline, consistency, and a willingness to see the enterprise from the perspective of those it serves. It requires the humility to redesign systems that create unnecessary burden and the courage to hold the organization to a standard of dignity even when speed or scale tempt shortcuts.

Hospitality is not softness. It is stewardship. It is strategy. It is the mature recognition that the enterprise endures only when the people it touches feel respected, supported, and cared for.

Serving Without Submission

Service is often misinterpreted as subservience; a softening of standards, a lowering of authority, a willingness to bend in order to please. But true service has nothing to do with self-erasure. It is a disciplined act of clarity: the commitment to meet the real needs of others without abandoning the structure, principles, or direction of the enterprise. Serving without submission requires strength, not compliance. It requires presence, not passivity. It is leadership expressed through care rather than control.

A leader who serves without losing themselves understands that hospitality does not mean saying yes to everything. It means creating environments in which people can succeed; customers, employees, collaborators; while maintaining boundaries that protect the mission. Service guided by clarity strengthens the enterprise; service guided by insecurity weakens it. When leaders conflate service with appeasement, they sacrifice standards in the name of harmony. The result is predictable: resentment, misalignment, and erosion of trust. But when leaders remain anchored in their principles while offering genuine care, service becomes a stabilizing force.

To serve without submission, the entrepreneur must develop a firm internal posture. They must know what the enterprise stands for; and what it will not tolerate. Only then can service become a strategic act rather than a reactive one. Boundaries are not barriers to hospitality; they are what make hospitality sustainable. Without boundaries, service becomes exploitation. With boundaries, service becomes a form of strength. It communicates: *We see you, we care, and we also know who we are.*

This balance becomes especially important in relationships where power is asymmetrical; client relationships, investor relationships, partnerships, and even internal dynamics. When leaders serve without clarity, they can be pulled into endless accommodation, shaped by the demands of others rather than guided by purpose. The enterprise becomes distorted by external pressure. But when the leader serves from a grounded position, they can listen deeply without absorbing every request, respond generously without compromising standards, and maintain authority without resorting to dominance.

This posture of grounded service has a profound impact on culture. Teams watch how leaders navigate pressure. When they see leaders contort themselves to please, they internalize that fear. When they see leaders impose without listening, they internalize that aggression. But when they see leaders offer care without compromising direction, they learn how to balance empathy with discipline, flexibility with conviction. They learn that service is not the opposite of leadership; it is a mature expression of it.

Customers, too, respond differently. They sense when service is performative rather than principled. They sense when the enterprise is bending beyond its capacity. The most enduring loyalty comes not from enterprises that seek to please everyone, but from enterprises that serve intentionally, consistently, and with structural integrity. Customers trust boundaries. They trust clarity. They trust leaders who know their limits and honor them.

Serving without submission is ultimately a question of identity. A builder who does not know themselves will either collapse under the demands of others or retreat into defensiveness. A builder who is anchored can open their hands without losing their footing. They can be generous without being depleted. They can serve without being bent out of shape.

In the long arc of building, those who can hold this balance create enterprises that feel both strong and welcoming; structures that honor others without shrinking themselves. Service becomes not an act of surrender, but an act of stewardship.

The Power of Generous Design

Generous design is the quiet force that separates enduring enterprises from merely functional ones. It is the practice of building systems, environments, products, and experiences that account not only for the explicit needs of others but also for the unspoken, the unseen, the easily overlooked. Generous design anticipates rather than reacts. It notices what others do not articulate. It removes friction before it becomes frustration. It shapes the environment so that people feel supported without knowing why. At its core, generous design is an act of respect.

Most organizations design from the perspective of efficiency; How fast can someone complete this task? How cheaply can this system operate? How do we optimize for scale? But efficiency alone does not create loyalty or resilience. People return to environments that make them feel cared for, and care is embedded in details. The small refinements, the quiet conveniences, the moments where someone's path becomes easier rather than harder; these accumulate into trust. Trust accumulates into endurance.

Generous design requires humility. It begins with the recognition that people often struggle silently. They may not know what to ask for. They may not have the words to describe their difficulty. They may not feel entitled to express discomfort. The builder who practices generous design assumes responsibility for seeing what others cannot or will not articulate. This becomes a discipline of observation: watching where confusion arises, where energy drains, where anxiety appears, where bottlenecks form. These observations become invitations to improve the environment.

This discipline can be applied at every scale. In product design, generous architecture considers how people feel as they interact with the offering; not simply what functions it provides. In organizational design, generous systems simplify workflows and reduce cognitive load so teams can focus on meaningful work rather than administrative noise. In leadership, generous communication clarifies expectations and reduces ambiguity so that people do not have to guess what is required of them. Each act of generosity strengthens the fabric of the enterprise.

Generous design also anticipates failure. It builds cushions for human error, clarity for moments of confusion, and support for inevitable seasons of strain. Instead of assuming perfection, it designs for reality; the messy, unpredictable nature of human behavior. This realism is not pessimistic; it is compassionate. It acknowledges that people thrive when systems help them recover quickly from setbacks rather than punish them for imperfections. Enterprises that embed this generosity into their architecture become more resilient because people feel safe enough to take risks and strong enough to adapt.

Importantly, generous design is not extravagance. It is not luxury for its own sake. It is precision; ensuring that every element of the enterprise serves a purpose rooted in care. The generosity is not measured in cost but in attention. A simple refinement can be more generous than an expensive feature if it honors the user's time, dignity, or emotional bandwidth. The entrepreneur who practices generous design does not ask, *What impresses?* but rather, *What supports?*

When generosity becomes a design principle, the enterprise takes on a distinctive quality. Customers feel it in the ease of their experience. Employees feel it in the clarity of their work environment. Collaborators feel it in the coherence of the relationship. This atmosphere is not accidental; it is engineered. And because it is engineered, it can be scaled without losing its essence.

Generous design is the architecture of hospitality made structural. It reveals a deeper truth about building: people remember not what was provided, but how they felt in the presence of the system. And the enterprises that endure are those that consistently make people feel considered, supported, and respected; even when no one is watching.

The Entrepreneur's Quiet Authority

Authority in the entrepreneurial world is often confused with noise; visibility, charisma, dominance, the ability to command a room or impose direction. But this form of authority is volatile. It depends on performance, on personality, on constant outward projection. The moment the entrepreneur withdraws, the authority weakens. The moment the performance falters, the structure destabilizes. Quiet authority, by contrast, is not rooted in display but in presence. It is the authority that emerges when a leader's actions, behaviors, and decisions consistently embody clarity, steadiness, and care.

Quiet authority is earned, not asserted. It grows from the builder's ability to hold standards without aggression, offer direction without ego, and listen deeply without losing conviction. People follow a leader with quiet authority not because they fear them or feel dazzled by them, but because they trust them. And trust is gained through consistency; through the leader's willingness to honor commitments, admit mistakes, and make decisions anchored in the enterprise's purpose rather than personal validation.

This kind of authority requires restraint. The entrepreneur must resist the impulse to fill every silence, answer every question, or control every detail. They must allow others to contribute rather than positioning themselves as the irreplaceable center. Quiet authority creates space. It invites others to step forward, to think, to lead. It communicates confidence not through intensity but through groundedness; a calm presence that steadies the environment rather than amplifying its volatility.

Quiet authority also protects the enterprise from the fluctuations of the builder's personality. When leadership relies on charisma or force, the organization becomes reactive to the leader's moods and insecurities. Teams become attuned not to the mission but to the leader's emotional weather. Quiet authority decouples leadership from emotional volatility. It provides a reference point that remains stable even when conditions are not. It ensures that the enterprise's rhythm is not dictated by the founder's adrenaline but by the structure's purpose.

This authority has a moral dimension. The host-leader understands that leadership is a form of stewardship. Their decisions affect lives, livelihoods, and futures. Quiet authority recognizes the weight of this responsibility without dramatizing it. The entrepreneur leads with seriousness, not self-importance. They understand that influence is not a right granted by title, but a trust earned through competence, empathy, and integrity. This moral weight disciplines the leader's instincts; it shapes how they speak, how they correct, how they praise, how they respond to crisis.

Importantly, quiet authority endures. Spectacle fades. Force burns out. But the authority rooted in presence, character, and service becomes stronger over time because it is reinforced by every interaction. People do not follow out of obligation or excitement; they follow out of conviction. They believe in the leader because the leader consistently demonstrates belief in them, in the mission, and in the structure's purpose.

Quiet authority is not about diminishing oneself. It is about removing everything that is unnecessary so that what remains is strong, intentional, and true. It is the authority of the host who creates safety rather than demands attention; the authority of the gardener who shapes indirectly through care; the authority of the builder whose steadiness allows others to rise.

In the long arc of entrepreneurship, it is this quiet authority; not charisma, not dominance; that creates enterprises capable of acting with coherence long after the founder leaves the room.

Scaling Hospitality Without Losing It

The greatest challenge of any hospitality-centered enterprise is scale. Care is easy to offer in small environments where the builder's presence shapes every interaction. Intimacy comes naturally when the team is small, the customer base is limited, and the founder can personally embody the standard. But as the enterprise grows, the atmosphere risks dilution. Systems replace intuition. Policies replace conversation. Efficiency begins to overshadow attention. What once felt personal can become procedural, and what once communicated dignity can become mechanical. The question, then, is not merely *how to grow,* but *how to grow without losing the ethos of hospitality that made the enterprise trustworthy in the first place.*

Maintaining hospitality at scale begins with designing culture, not relying on personality. The founder's personal warmth cannot be the foundation; it is not replicable. What *can* be replicated are principles: clarity, presence, respect, anticipation of needs, and the discipline of care. These must be embedded into the organization's systems, language, training, and decision-making frameworks. When hospitality becomes a shared standard rather than an individual trait, it can survive expansion because it lives in the structure, not merely in the founder.

Systems must be built to carry the weight of care. This does not mean scripting every interaction or mechanizing empathy. It means creating processes that reduce friction for customers and employees, clarifying responsibilities, simplifying workflows, and ensuring that no one is left guessing what the experience should feel like. Hospitality thrives when structure supports people rather than burdening them. At scale, care becomes operational: response times, design language, onboarding rituals, communication norms; all become carriers of hospitality.

Scaling hospitality also requires rigorous hiring. Skill alone is insufficient. The enterprise must select people who understand how to hold others with respect, who can express clarity without aggression, who value dignity as much as efficiency. These individuals become culture carriers. They embody the principles in their everyday decisions, modeling the posture of hosting for those who join later. If hiring prioritizes technical performance while neglecting character, hospitality collapses long before the enterprise reaches maturity.

Leaders must also practice layered stewardship. In early stages, the founder hosts the team; as the organization grows, leaders must host their departments; managers must host their teams; employees must host customers and each other. Hospitality cascades. It becomes a chain of care. When each layer of the enterprise models hosting for the next, intimacy does not disappear; it redistributes. Scale becomes an expansion of hospitality, not a dilution of it.

Yet scaling hospitality requires vigilance. Growth introduces pressures; financial, operational, competitive; that tempt the organization to prioritize speed over presence, volume over value, compliance over dignity. The enterprise must guard against this drift by continuously returning to the core question: *Does this system, decision, or process honor the people we serve?* When the answer is no, the structure must be recalibrated. When hospitality becomes negotiable, it soon becomes obsolete.

Finally, the builder must accept that intimacy will evolve. It cannot remain identical to its early form. What once was personal may become environmental; what once was direct may become structural. This is not loss but transformation. True hospitality does not depend on proximity; it depends on intention. An enterprise can scale to thousands and still feel personal if its systems, culture, and decisions consistently communicate, *You are seen. You are valued. Your experience matters.*

Scaling hospitality is not about preserving a smallness of operation. It is about preserving a largeness of heart; codified, disciplined, and distributed across a growing structure. When done well, scale amplifies hospitality rather than eroding it.

Building Beyond the Builder

Every builder eventually confronts a truth that alters the trajectory of their work: an enterprise designed to survive only in the builder's presence is not an enterprise but an extension of the builder's identity. It cannot outlive them because it was never built to. Enduring structures, by contrast, are created with intentional distance between the founder and the foundation. They are engineered to grow, evolve, and adapt long after the builder steps aside. This is the movement from ownership to legacy; from building *for oneself* to building *beyond oneself.*

To build beyond the builder, the enterprise must be anchored in principles rather than personality. Personal charisma, instinct, and momentum may be powerful in early stages, but they cannot form the long-term architecture of a resilient organization. Principles can. Clear purpose, disciplined systems, shared stewardship, and a culture rooted in dignity; these elements create continuity even when leadership changes. They allow the enterprise to remain recognizable to itself over time, preserving its identity while still evolving with its environment.

This shift requires the builder to relinquish a subtle but dangerous fantasy: that the organization's meaning depends on their ongoing involvement. Builders who cling to centrality restrict the enterprise's growth. They become bottlenecks, not anchors. Everything must be approved by them, shaped by them, justified to them. Decision-making slows. Capabilities weaken. Teams become dependent rather than empowered. The enterprise becomes a monument to the founder's significance instead of a living system capable of serving many generations.

Building beyond the builder demands a different kind of courage; the courage to be unnecessary. The founder must intentionally design themselves out of critical functions, transferring knowledge, authority, and responsibility into the structure and into the people who inhabit it. They must cultivate leaders capable of carrying the mission forward without replicating the founder's personality. This is not abandonment of responsibility; it is the highest form of it. The builder becomes a custodian rather than a guardian, preparing the organization to flourish independently.

This independence also protects the enterprise from the volatility of individual identity. Builders evolve. Their passions shift. Their energy rises and falls. Their lives move through seasons that may no longer align with the enterprise's needs. When the structure is built to survive these fluctuations, the organization does not collapse under the rhythms of a single life. It continues its work because its purpose is larger than the person who initiated it.

Customers and teams sense the difference. In founder-dependent structures, people look upward for answers, waiting for direction or permission. In founder-transcendent structures, people look inward; to the mission, to the culture, to the collective intelligence that has been developed over time. This creates resilience. It ensures continuity of service. It allows the enterprise to adapt to new markets, new generations, and new realities without losing its center.

Building beyond the builder also transforms legacy. A founder who ties their identity to the enterprise's operations risks becoming an obstruction in its evolution. But a builder who sees themselves as the first steward; one of many across time; builds a lineage, not a monument. Their legacy is not the applause they receive but the longevity of the structure they shaped. Endurance becomes the proof of their leadership.

Ultimately, building beyond the builder requires humility and vision. It asks the entrepreneur to prioritize impact over personal importance, continuity over control, and service over recognition. When the builder is no longer the center, the mission becomes the anchor. And in that realignment, the enterprise finally becomes capable of what it was always meant to do: serve long after the builder's hand is no longer guiding it.

Closing Meditation

Allow the noise of achievement to fall away for a moment; the metrics, the milestones, the performance of success. Set aside the impulse to build something that reflects well on you, or remembers you, or elevates your name. Let the ambition to be seen soften. In its place, call forward a quieter question: *What does it mean to build something that serves?*
Not something that glorifies the builder, but something that dignifies the people who enter it.

Take a slow breath and imagine the enterprise as a room you are preparing. People will walk into this room carrying their uncertainties, ambitions, fears, talents, and needs. Some will arrive seeking direction; others seeking belonging; others simply seeking a place where their work matters. As the builder, your task is not to stand in the center of the room, drawing attention. Your task is to shape the room so they can inhabit it fully. This is hosting; leadership expressed through presence rather than performance.

Reflect on where you have built for admiration rather than service. Notice the structures designed to display your identity rather than hold the weight of others. Notice the decisions driven by ego rather than purpose. There is no shame in recognizing these patterns; they are nearly universal. But growth begins with the willingness to release them. Building for others requires subtracting the impulse to make the enterprise about yourself.

Consider the gentler strength that emerges when you shift from hero to host. Authority becomes quieter, steadier, more trustworthy. Decisions become clearer because they are anchored in service rather than self-preservation. The enterprise becomes lighter because it no longer needs to carry the burden of your identity; it carries only the responsibility of its mission. You become freer as well. You no longer need to be indispensable; you only need to be intentional.

Let your attention settle now on the people you serve; the customers who trust you, the employees who rely on you, the collaborators who build alongside you. Host them with seriousness. Shape the environment so that they feel safe enough to contribute and supported enough to grow. Build systems that honor their time, their effort, and their humanity. Craft experiences that reflect thoughtfulness rather than spectacle.

Finally, hold this truth: the most enduring enterprises are not monuments to the builder's greatness but vessels of the builder's care. They outlive the founder not because they immortalize the founder, but because they serve with clarity long after the founder has stepped away.

As you move forward, carry the posture of the host; attentive, grounded, disciplined in service, generous in design. Build not for applause, but for continuation. Build not to be remembered, but to make something worth remembering.

Your work becomes legacy not when it glorifies you, but when it nourishes others.

Chapter 9

Transparency as Light

The Corrosion of Obscurity

There is a particular decay that sets in when a builder chooses concealment over clarity. It is slow at first; imperceptible, even; but it spreads. Obscurity in leadership may begin as an attempt at control, or as a buffer against conflict, but left unchecked, it corrodes the structure from within. Not because all things must be known at all times, but because what is hidden without purpose eventually loses alignment with the whole. A concealed decision, a veiled motive, a pattern of quiet omissions; these form the invisible fractures that widen over time.

What begins as strategic withholding often becomes habitual opacity. The intention might be to spare the team from distraction, or to preserve optionality in the face of uncertainty. But the effect is the same: doubt proliferates where light is withheld. Teams begin to second-guess intentions. Coherence weakens. Morale drifts. Soon, what was obscured to buy time begins to cost trust; and then authority. When builders routinely choose to protect themselves from discomfort by cloaking reality, they train the culture to do the same.

The danger is not simply in what is hidden, but in what happens when hiding becomes the default. It creates distance: between those who know and those who guess, between the reason for a decision and the labor to execute it. When the why behind a choice is never shared, when people are expected to align without understanding, something foundational is lost. Obscurity unravels a team's internal compass. It replaces shared purpose with quiet compliance.

Transparency is not about overexposure. It is not the reckless publishing of every thought or fear. It is about designing an environment where truth is not feared, where clarity is not postponed, and where decisions, even difficult ones, are accompanied by the dignity of explanation. Builders do not owe their teams perfection, but they owe them light. When we obscure by habit, we erode by design.

To lead is to illuminate. To build is to hold nothing vital in the dark. The moment the enterprise begins to shield itself from its own people is the moment it begins to lose its integrity. And without integrity, no structure; no matter how well-funded or cleverly designed; can endure.

Transparency as an Act of Strength

There is a common misconception in leadership that transparency is a form of weakness; an overexposure, a surrender of strategic position, a kind of naive idealism incompatible with serious building. In reality, the opposite is true. Transparency, when applied with discipline, is not vulnerability; it is precision. It is the deliberate act of inviting alignment, of refusing to obscure reality in order to protect ego or mask indecision. It is strength exercised through clarity.

The mature builder understands that clarity is not a luxury; it is infrastructure. You cannot architect coherence while hoarding truth. You cannot expect others to act with integrity if you do not model it in your decisions, your reasoning, and your visibility. To be transparent is not to share everything; it is to share what matters, without distortion, and without deflection. It is to create a culture where people are trusted with the truth and are not infantilized by the illusion of certainty.

But transparency must be trained. Left unrefined, it can become a kind of performative confession; noise masquerading as openness. Builders who confuse transparency with unfiltered emotion often destabilize what they mean to stabilize. Just as dangerous are those who swing the other way: leaders who mask cowardice as discretion, who invoke confidentiality as a shield for avoiding discomfort, and who weaponize silence under the guise of maturity. True transparency lives between these two extremes. It is sober. Intentional. Earned.

To practice transparency is to name reality without panic. It is to explain decisions not to justify them, but to allow others to see the map you are using to navigate. It builds context, not consensus. It creates shared understanding even when there is disagreement. And it reinforces the truth that trust is not given; it is built, slowly, through repeated acts of openness under pressure.

The transparent leader is not always liked. But they are trusted. Their teams may not agree with every move, but they are rarely confused. And over time, that clarity becomes an advantage; not just operationally, but morally. The organization becomes safer, not softer. Accountability deepens. Mistrust loses oxygen. And what remains is a structure that can breathe; because nothing essential is being suffocated to protect the builder's pride.

The Builder as Illuminator

The true role of a builder is not merely to organize people or deploy capital. It is to illuminate. To cast light into places where confusion lives. To make visible the path others could not see, and to do so without spectacle or ego. The builder does not create from noise; they create by revealing order, by bringing structure to what was formless. Illumination is not about drawing attention to oneself; it is about helping others see what matters, and why.

Leadership, at its most grounded, is the discipline of clarity. Not the kind that comes from charisma or clever phrasing, but the kind that comes from patient design. A builder who illuminates does not hide behind titles or jargon. They do not use abstraction as insulation. Instead, they communicate in ways that orient. They make the invisible visible; structures, expectations, causes, consequences. And they do this consistently, especially when stakes are high.

In this way, the builder becomes a kind of architect-lighthouse. Their job is not just to decide, but to allow others to move with confidence through the terrain of complexity. When clarity is withheld, anxiety rises. When meaning is hidden, morale dissipates. But when the builder takes seriously their role as a source of light; not control, not perfection, but light; coherence spreads.

Yet there is a cost to this discipline. To illuminate, one must also accept responsibility for what the light reveals. Sometimes it reveals error. Sometimes it reveals inefficiency, or conflict, or consequences we would rather not see. And still, the builder shines the light. Because hiding those truths does not protect the team; it weakens them. And it hollows the builder's credibility over time.

Illumination is not an aesthetic. It is a duty. It is not about looking honest; it is about refusing to obscure. When others cloak themselves in mystique, in selective access, in plausible deniability, the mature builder instead names things clearly. Not because they seek validation, but because they understand that clarity, repeated over time, becomes the foundation of trust.

A leader who chooses illumination over image becomes something rare: a point of orientation in a disoriented system. Not by shouting, not by dazzling, but by being relentlessly clear; and staying clear when it would be easier to hide.

Light as Strategic Discipline

Transparency is not a one-time gesture. It is a discipline; a repeatable commitment to clarity even when silence would be easier, or more politically convenient. In the architecture of resilient companies, light is not an accessory; it is a structural element. Without it, things do not just grow dim; they come apart. Coherence dissolves when communication becomes erratic. Trust fades when visibility is inconsistent. Transparency, rightly understood, is what fortifies the entire system against internal drift.

Most leaders value trust, but few are willing to earn it in the quiet, unglamorous way transparency requires. They want loyalty without exposure, alignment without disclosure. But trust cannot be manufactured through slogans or culture decks. It is built through a pattern of consistent illumination; explaining not just the "what," but the "why," naming trade-offs, sharing context, and doing so when it matters most. When light is present, decisions become understandable even when they are hard. Without it, even good decisions appear suspicious.

Transparency doesn't mean broadcasting every internal detail. It means making truth structurally accessible; through systems, through habits, through language that makes people feel included rather than inspected. In organizations that practice transparency as strategy, people understand how decisions are made. They see patterns. They trust that what is said privately will match what is reinforced publicly. These are not soft skills. They are cultural infrastructure.

The disciplined use of light also has another effect: it preempts distortion. When leaders are clear early and often, they prevent the rumors and interpretations that flourish in dark spaces. Gossip thrives in opacity. Mistrust festers in silence. But when a company's rhythm includes regular, thoughtful communication; when people can anticipate when and how they'll be informed; they relax. Not because everything is perfect, but because nothing is being hidden.

It is easy to be transparent when things are going well. The test comes when there is tension, when results are uneven, when change is imminent. That's when light must become non-negotiable. Because in those moments, it is not information people crave; it is orientation. And orientation cannot be delivered without strategic, deliberate clarity from those who lead.

To build a resilient system is to build one that assumes light will be present. Not as performance, but as protocol. Not to flatter the ego of the leader, but to dignify the intelligence of the people. Transparency, held as discipline, makes the system stronger than any one person within it.

Transparency in Decision-Making

The clarity of a decision is rarely found in the outcome; it is found in the reasoning that shaped it. Yet in many organizations, decisions are delivered as verdicts: final, unaccompanied, unquestionable. They arrive fully formed and isolated, leaving others to interpret the logic, to speculate on the intent, or worse, to simply comply without connection. In this environment, decision-making becomes a performance, not a process. Trust becomes fragile. Initiative erodes. And culture drifts into quiet resignation.

The transparent builder approaches decision-making differently. Not by opening every deliberation to democratic vote, but by choosing to reveal the logic that guided the path. Transparency in decisions is not about consensus; it's about coherence. It means that even when people disagree, they can see the map. They understand how trade-offs were weighed, why a direction was chosen, and what principles were prioritized in getting there.

This doesn't just improve morale. It strengthens operational intelligence. When people are routinely exposed to the reasoning behind decisions, they begin to think with the same lenses. They develop instinctual alignment. They don't have to ask what the founder would do; they've been shown how to think. And over time, this becomes a cultural multiplier. Clarity compounds.

Systems must be built to support this kind of transparency. It cannot depend on mood or bandwidth. Builders who wish to scale clarity must embed it into the cadence of how they lead; how they share updates, how they frame pivots, how they narrate strategy. A decision communicated without context might move the company forward temporarily. But a decision that brings others into the logic behind it moves the culture forward permanently.

At the core of this practice is respect. Transparency in decision-making is an act of honoring the intelligence and stake of those who are building alongside you. It assumes your people do not need to be shielded from the truth, only trusted with it. When leaders hoard reasoning, they may preserve mystique; but they sacrifice alignment. And without alignment, no execution plan can hold.

The builder who explains their decisions; even imperfectly; builds something far stronger than control. They build understanding. And understanding is what allows an organization to think, and act, and adapt together; without needing to be told what to do.

Guarded Openness: Transparency with Discernment

Not everything should be said. Not everything should be shared. And not every moment is a call for clarity. This is the paradox of transparent leadership; it is not a doctrine of disclosure, but a discipline of discernment. The goal is not to flood the room with light, but to ensure that light reaches where it's needed. This is what separates mature transparency from careless exposure: knowing when clarity serves alignment and when silence preserves integrity.

Openness without discernment is not leadership; it's leakage. Builders who confuse transparency with emotional dumping destabilize their teams. They mistake honesty for immediacy, believing that every passing fear or unresolved tension must be announced. But unprocessed emotion, when projected outward, does not build trust. It burdens others with the weight of uncertainty without offering the frame to hold it.

At the same time, guardedness can become its own pathology. Some leaders, afraid of being misinterpreted or misquoted, default to silence. They shroud even basic truths in confidentiality. They assume that keeping others in the dark is the safest way to maintain control. But this instinct, though common, breeds suspicion. And over time, it fractures the relational bonds that any enduring structure depends on.

The discipline of guarded openness lies between these two errors. It asks the builder to constantly assess what must be revealed for the sake of coherence; and what must be held, for now, in order to protect timing, context, or people. It requires deep internal clarity. You cannot be selectively transparent unless you've done the work to know your own motivations. If the withholding is coming from fear, pride, or manipulation, it will show. But if it is grounded in protection, not control; in care, not concealment; then silence can serve the mission without undermining it.

Guarded openness also means giving shape to the things you cannot yet share. When timelines shift, when decisions are in flux, when there is complexity behind the curtain; it is still possible to narrate that tension without pretending it isn't there. Transparency doesn't always require specifics. Sometimes it simply requires acknowledgement.

The builder who masters this balance builds trust not through volume, but through precision. Their transparency is not reactive. It is principled. Their team doesn't need every answer, but they learn to trust that when it matters, they won't be left in the dark.

The Costs of Concealment

Concealment rarely announces itself as danger. More often, it presents as pragmatism; a quiet deferral of explanation, a decision to wait, to protect, to simplify. In the moment, it feels efficient. But what is hidden today does not stay neutral. It accumulates weight, distorts relationships, and alters the culture beneath the surface. The cost of concealment is rarely visible on the balance sheet, but it always shows up in the foundation.

Teams begin to sense what is being left unsaid long before they can name it. They notice inconsistencies in message. They detect shifts in energy. They feel gaps between action and explanation. Over time, those patterns create an undercurrent of uncertainty. People begin to fill in the blanks with their own stories. Mistrust grows in the vacuum. Decisions start to feel less principled and more political. And soon, what was once a unified structure begins to fragment.

Leadership that relies on concealment slowly hollows itself out. It loses the moral authority that transparency earns. Influence becomes positional rather than principled. People begin to comply rather than commit. The culture shifts from ownership to self-preservation. Even well-meaning concealment corrodes over time;

not because of malice, but because of misalignment. When the inside and outside of a company no longer match, the tension is felt everywhere.

There is also the personal cost. Builders who default to concealment often become isolated. They carry the burden of unspoken decisions. They become surrounded not by partners, but by executors; people trained to implement, not to think. And without feedback, without shared reasoning, the builder becomes trapped in their own design. What started as a way to stay in control becomes a barrier to clarity, agility, and evolution.

None of this is to suggest that everything must be revealed at once. But it is to say that concealment, when used as a pattern rather than a practice of discernment, always exacts a price. It weakens the connective tissue of the team. It signals that truth is conditional. And it teaches others that safety lies in silence, not in shared understanding.

The enduring builder refuses to normalize this. They recognize that transparency is not about ease; it is about integrity. They choose to speak when it would be simpler to hide. Not to be praised for honesty, but to build a structure that can hold real weight. Because in the end, what we hide to preserve, we often lose anyway.

Transparency and the Strength of Teams

A team becomes strong not by shielding itself from complexity, but by being invited into clarity. Strength is not forged in silence; it emerges when people understand the shape of the work, the stakes of their choices, and the reasons behind the path they are walking together. Transparency, when practiced with consistency and care, becomes the force that binds a team in shared purpose. It removes the guesswork. It deepens mutual respect. It reinforces the truth that alignment is not demanded; it is earned.

Many leaders misunderstand transparency as a risk to authority. They fear that by revealing uncertainty or trade-offs, they will lose control. But in reality, transparent environments do not weaken leadership; they distribute intelligence. Teams that are routinely trusted with context become sharper. They ask better questions. They anticipate needs. They understand where they fit into the broader movement of the whole. And in times of pressure, they adapt more fluidly because they are not waiting for permission; they are already oriented.

Transparency also shapes how teams hold each other. When openness is modeled at the top, it trickles into how colleagues communicate. Accountability becomes cultural, not just procedural. Feedback is shared earlier, not just when something breaks. There is less posturing and more substance. People stop managing optics and start managing outcomes. And most critically, trust compounds; not just in the leader, but in one another.

This kind of culture does not happen by accident. It is built through thousands of small acts: context shared before it's demanded, mistakes acknowledged without excuse, intentions clarified before they are misinterpreted. The leader's job is not to create perfect transparency, but to ensure the conditions for it exist. That means creating forums for information to flow. It means setting a tone where questions are welcome and not punished. It means reinforcing that silence is not safety, and that withholding is not power.

Strong teams are not the product of strong personalities; they are the product of transparent environments. When people understand why things are the way they are, they stop bracing for impact. They stop building defensive postures. And they start leaning into the work itself; with steadiness, with confidence, and with a sense that they are part of something coherent and real.

In the end, transparency is not just a leadership trait; it is a cultural transmission device. It teaches the team how to think, how to act, and how to move through difficulty without splintering. It is not a tactic. It is strength.

Illumination as Legacy

The mark of a lasting builder is not the size of what they constructed, but the clarity they left behind. When we speak of legacy, we often think of tangible things; companies, systems, capital, scale. But what remains long after a founder is gone is something quieter, less measurable: the degree to which others can still see clearly because of how they once led. Illumination; consistent, disciplined, principled; is the most durable form of impact.

A leader who builds with light makes it easier for others to carry on. Their reasoning is accessible. Their values are evident. Their decisions are intelligible in hindsight, not mysterious. They leave behind not just what they built, but how they built it. And that *how* becomes the culture's inheritance. Teams can carry forward that clarity even after the original voice is no longer in the room.

Builders who rely on opacity; who centralize insight, who guard rationale, who shield their thinking; may preserve control in the short term, but they orphan their organizations in the long run. Without illumination, succession becomes brittle. Without context, principles degrade into dogma. What was once coherent begins to drift because no one truly understood its inner shape.

Illumination requires effort. It means documenting not just outcomes, but the architecture of thought behind them. It means inviting others into decisions before they are final. It means codifying the ethos of the structure so that the people within it are shaped by more than their tasks. This is not about legacy as ego; it's about continuity. A system illuminated from the inside does not depend on memory to survive. It carries its principles forward because those principles are embedded in how people speak, act, and decide.

And illumination does more than preserve; it inspires. A team that knows *why* something is done can evolve that *why* as conditions change. They are not frozen in reverence. They are equipped to adapt without losing the thread. That is the true power of a well-lit structure: it endures *and* it evolves. It knows how to honor its source without becoming trapped by it.

The legacy of illumination is not noise. It is not spectacle. It is not a carefully curated personal brand. It is the quiet strength of having made things clearer; for others, for the culture, and for the work to go on long after your hand is no longer on the helm.

Closing Meditation

Light is not an aesthetic. It is a discipline.
It is what remains when the noise has receded; when urgency fades, when control is no longer possible, when structure must stand on its own. Transparency, practiced with steadiness and discernment, is not a tactic for smoother communication. It is the architecture of trust. It is the soul of continuity.

To build with light is to accept that not all clarity is comfortable. It means naming truths before they are safe. It means allowing others to see not just your intent, but your process; your logic, your boundaries, your evolution. It means rejecting the myth that leadership must be shrouded in mystique. And it means trusting that people, when offered real context, will rise to meet it.

Opaque systems may look efficient. They may move faster in the short term. But they do not scale coherence. They do not foster resilience. And they do not survive disruption well; because no one knows how to think when they're gone. The systems that last, the teams that hold, the legacies that breathe; are those built in light.

The mature builder understands this. They do not equate transparency with weakness. They do not confuse silence with strength. They illuminate; not to be seen, but so others can see. They create with the awareness that what is unclear today will become unstable tomorrow. And they commit, over and over again, to clarity; not as performance, but as a sacred form of service.

In the end, what we illuminate outlives us.
It guides without demanding.
It teaches without shouting.
And it proves, long after we are gone, that leadership was never

about having all the answers;
only about refusing to hide the ones that mattered.

Chapter 10

Stewardship of Scale: Growing Without Eclipsing Purpose

The Myth of Scale as Success

The modern myth equates size with success. Bigger is presumed to be better, louder is mistaken for stronger, and scale is treated as evidence of permanence. But size does not mean resilience. It does not imply clarity. It does not guarantee endurance. Scale can project the image of security while hiding the rot beneath the surface. And in many enterprises, it does just that; masking the fragility that grows in parallel with unchecked expansion.

The temptation to chase scale is rooted in vanity. It flatters the ego of the builder, offering the illusion that reach equates to relevance. But what scale actually does is amplify what is already true. If the foundations are solid; clear culture, coherent mission, principled leadership; then growth can reveal that strength. But if the structure is hollow, expansion only exposes that weakness more dramatically. Scale is not a force of transformation. It is a magnifier.

Many enterprises become large before they become wise. Their visibility outpaces their maturity. Their audience grows faster than their internal cohesion. What looks like triumph from a distance is often a fragile lattice up close; one stressor away from collapse. What appears to be a monolith may, in truth, be brittle. Under pressure, it fractures not because of its size, but because its size outpaced its stewardship.

True strength, then, is not measured in magnitude but in coherence. The question is not how far something has spread, but whether its essence holds under strain. An organization ten times the size of its former self but devoid of its founding discipline is not stronger. It is merely more vulnerable in more directions.

The serious builder refuses to chase growth for its own sake. They know that expansion without stewardship is not progress; it is drift. Growth without clarity corrodes mission. Scale without design accelerates failure. What matters is not the volume of what is built, but the integrity of its architecture. The builder who forgets this may gain applause but will lose endurance. The one who remembers will grow deliberately, not recklessly. Slowly, not loudly. With purpose, not performance.

In the end, the question is not how much you built. It is how deeply it held when stretched.

Growth as a Test of Discipline

Growth does not create strength; it reveals the presence or absence of discipline. The more something expands, the more pressure it exerts on the systems, people, and values that once held it together. In this way, scale is not an accomplishment but a test. It is the mirror that exposes whether the structure was built with foresight or simply fueled by momentum.

Many builders confuse acceleration with mastery. They treat growth as proof of correctness, not realizing that expansion often conceals the very flaws that will one day cause collapse. Unrefined decision-making, brittle culture, vague principles; these do not disappear at scale. They multiply. Growth magnifies the unexamined. It intensifies dissonance. And without disciplined oversight, the builder becomes a passenger in a vehicle they no longer control.

Discipline at scale looks different than discipline at the beginning. In the early days, discipline is scrappy; it means holding a vision when others don't see it. Later, it becomes more complex: preserving focus amid competing demands, enforcing boundaries without becoming rigid, and resisting the drift toward chasing every available opportunity. The larger the enterprise becomes, the more tempting it is to dilute the original standard for the sake of speed, consensus, or ease. Discipline resists this. It remembers the reason for building, and it governs accordingly.

Growth that is not governed becomes chaotic. Momentum, once a gift, begins to pull the enterprise in directions it never intended to go. Systems become bloated. Communication grows noisy. Leadership becomes reactive. In the absence of discipline, growth turns from a blessing into a burden that deforms the very thing it was meant to advance.

This is why the builder must grow slowly, even when the market rewards speed. They must scale only what is ready to be scaled, not what is currently popular. They must reinforce what holds, rather than decorate what dazzles. And above all, they must refuse to let growth itself become the goal. Scale is only meaningful when it preserves, and even strengthens, the integrity of the original design.

The discipline of scale is not about perfection; it is about protection. Not protection from change, but from drift. The serious builder treats growth not as a celebration, but as a responsibility. Every new layer adds complexity. Every new reach tests coherence. Every step forward must be matched by the strength to hold what has been built.

The Builder as Steward, Not Owner

Ownership is a seductive idea. It offers the illusion of control, of permanence, of authorship over what has been built. But at scale, the mindset of ownership becomes dangerous. It fosters possessiveness instead of perspective. It narrows vision. It converts leadership into dominion. And in doing so, it erodes the very clarity that once made the builder effective. The shift that must occur is subtle but essential: the builder must become a steward, not a sovereign.

Stewardship is not weakness. It is strength governed by humility. To steward something is to understand that it does not belong to you, even if you created it. It means recognizing that the purpose of the enterprise exceeds your own preferences, and that the people, systems, and ideas within it deserve protection and care; not manipulation. The steward does not tighten their grip as things grow.

They widen their awareness. They ask not "What do I want?" but "What does this structure need to endure?"

Growth makes this shift more urgent. As the enterprise expands, the leader's role must evolve. What was once a founder's domain becomes a shared ecosystem. Control becomes decentralized. Decisions multiply. And without a stewardship mindset, the builder can fall into panic; trying to reassert dominance through micromanagement, secrecy, or over-optimization. But none of these tactics preserve the mission. They only distort it.

Stewardship is about protecting the purpose, not clinging to power. It is the discipline of ensuring that scale does not eclipse clarity. The steward knows they cannot be everywhere. But they can build a culture that moves in alignment even in their absence. They can model the values that shape how decisions are made at every level. And they can relinquish control without abandoning responsibility.

This is not about self-erasure. It is about identity that transcends ego. The builder's role at scale is no longer to do everything; but to ensure that everything remains connected to the original intention. That requires vigilance, but also trust. Authority, but without possessiveness. Vision, without vanity.

To steward is to walk with reverence. To know that what has been built is temporary, and that its strength lies in how well it can be carried forward by others. The enduring builder is not remembered for how tightly they held the reins; but for how carefully they protected the reason it all existed in the first place.

Maintaining Coherence as You Grow

Growth is not inherently destabilizing. But without design, it almost always leads to drift. The more a structure expands, the greater the risk that its essence becomes diluted; its purpose scattered, its language blurred, its core distorted by distance from the original vision. What was once a unified act of building becomes fragmented across teams, functions, and geographies. The mission remains printed on the wall, but it is no longer alive in the decisions being made. Coherence dissolves quietly; until suddenly, it is gone.

Maintaining coherence is not a matter of repeating slogans or enforcing loyalty. It is a deeper form of continuity. It means that as the enterprise grows, it retains a felt sense of why it exists. Its choices remain tethered to its original promise. Its people speak a shared internal language. Its systems reinforce values rather than distract from them. Coherence is what makes a ten-person company feel the same in spirit when it becomes a hundred; or a thousand; not identical, but aligned.

The builder's task is not to prevent change, but to preserve signal. Coherence is not about resisting adaptation. It is about ensuring that as the structure changes shape, its center remains intact. That means translating purpose into systems, rituals, and hiring. It means training new leaders not just in how to operate, but in how to think. It means saying no to growth that would stretch the enterprise into incoherence, even when the numbers say yes.

There will always be pressure to expand faster than clarity allows. Markets reward scale. Stakeholders push for speed. But the builder must resist the seduction of visibility at the cost of internal truth. To scale without coherence is to build noise into the system. It may look impressive, but it will not last. The fractures will show; first in small misalignments, then in cultural erosion, then in collapse.

Coherence is not maintained by accident. It requires constant tending. The serious builder makes this part of the architecture. They do not assume alignment will persist; they build mechanisms to protect it. They reinforce meaning at every layer. And they are willing to contract if growth threatens to erase the core.

To grow without losing yourself is rare. To lead others into scale without diluting what made the work sacred in the first place is rarer still. But it is possible. And it begins by treating coherence not as a byproduct, but as a condition for everything else.

Cultural Integrity at Scale

Culture is not what you say; it's what you permit. It's what people learn to expect from each other in moments of tension, uncertainty, and speed. In small organizations, culture often survives on proximity: values are modeled directly, behaviors are corrected in real time, and alignment is reinforced through daily contact. But at scale, proximity fades. The founder's presence becomes diffused. Assumptions replace conversation. And if culture is not intentionally preserved, it begins to warp under the weight of growth.

Cultural integrity means preserving not just the mood of a company, but its ethics, its way of working, and its treatment of people. It is the sum of the unspoken rules that shape how decisions get made. When left unguarded, scale introduces mutations; new layers of bureaucracy, power dynamics, and competing agendas that quietly pull the culture away from its center. This drift rarely announces itself. It appears subtly, in how feedback is handled, how priorities shift, and how quickly people learn to keep their heads down instead of speaking the truth.

The serious builder recognizes this early. They understand that culture is not a vibe; it is a discipline. It requires design. It must be codified, reinforced, and modeled, especially when the company grows faster than new hires can be truly immersed in its ethos. Leaders at every level must be taught to carry the culture forward; not through slogans, but through decisions. Every promotion, every firing, every trade-off is a cultural signal. If those signals become inconsistent, no amount of narrative can compensate for what people experience.

Cultural integrity also demands that the builder confront the temptation to tolerate misalignment in exchange for performance. High output from someone who violates core principles may serve short-term goals, but it poisons the culture in the long run. One unaddressed contradiction becomes permission for a hundred more. Growth puts pressure on values; but that pressure is the test, not the excuse.

To preserve culture at scale, the builder must be relentless in defining what matters; and ruthless in protecting it. That doesn't mean resisting change. It means curating change. Culture must evolve, but it must evolve coherently. It must stay anchored in the original commitments, even as the structure stretches.

In the end, cultural integrity is what ensures that growth is not merely an expansion of surface area, but a deepening of character. It is what allows an organization to grow not just in reach, but in substance. Without it, the structure may rise; but it will always be at risk of collapsing under the weight of what it abandoned along the way.

Scaling Systems Without Scaling Complexity

As an organization grows, it becomes tempting to meet complexity with more complexity; more layers, more processes, more tools, more policies. But systems that scale well do not become heavier. They become sharper. They expand in precision, not in bureaucracy. They carry more weight with less friction. The mature builder understands that scaling systems is not about adding volume; it is about distilling function.

Complexity, left unmanaged, becomes a tax on momentum. Every extra layer slows decision-making. Every new tool demands maintenance. Every added process introduces the risk of misalignment. Over time, the very systems designed to enable growth begin to strangle it. What once served clarity now serves confusion. What once enabled action now enforces hesitation. This is how companies lose their edge; not from external threat, but from internal drag.

To scale effectively, the builder must learn to simplify without weakening. That begins with knowing what the system is meant to protect. Not all friction is bad; some rules safeguard integrity. But many systems grow for the wrong reasons: to protect egos, to avoid discomfort, to preserve appearances. The serious builder resists this. They ask: Does this system clarify or obscure? Does it empower or obstruct? Does it align with the culture, or distract from it?

Scaling systems well requires a mindset of subtraction. It asks the builder to remove what no longer serves, to streamline what has become bloated, and to resist the comfort of overengineering. It means choosing principles over preferences, function over flash. A strong system is one that can be explained simply and used instinctively. If people need a manual to navigate basic operations, the system has failed.

Technology often accelerates this problem. Tools meant to simplify communication can instead fragment it. Platforms designed for insight can flood teams with noise. Automation, when applied without clarity, doesn't scale intelligence; it scales inertia. The solution is not to resist tools, but to wield them with discipline. Systems must serve the mission; not become the mission.

In scaling, the builder must remember that elegance is strength. A clean, coherent system outperforms a sophisticated but bloated one every time. Precision, not volume, is what carries momentum through growth. And restraint; not accumulation; is what ensures the structure remains agile, responsive, and durable.

Growth that outpaces system design leads to collapse. But system design that honors simplicity; held with care, adjusted with purpose; allows the enterprise to grow with grace, not weight.

The Temptations of Growth

Growth seduces. It offers the thrill of momentum, the validation of numbers, the illusion of arrival. It flatters the builder into believing that expansion is always progress, that more is always better, and that scale is its own justification. But growth is not neutral. It comes with temptations that, if unexamined, will distort the enterprise and hollow the mission it was meant to serve.

The first temptation is to equate visibility with value. As the organization gains attention, it becomes easy to mistake applause for alignment. Public perception becomes a metric. Recognition replaces reflection. The builder, once grounded in purpose, begins to chase scale not as a means, but as an end. They expand into markets they don't understand, chase partnerships that dilute the brand, and stretch the team beyond its center of gravity; all in service of staying visible.

Then comes the temptation of vanity metrics. Numbers that look impressive but say nothing about health. User counts, revenue spikes, valuation increases; these become substitutes for real indicators of coherence, sustainability, and cultural integrity. Leaders start managing the optics rather than the operations. Teams become reactive. Goals become shallow. And before long, the company is growing in every direction except inward.

Another lure is the comfort of momentum itself. When things move quickly, reflection feels inefficient. But pace without pause is not mastery; it is drift. Builders begin to accept success on momentum's terms. They tolerate mediocrity in exchange for speed. They stop asking the harder questions: Does this expansion serve the mission? Is this product aligned with our values? Are we still recognizable to ourselves?

Perhaps the most dangerous temptation is to believe that growth grants immunity; that the rules of discipline no longer apply, that what once required vigilance can now be assumed. But scale does not erase risk; it magnifies it. What goes unexamined at ten people becomes a crisis at a hundred. What is tolerated in one department becomes normalized across the culture.

Resisting the temptations of growth requires anchoring. The builder must return, again and again, to the founding questions: Why are we doing this? What must remain true no matter how large we become? What are we unwilling to trade for more?

The world rewards expansion. But the structure rewards integrity. The builder who stays grounded in purpose; who sees through the noise of growth and chooses clarity over conquest; will build something not just big, but worthy.

Stewardship of People Through Growth

As the enterprise expands, it's not just systems and structures that must evolve; it's people. And the greatest responsibility a builder holds is not simply to grow the business, but to grow those within it. Scaling an organization without scaling its people is a betrayal of stewardship. It breeds disconnection, resentment, and waste. Growth, done well, develops new stewards. Growth, done poorly, leaves people behind.

In the early stages, leadership is often intimate. Builders know their teams personally. Communication is direct. Feedback is fluid. But as the structure widens, that intimacy thins. Layers form. Relationships shift. What once worked informally now needs intentional design. If the builder fails to tend to the development of others, they find themselves surrounded by executors instead of leaders; people who carry out orders but cannot carry the mission forward.

Stewardship of people begins with recognition: not everyone grows at the same pace, but everyone deserves the chance to grow. It means identifying potential early, not just in performance but in alignment; those who think with the culture's ethos, who hold the mission with care, who lead without needing credit. These are the next stewards, and they must be cultivated deliberately. That means training not just in tasks, but in judgment. Not just in roles, but in responsibilities.

As growth continues, the pressure to prioritize efficiency can override the commitment to development. Hiring becomes transactional. Onboarding becomes mechanical. Feedback loops shrink. But the builder who is serious about scale resists this drift. They understand that investing in people is not a distraction from growth; it is the only way to sustain it. The culture must not only include room for learning; it must demand it.

This is also a test of the builder's ego. As the organization matures, leadership must be distributed. Others will make decisions. Others will carry the vision into places the founder will never see. The question is not whether they will get it perfect; but whether they will get it true. The builder must release the need for control and replace it with a trust in the culture they've shaped. That trust must be earned, not assumed.

True stewardship of people means preparing them to operate with autonomy, with discernment, and with integrity. It means creating leaders who do not mimic the founder, but who extend the founder's values into new domains. It is the long game. And it is the only game that matters when the goal is to build something that lasts beyond the builder's shadow.

Sustainable Expansion: Knowing When to Stop

Few forces are more difficult to resist than the momentum of success. Once growth begins, it seems to justify itself. Each new market, product, or opportunity appears as an obligation; something that must be pursued, simply because it can be. But sustainable expansion is not about how far you can go. It is about knowing when further is no longer better. The builder must be able to stop; not from exhaustion, but from discernment.

Endurance requires restraint. Just as the body cannot inhale forever, an enterprise cannot expand infinitely without losing form. Growth has natural limits; cultural, operational, moral. When those limits are ignored, the structure begins to deform. The team becomes stretched, the systems overburdened, the mission diluted. What once felt focused now feels scattered. And the builder, once energized by creation, becomes consumed by containment.

Stopping; or choosing not to grow further; is not an act of failure. It is an act of stewardship. It means the builder has seen clearly the difference between ambition and appetite. They understand that more reach does not equal more relevance. That another product line, another office, another partnership is not necessarily additive. It may in fact be subtractive; pulling energy, time, and attention away from what truly matters.

The pressure to ignore this is constant. Investors want scale. Markets reward expansion. Teams seek opportunity. And the builder's own ego may crave continued forward motion. But the serious builder must weigh each step against the integrity of the whole. They must ask: Does this serve the structure? Does this preserve our coherence? Does this grow our impact or just our surface area?

There is wisdom in knowing where to stop; not because the path ahead is impassable, but because the current terrain is sufficient. There is wisdom in refining rather than inflating, in deepening rather than extending. The builder who can pause; who can say "this is enough"; builds something that can breathe.

Sustainable expansion is not the absence of growth. It is the presence of wisdom. It is the clarity to know what should grow, and what must be held as it is. It is the rare courage to prioritize longevity over leverage, and mission over movement.

In the end, knowing when to stop is not about halting ambition. It is about anchoring it. Growth becomes meaningful only when it honors the capacity of what has been built; and the purpose it was built to serve.

Closing Meditation

Growth is not a reward. It is a responsibility. It does not elevate the builder; it tests them. It asks whether the clarity that birthed the structure can hold under pressure. Whether the purpose that once guided early decisions can survive the allure of acceleration. Whether the culture that once moved in unison can still breathe in a larger body. The question is not how high the structure stands, but how deeply its foundations remain intact as it rises.

To build at scale is not to command more. It is to protect more; more people, more complexity, more meaning. Scale demands vigilance. It demands refusal. It demands the capacity to pause expansion in order to preserve coherence. The builder who forgets this chases magnitude and loses the mission. The builder who remembers it becomes something rarer: a steward of form, not just force.

This is the spiritual posture of the mature entrepreneur; not domination, not conquest, but care. To tend what grows without distorting it. To distribute leadership without diluting responsibility. To cultivate culture without ossifying it. And above all, to know that stopping is not a failure of ambition, but a sign of wisdom.

In a world that worships scale, the real discipline is to build something that grows only as far as it can remain true. That discipline is what makes expansion sacred; not because it glorifies the builder, but because it dignifies the work. It ensures that growth becomes not a monument to ego, but a vessel of purpose.

Let growth come; but let it come with coherence. Let it stretch; but not splinter. Let it move; but always from a place of rootedness. Because when we scale with stewardship, we do not just build bigger; we build longer. We build quieter. And we build with the kind of strength that does not demand to be seen, only to endure.

Chapter 11

Scars as Credentials: Wisdom Through Wounding

The Myth of Unbroken Success

The stories we are sold about success are almost always clean. They shine. They ascend. They resolve neatly, free of blemish or blood. And yet anyone who has built seriously knows: these are not stories of reality. They are carefully edited performances, sold to audiences who prefer illusion over instruction.

The true builder understands that uninterrupted triumph is not the norm; it is a myth. Worse, it is a dangerous myth. Because it conditions founders, creators, and entrepreneurs to believe that any disruption, any wound, any failure is evidence of deficiency rather than the proof of pursuit. It breeds shame in the face of the inevitable. It causes silence where there should be reflection. And it encourages a shallow version of success that crumbles under real weight.

The longer one stays in the act of building, the more scars they collect; not as symbols of recklessness, but as evidence of contact with the real. Collapse, missteps, losses; these are not signs of weakness. They are the contour lines of a terrain that only the committed cross. The builder who has not been broken has either not risked enough, or not lasted long enough to matter.

Wounds, therefore, are not anomalies in the arc of building. They are the arc. They shape the spine of serious experience. They signal not a deviation from the path; but the very moment the path becomes real.

Wounds as a Rite of Passage

In every serious path of mastery, there comes a moment when something breaks; something you built, something you believed, something you thought would hold. That break is not a failure in the journey; it is the initiation into it. The wound is not incidental to the work. It *is* the work.

To endure a real wound in the act of building is to pass through a threshold. Before it, you are rehearsing; testing ideas, playing with frameworks, gathering praise or rejection without full consequence. After it, you know what the stakes are. You've paid something real. You've crossed from curiosity to conviction.

But not all wounds are created equal. An injury is still open, still raw, still unintegrated. It consumes energy and narrows perspective. A scar, by contrast, is closed. It has been processed. It has taught. The builder who carries scars rather than injuries is not untouched; they are changed. Not bitter, but clear. Not hardened, but disciplined.

The rite of passage occurs in the integration. Not merely being hurt, but learning what the hurt revealed. Not simply surviving collapse, but mining the collapse for truth. The builders who emerge with scars; not just losses; are those who made meaning out of pain. They found shape within destruction. They re-entered the act of building not as idealists, but as initiates.

This is not to glorify suffering. It is to recognize that seriousness has a price. To build anything of consequence is to eventually reach a point where belief is tested, systems fail, and illusions fall away. That point is not the end. It is the door.

Only those who pass through it; not around it; become the kind of builders who last.

What Scars Teach That Success Cannot

Success, for all its rewards, teaches incompletely. It can affirm competence, validate decisions, and strengthen morale. But it rarely teaches depth. It rarely provokes real reflection. Success is seductive precisely because it doesn't demand examination. It allows builders to coast on momentum, to confuse fortune with foresight, and to mistake favorable conditions for personal mastery.

Scars teach what success conceals. They illuminate fault lines. They expose the limits of strategy, the blind spots of character, the fragility of plans. When something breaks; truly breaks; it forces a confrontation with reality that no win ever will. And it is only in that confrontation that a builder begins to know themselves. Not their persona, not their pitch, but their actual substance.

Scars mark the moments where theory failed and reality intervened. They are not abstract lessons. They are memories embedded in the body; in how one makes decisions, how one paces a team, how one listens more carefully the second time around. They convert confidence into caution, and caution into wisdom. They replace the arrogance of certainty with the discipline of attention.

More than anything, scars reveal what endures. When the false narratives collapse, when the metrics stop growing, when the crowd disperses; what remains? What values held? What people stayed? What part of you didn't shatter under pressure? Those are the answers only scars can give. Not because they're sentimental, but because they're earned.

A builder marked by success alone is incomplete. But a builder marked by scars; scarred and still standing, scarred and still building; carries a different kind of authority. Not louder, but quieter. Not performative, but grounded. They do not preach. They witness.

And in that witnessing, they carry forward a truth that others can recognize, even if it's never spoken: I have been there. I have lost. I have learned. And I am still here.

Pain as the Teacher Success Conceals

Pain does what praise cannot. It clarifies. It purifies. It strips away the excess until only what matters remains. While success multiplies options, pain forces choices. It reveals which convictions are real and which were merely convenient. It shows what the builder can live without; and what they can't.

Success often conceals weak foundations. Momentum can obscure fragility. Popularity can excuse incoherence. Teams may hold together under prosperity, but their true character is only revealed under pressure. Pain interrupts the illusion. It disorients just long enough to expose the fault lines. And in doing so, it offers a kind of brutal mercy: the chance to rebuild on something true.

But pain doesn't automatically teach. It only becomes teacher when the builder chooses to learn. There are those who run from it; who mask it, numb it, blame others for it, or become consumed by it. They miss the lesson. They confuse being wounded with being wronged. And they often return to building too quickly, eager to recover momentum without integrating meaning.

The serious builder does something else. They stay with the discomfort. They trace the pain to its origin. They ask harder questions: Where did I drift? What did I ignore? What did I protect that should've been dismantled? And what did I sacrifice that I should've held sacred?

It's in these moments that the builder's ambition is refined. No longer driven by projection or pressure, they return to purpose. Pain becomes the crucible; not just of better systems or sharper strategy, but of deeper alignment. It creates a kind of negative clarity; what must never happen again, what must never be compromised, what the builder is finally ready to name and face.

Success has its uses. But only pain reveals what success hides. It is not a punishment. It is an invitation; to integrity, to depth, to a form of leadership that is less about control and more about consequence.

The builder who accepts that invitation becomes something else entirely. Not just experienced, but wise.

The Difference Between Hurt and Harm

Not all pain is destructive. Some wounds are necessary. Some discomforts are part of the process of growth, discipline, and transformation. The key is learning to distinguish between *hurt* and *harm*; between the friction that refines and the force that fractures.

Hurt is what happens when something real is at stake. It's the strain of taking responsibility, the sting of hard feedback, the exhaustion of doing things the right way when shortcuts abound. It's the pain of care; of being invested, of choosing integrity even when it costs. Hurt signals friction with reality, but it doesn't erode the self. In fact, when held correctly, it strengthens it.

Harm is different. Harm degrades. It confuses. It twists what is valuable into something fearful or numb. It disconnects builders from their sense of purpose and from each other. Harm results from systems that reward denial, from leadership that operates in manipulation or neglect, from cultures that punish honesty. Where hurt is friction, harm is erosion. Where hurt teaches, harm silences.

For the builder, recognizing this distinction is crucial. There will be seasons of difficulty where the work is heavy and the risk is real; but not all of it is harmful. What matters is how the pain interacts with purpose. If the struggle leads to clarity, depth, and resilience, it is a wound worth bearing. If the struggle leaves only confusion, depletion, and bitterness, it must be addressed, not endured.

This also applies inward. Builders must be careful not to romanticize hurt, nor normalize harm. Enduring doesn't mean ignoring. Resilience isn't about tolerating the intolerable. There is a line between being tested and being damaged; and part of wisdom is learning when to stay in the fire, and when to walk away.

Many don't make the distinction soon enough. They glorify pain as proof of seriousness and wear their injuries as credentials, never realizing they've internalized harm as identity. They grow protective, cynical, and rigid. But the mature builder moves differently. They process hurt without becoming hard. They acknowledge harm and make different choices. They carry scars, yes; but not open wounds.

To build well over time, this discernment is essential. It allows the builder to accept necessary pain without becoming a martyr to it. It allows them to lead others with compassion, rather than projection. And it ensures that their own endurance is not bought at the cost of their inner coherence.

Wounded Builders and Their Quiet Strength

Builders who have suffered do not build the same way twice. The second time is quieter. Slower. More deliberate. They no longer confuse noise with momentum or applause with alignment. They've seen what breaks when things are rushed. They've learned what matters after everything that didn't has been stripped away.

The wounded builder carries a kind of strength that's easy to miss. It isn't charismatic. It doesn't flash. It isn't the loudest voice in the room. But it's the one that holds when the room begins to shake. Their strength isn't in domination; it's in discipline. It's the patience to say no when others are racing forward. It's the calm to withstand ambiguity without collapsing into panic. It's the clarity to make decisions that hold up years later, not just for the next quarter.

This quiet strength is earned. Not gifted, not studied, but *earned*; through collapse, repair, and return. Through the painful process of integrating lessons that came at high cost. The wounded builder no longer chases every opportunity. They curate. They protect. They understand that endurance requires not just energy, but wisdom. And wisdom is not gained through reading; it is carved through experience.

Such builders are also more compassionate. They've seen how easy it is to fall out of alignment, how quickly clarity can slip under pressure. They don't mistake weakness for incompetence, nor struggle for failure. They recognize the signals others miss. And because they've been there, they lead differently. With fewer commands. With more presence. With less need to be seen, and more focus on what must be done.

This doesn't mean they've become timid. It means they've become serious. They know what they're risking. They know what collapse costs. And so when they choose to build again, it is not out of naïveté or hunger for validation. It is out of conviction; rooted, grounded, and clean.

The quiet strength of the wounded builder isn't measured in charisma or dominance. It's measured in how much noise they can stand without reacting. How much pressure they can absorb without passing it on. How much truth they can hold without flinching.

And when they speak, it matters. Not because they command authority; but because they've walked through fire and chosen to stay human.

The Courage to Build Again

To build something is brave. But to build again; after collapse, after loss, after humiliation; that requires a different kind of courage. It's not the courage of momentum. It's the courage of memory. Of returning to the work not with the energy of innocence, but with the gravity of experience. Many walk away after their first fall. Some return too quickly, trying to erase the past with a louder future. Few pause long enough to integrate, then build again; not out of compulsion, but out of clarity.

Starting over after deep failure forces a reckoning. The world may forget, but the builder remembers. The risks, the cracks, the cost of every misstep. And with that memory comes hesitation; not weakness, but wisdom. The second time around, things move slower. Caution replaces urgency. Precision replaces noise. There is no appetite for the chaos that once passed for ambition.

But hesitation alone is not enough. Rebuilding also demands re-commitment. It asks whether the builder still believes; still believes in the work, in their ability to carry it, in the possibility of making something worth enduring. That belief doesn't come cheap the second time. It must be re-earned, step by deliberate step. And that's what makes this return sacred. It's not about rebounding; it's about re-entering with eyes open.

The builder who has the courage to start again carries a different center of gravity. They're no longer building to prove something. They're building because the work is true. They're no longer obsessed with outcomes. They're devoted to process. There's less noise, fewer performances, and a deeper intimacy with reality.

This kind of courage doesn't posture. It doesn't need slogans. It shows itself in steady hands, in sharp boundaries, in quiet refusals. The courage to build again means saying yes to risk; not blindly, but knowingly. It means holding the memory of collapse without letting it paralyze the future. It means choosing to return, not because it's safe, but because it's right.

Few endure the first fall. Fewer still endure the second ascent. But those who do; who rebuild without bitterness, without bravado; become the builders others look to in crisis. Not for rescue, but for example. They've proven what matters: not how high you climb, but how cleanly you return.

The Witness of Scars

Scars are silent witnesses. They don't speak, but they signal. They carry stories too layered for quick telling; stories of collapse, recovery, endurance. To those who know how to read them, they offer credibility that no résumé or reputation can match. Scars don't boast. They don't market. But they command attention because they imply survival; and not just of any hardship, but of the kind that reshapes a person without undoing them.

There is a particular trust that forms in the presence of someone visibly marked by experience. It's not just that they've failed. It's that they've failed and returned without bitterness. That they've faced the chaos, integrated the damage, and chosen not to become cynical. That they still believe in what they're doing; not out of naivety, but because they've paid enough to know what's worth continuing.

In leadership, this is especially potent. Teams don't just need inspiration; they need to know that when pressure mounts, when the unexpected strikes, when momentum breaks, the person at the helm won't unravel. They need to see someone who's bled before and doesn't panic at the first sign of fracture. Scars, in this way, offer calm. They communicate resilience without needing to be declared. They say: *I've stood where it's dark. I know the way through.*

But this witness is not automatic. It depends on how the scar was earned; and how it was integrated. Those who hide their scars deny others the benefit of their experience. Those who wear them as weapons, demanding recognition, turn survival into performance. The serious builder does neither. They carry their scars with dignity. Quietly. With precision. They let the lessons shape them, not showcase them.

What makes scars powerful is not that they are visible, but that they are *true*. They point to places where the builder was broken open; and chose to rebuild with clarity, not concealment. They mark moments where identity was tested, stripped, refined. And for others navigating their own wounds, these scars serve as unspoken permission to keep going. To recover without shame. To grow without pretending it was painless.

The builder who carries scars well becomes more than a leader. They become a reference point; for what survival can look like without collapse of character, and what wisdom feels like when it has truly been lived.

From Injury to Integrity

Every injury carries a choice: remain damaged, or become disciplined. Some wounds linger because the builder never paused long enough to understand them. They stayed open; raw, reactive, festering beneath momentum or masked by bravado. But injury, when met with intention, can become something else entirely. It can become integration. And over time, integration becomes integrity.

The path from injury to integrity is not linear. It doesn't begin with optimism. It begins with rupture; something broke: a plan, a partnership, a self-perception. In that aftermath, the temptation is to patch things quickly, to move on without reflection. But what's unexamined becomes repeated. And what's repeated becomes a pattern, not a lesson. Builders who fail to convert injury into insight often find themselves reliving the same collapse in new forms; new ventures, new roles, new relationships; still carrying the same unresolved wound.

Integrity emerges when the wound is held with care, not hidden with shame. It's the slow, demanding work of asking: What did this injury expose? What part of me allowed it, ignored it, caused it, or refused to see it coming? What boundary was missing? What truth was avoided? And what value will not be compromised again?

Through this questioning, the injury becomes more than a scar. It becomes structure. The pain that once disoriented now sharpens discernment. The collapse that once seemed like an end becomes a foundation for something cleaner. Integrity isn't moral posturing. It's coherence. It's when your choices, your systems, your leadership all align because the lessons of pain have been absorbed and applied.

This is not about perfection. Builders who have known injury don't pretend to be invincible. But they also don't move recklessly. Their pace is slower, their yes carries weight, their no is firm without apology. They operate with a kind of internal clarity that can't be faked. It's not about being right; it's about being real.

What was once an injury is now a compass. What was once a fracture is now a frame. The harm that once threatened to undo the builder has become a reason they are trusted; because they've rebuilt, not just the venture, but themselves. That is integrity; not purity, not flawlessness, but the integration of everything survived, into everything now chosen.

Closing Meditation

Scars are not decorations. They are not meant to be admired or explained. They are meant to be carried. Quietly. Fully. As part of the architecture of who the builder has become. They speak not of perfection, but of presence; of someone who did not retreat from what broke them, who did not outsource their healing, who did not mask their collapse with noise. They speak of someone who stood in the wreckage long enough to learn something no success could teach.

In the end, it is not the absence of injury that makes a builder trustworthy. It is how they've responded to it. Whether they've integrated it, or buried it. Whether they've used it to deepen their craft, or to justify their distance. Whether they've allowed it to turn them bitter, or to strip away everything false.

What lasts is not brilliance. What endures is not charisma. What draws others near; especially in uncertain times; is the quiet gravity of someone who has been through something and still chooses to build. Someone whose integrity was not inherited or learned in theory; but earned, the hard way.

There is no shame in being wounded. The shame would be in letting the wound go unexamined. In missing the invitation it carries. In rushing past the very moment that could've made you whole.

Scars don't mean you lost. They mean you stayed. You stood in the fire. You didn't flinch. And what was burned away wasn't you; it was what couldn't last.

You remained. You rebuilt. And now, when others falter, it is you they'll look to; not for comfort, but for example.

Chapter 12

Destruction as Precursor to Creation

Collapse as Clearing

Collapse is often framed as failure. A sign that something was broken, mismanaged, or unworthy. But serious builders come to understand collapse differently. Not as an end, but as an invitation. A reordering. A clearing of what can no longer be carried. What appears on the surface as destruction often reveals itself, over time, as the start of something far more true.

Every structure; personal, professional, cultural; contains within it the seeds of its own undoing. The compromises made for growth. The assumptions left unchallenged. The beliefs too rigid to evolve. When those tensions are left unresolved, collapse doesn't happen suddenly. It accumulates. Quietly. And then all at once. What's lost in that moment is not just stability; it's identity, strategy, certainty. But what's uncovered is something harder to reach without that collapse: honesty.

There is a strange mercy in collapse. It strips away what was performative. It clears the debris of outdated systems, untrue stories, and unsustainable dynamics. It confronts the builder with what is essential and what was never real. Collapse simplifies; violently, perhaps, but with clarity. It removes the option to pretend.

For the builder willing to see it, collapse becomes a form of precision. It says: this part no longer serves. This system cannot carry what you're asking it to. This relationship, this model, this self-concept; it has expired. Collapse does not negotiate. But it tells the truth.

To frame collapse as failure is to miss its intelligence. It may come with pain, but it comes bearing vision. It forces questions the builder would never ask when things are working. It removes options the builder would never relinquish voluntarily. It creates a blank space where choice is possible again; not from comfort, but from necessity.

What rises from that space will not be the same. Nor should it be. Collapse has done its work; not by ending the story, but by demanding that it be rewritten with cleaner lines.

The Myth of Constant Growth

Modern business culture idolizes growth. Scale is treated as proof of success, acceleration as evidence of intelligence, and expansion as a moral imperative. But this obsession with unbroken growth is both unnatural and unsustainable. In nature, nothing grows forever. In life, no cycle moves only forward. To demand constant growth is to reject rhythm; and to reject rhythm is to invite collapse.

The myth of constant growth trains builders to fear stillness. It teaches them to interpret contraction as failure, plateau as weakness, and decline as incompetence. It severs the builder from the natural cadence of all lasting things: the breath-like cycle of expansion and release, emergence and retreat, blooming and pruning.

This mindset creates businesses that are bloated, reactive, and fragile. When growth becomes the only metric that matters, depth is sacrificed. Culture is sacrificed. Discernment is sacrificed. Builders stop asking whether growth is aligned; and start chasing it for its own sake. The structure grows, but coherence thins. Teams expand, but the mission blurs. What once moved with clarity now moves with compulsion.

Sustainable building does not reject growth; it reframes it. Growth is not a straight line. It is a pulse. There are seasons for forward motion and seasons for grounding. There are phases where systems should be refined, not stretched. Phases where culture needs tending, not scaling. Wisdom lies in knowing the difference.

The mature builder releases the fantasy of perpetual expansion. They understand that growth without contraction is distortion. That the pauses are not interruptions; they are part of the pattern. They allow space for integration, rest, and recalibration. They know that in the absence of contraction, growth becomes cancerous. More is not always better. Sometimes, more is what breaks it.

When the myth of constant growth is abandoned, something more durable appears in its place: rhythm. A way of building that honors seasons. A form of leadership that knows when to press forward and when to pull back. A commitment to creation that leaves room for destruction; not as failure, but as part of the dance.

Letting It Burn: When Holding On Becomes Harm

There comes a point in every builder's journey where the thing they created becomes the very thing holding them back. The product that once made sense is now clutter. The system once praised becomes brittle. The partnership, the identity, the strategy; all begin to fray. But because they were hard-earned, they are hard to release. So instead, they are protected. Prolonged. Justified. And in doing so, the builder crosses a line; where holding on no longer preserves value, it creates harm.

Letting something die is not the same as giving up. Sometimes, the most disciplined act is not to fix, but to let the structure burn. Not recklessly, but consciously. Not in bitterness, but in clarity. Because there is such a thing as loving something beyond its usefulness. There is such a thing as guarding something that no longer aligns. And every moment spent preserving what no longer fits is a moment stolen from what wants to emerge.

The serious builder knows the signs. Energy begins to drain. Meetings spiral into maintenance. Feedback is filtered to protect the illusion. Creativity stalls, and culture calcifies. What once felt alive now feels like a museum exhibit; preserved, curated, admired, but inert. And still, many keep it going. Out of duty. Out of pride. Out of fear of being seen as unstable or ungrateful. They convince themselves that endurance is nobility. But sometimes, endurance is avoidance.

Letting it burn is not about destruction for its own sake. It's about acknowledging that every structure has a lifespan. That some systems are meant to be seasonal. That not everything we build is supposed to last forever. In fact, trying to make it last beyond its time dishonors what it was at its best. It distorts the memory. It burdens the future.

There is grace in knowing when to release. And power in trusting that what burns may feed the soil for what comes next. This is not failure. This is the discipline of ending well. Of surrendering not because it's easy, but because it's right.

Sometimes, the most sacred work a builder can do is to walk away from what once served, light the match, and watch with reverence as the flame clears the path forward.

Sacred Ruin: Making Space for the Unmade

There is a kind of destruction that feels like desecration; chaotic, senseless, rageful. But there is another kind: intentional, clean, almost reverent. Not an act of violence, but of clarity. This is sacred ruin. The deliberate dismantling of what no longer serves, in order to make space for what does not yet exist. It is not loud. It is not impulsive. It is the quiet, strategic undoing of what once had meaning but now has mass.

Most builders fear ruin because they see only loss. But sacred ruin reframes the act. It treats ruin not as erasure but as return; to essence, to alignment, to simplicity. It is the moment when structure yields to soil, when ego yields to design, when permanence yields to possibility. Ruin becomes sacred when it is not driven by reaction, but by integrity. When the decision to tear down is made not in despair, but in discipline.

This process demands more from the builder than creation ever did. It requires stillness in the face of uncertainty. Courage in the face of external judgment. It requires confronting everything one once called "mine" and asking; does this still belong? Not everything does. Even the most inspired vision, if clung to too long, can become obstruction.

What makes ruin sacred is not the collapse, but the posture within it. The willingness to witness the fall without rushing to rebuild. To sit inside the cleared space and allow it to be empty. To resist the urge to fill it with the familiar. Sacred ruin is uncomfortable because it strips away identity. Without the role, the product, the structure; who is the builder now? The temptation is to rebuild immediately, to reclaim status, to reassert relevance. But wisdom holds the line. Wisdom waits.

From the outside, this waiting may look like failure. But from the inside, it is preparation. It is respect. It is an act of making room for something that is not yet visible, but deeply needed. And only in the absence of clutter; mental, emotional, structural; can that new clarity emerge.

Sacred ruin is not the end of the story. It is the page intentionally left blank.

What Falls, Reveals

When a structure collapses, what's exposed isn't just failure; it's truth. Beneath the wreckage, patterns become visible. Fault lines surface. Dynamics that were once ignored or rationalized are suddenly undeniable. Collapse doesn't just destroy; it illuminates. It reveals what was always there but concealed by momentum, performance, or sheer will.

Often, what falls was already unstable. The collapse is just the moment we can no longer look away. And in that moment, something vital is offered: the chance to see the thing for what it really was. Not what we hoped it would be. Not what we told others it was. But what it actually became.

This is one of the quiet gifts of destruction. It clears away the noise and exposes the foundations; what they were made of, how they were treated, and whether they could carry the weight they were given. It reveals who showed up when things were hard. Who disappeared. What values held, and what values were for sale. It shows how strong the mission truly was when the scaffolding was gone.

For the builder, this is not a time for defense. It is a time for witness. Not everything that collapses should have survived. Not every role deserved to be preserved. Sometimes, the most painful part is realizing that the fall was long overdue; and that you, too, participated in prolonging it.

But this is not about blame. It's about honesty. When the dust settles, the question isn't "How did this happen to me?" It's "What was this trying to show me?" The structure has spoken. The mask has slipped. What remains is unvarnished reality; and the rare opportunity to build again, this time without delusion.

This act of witnessing; of seeing what the collapse reveals without flinching; is a kind of rite. It separates the builder from the performer, the mature from the merely ambitious. It's a moment where the next phase of leadership begins. Not with noise, but with vision. Not with new ideas, but with honest soil.

Because only when we've truly seen what was can we begin to imagine what might be built more cleanly, more coherently, and more enduringly than before.

Surrendering the False to Reclaim the True

Every builder, at some point, constructs around something false. A borrowed ideal. A market expectation. A persona crafted to impress investors, clients, or even themselves. It's rarely intentional. It begins subtly; in decisions made to preserve image, in compromises justified as temporary, in silence maintained to avoid conflict. Over time, these small departures accumulate, until the structure that emerges no longer reflects the clarity that once inspired its creation.

Collapse unmasks this. Not with cruelty, but with precision. It strips away what was propped up rather than rooted. And in the aftermath, the builder is left facing the uncomfortable truth: some of what was lost never truly belonged. Some of what was defended was never really alive. The collapse wasn't just about market forces or timing; it was about misalignment.

To move forward, something deeper must occur. The builder must surrender the false; not just intellectually, but emotionally. Letting go of the performance. Releasing the identity built around appearances. Naming what was never really true, even if it once felt necessary. This isn't a public gesture. It's a private reckoning. And it doesn't happen all at once. It happens in layers, each one revealing a clearer view of what's been compromised, and what must now be reclaimed.

This surrender is not weakness. It's strength of the rarest kind: the ability to return to essence. To rebuild not from ambition, but from alignment. To say no to strategies that impress but do not endure. To reject roles that generate status but drain integrity. To remove the ornaments and return to form.

What's reclaimed in this process is often quieter than what was surrendered. It doesn't sparkle. It doesn't scale quickly. But it feels clean. It holds. It allows the builder to stand inside their structure without contradiction. That feeling; of coherence; is more powerful than momentum. It's what makes longevity possible.

Reclaiming the true is not about nostalgia. It's about listening to what's always been there, buried beneath layers of noise. It's about choosing to build not for approval, but for truth. And in doing so, the builder becomes trustworthy again; not just to others, but to themselves.

Why Not Everything Is Meant to Survive

There is a quiet cruelty in the idea that everything we build must last. It suggests that permanence is the only proof of value. That endurance is the only valid outcome. But not everything is meant to survive; and insisting otherwise burdens both the builder and the structure with expectations they cannot carry.

Some creations are meant to teach, not last. Some partnerships are meant to catalyze, not continue. Some phases of identity are meant to shed, not sustain. When we demand survival from everything, we confuse purpose with permanence. We mistake duration for depth. And we end up clinging to what has already completed its work.

Survival is not always success. In fact, many of the most bloated and brittle systems in business and culture are those that refused to die when their time came. They limped forward, protected by nostalgia, inertia, or fear, draining the energy that could have nourished something new. The builder who insists on keeping everything alive becomes less a creator and more a caretaker of decay.

Letting things end is not a failure of commitment. It's a refinement of it. It's an act of respect; to the work, to the people it served, and to the future that now needs room. This doesn't mean being reckless or impatient. It means being honest. It means asking: Is this still aligned? Is this still alive? Or are we keeping it breathing out of fear of what its death would ask us to confront?

The most disciplined builders carry a quiet willingness to release. They understand that pruning is not destruction. It's design. That loss is not the opposite of success; it's part of the rhythm that makes success possible. They choose what to let die so that what deserves to live can actually thrive.

Not everything you build will last. It shouldn't. The goal is not permanence. The goal is coherence. And when coherence requires an ending, let that ending come; not as failure, but as fulfillment.

The Builder's Choice: Grieve or Cling

When something ends; an idea, a venture, a season; the builder is faced with a choice: grieve, or cling. One leads to freedom. The other to distortion.

Grief is not weakness. It is the honest recognition that something mattered. That energy was given, belief was invested, and meaning was shaped through effort and time. To grieve what ends is to honor what was; without needing to drag it forward into what will be. It allows the builder to carry memory without carrying mass. To integrate the lessons without preserving the form. Grief clears the space without denying its history.

Clinging, by contrast, is a refusal. It's a fixation on what should have lasted. It's a rewriting of the story to avoid the truth of its ending. Clinging turns collapse into a personal indictment. It insists that survival is always deserved, and that letting go is betrayal. The builder who clings becomes a curator of ruins, not a creator of futures. Their energy bends backward. Their clarity narrows. And slowly, the weight of what they won't release begins to shape everything they try to build next.

This choice; grieve or cling; is not just emotional. It's strategic. A builder who can grieve moves forward with cleaner judgment. They are not haunted by what could have been. They are not secretly trying to replicate a former identity. Their decisions emerge from the present, not from a refusal to let the past dissolve. They build what's needed now, not what once worked.

But grief takes time. And courage. It asks the builder to feel what they would rather skip. To sit in ambiguity. To not know what's next. Clinging, though painful, offers false comfort: a sense of movement, a story to repeat, a familiar role to perform. That's why it's seductive. But it's also why it corrupts.

In the end, grief doesn't erase the past; it integrates it. And only through that integration can the builder re-enter the creative process with clarity and integrity. Clinging postpones that work. Grief completes it.

To build well after loss, the builder must first become empty. Not numb, not hardened; empty enough to begin again without carrying what was never meant to follow.

The Hidden Intelligence of Ruin

Ruin feels senseless while it's happening. It arrives uninvited, unplanned, and often unexplainable in the moment. Systems fail. Partners leave. Momentum evaporates. Identity disorients. And in that storm, the builder is left grasping for cause and control. But what looks like chaos on the surface often carries a deeper order; an intelligence that only reveals itself in hindsight.

Ruin, when approached with awareness, rearranges what we cannot; or will not; rearrange on our own. It reorders priorities, redefines identity, and restores boundaries that success had blurred. It strips away the noise that clouded discernment. It dissolves the illusions that once drove action but no longer serve. This intelligence isn't gentle. It doesn't ask permission. But it acts with clarity. It arrives when the gap between what is real and what is performed has grown too wide to sustain.

The builder's task is not to understand ruin in the moment; it's to survive it cleanly enough to see its logic later. To stay present without panic. To resist the urge to fix too quickly. To allow the collapse to complete its work without rushing to rebuild on the same cracked foundation. Ruin is intelligent, but only for those willing to listen.

What makes ruin intelligent is not that it spares the builder from pain. It's that it gives the pain purpose. It forces alignment. It breaks what needed breaking. It removes what would not have been willingly surrendered. And in doing so, it clears space for what is truer, leaner, more essential.

This is not mystical thinking. It is structural. It is what happens when long-avoided decisions finally come due. When the architecture of a life or business, built on unsustainable logic, collapses under its own contradictions. Ruin may look like failure, but often it is reality asserting itself; non-negotiable, exacting, and ultimately, merciful.

When the builder sees this, a shift occurs. They stop fighting the fall. They start listening to it. They begin to see not just what's being lost, but what's being revealed. And in that revelation is the blueprint; not for restoration, but for reinvention.

The Seed in the Ash

In the aftermath of collapse, when the noise subsides and the structure is gone, what remains is often overlooked: silence, stillness, and ash. The ash looks like the end. The end of momentum, of identity, of relevance. But hidden within it, if one is paying attention, is something else. Something small. Something alive. A seed.

The seed is not a return to what was. It's not the preserved remnant of a former glory. It is the beginning of something new; something that could only emerge after the fall. It carries a different logic. It's quieter. It doesn't demand to be planted immediately. It waits. It asks the builder to slow down, to listen, to resist the urge to rebuild in the same shape out of habit or fear.

To recognize the seed is to accept that the ash was necessary. That the fire did not destroy indiscriminately; it refined. And in doing so, it made room for what the previous structure would never have allowed to grow. The seed is possibility; but not abstract hope. It's a grounded invitation. It asks: What can be built now that wasn't possible before? What can rise that won't repeat the mistakes of what fell?

This is not about reinvention as branding. It is reinvention as integrity. As a return to values that were overlooked, or a discovery of truths never named. It's about starting again, not with ambition, but with awareness. The seed does not promise speed or scale. It promises coherence; if the builder has the patience to let it root.

Many miss this. They sift through the ash looking for salvage. For pieces of the old to polish and reuse. But the serious builder learns to look elsewhere. They don't fear the emptiness. They understand that from this emptiness comes direction. Not a blueprint, but an instinct. And slowly, with discipline and attention, a new structure begins to take shape; one not built on fear, but on truth.

The seed doesn't announce itself. It doesn't need to. It waits for those with the presence to notice it and the courage to plant what will not resemble what came before.

Chapter 13

Grit Without Grasping: Endurance as Gentle Power

The False Heroism of Force

The modern imagination still worships force. We are taught to admire those who power through, push harder, override limits. The image of the tireless builder; outworking, outlasting, refusing to yield; remains a cultural icon. But beneath the surface, that image is hollow. Force may look heroic in the short term, but over time, it distorts. It severs us from rhythm. It erodes nuance. And it rewards a kind of brute perseverance that confuses exhaustion for integrity.

Force becomes seductive because it produces quick results. It commands attention. It implies strength. But it does so at a cost: it narrows our range. It blinds us to other forms of power. The builder who relies on force becomes reactive. They confuse resistance with meaning. Every obstacle becomes a battlefield. Every silence, a threat. Every delay, an enemy to overcome. And in this posture, they cease to listen; to others, to reality, to themselves.

The deeper problem is that force rarely builds what lasts. It demands constant energy. It creates brittle systems that rely on momentum rather than coherence. It may achieve short-term wins, but it struggles to sustain. And worse, it trains the builder to believe that control is the same as creation. That effort, by itself, guarantees outcomes. But endurance is not measured by how much pressure we can apply. It's measured by what kind of pressure we can absorb; without distortion, without disconnection, without becoming something we no longer recognize.

What looks like strength is often strain. What looks like heroism is often panic dressed as discipline. And what's praised as grit is sometimes a refusal to feel what must be felt. There is a strength in force; but it is not the only kind. Nor is it the kind that carries us the furthest.

The serious builder must unlearn the worship of force. They must trade the drama of intensity for the steadiness of rhythm. Not because they are weaker; but because they are ready to build what doesn't need to shout in order to last.

The Misuse of Grit in the Modern Myth

Grit, once a quiet virtue, has become a noisy slogan. It is cited as the defining trait of winners, the secret sauce of the relentless, the badge of those who refuse to quit. But in the hands of the modern myth, grit has been distorted. It has become a justification for overwork, for emotional suppression, for stubbornness disguised as resilience. We've hollowed it out. What was once inner strength is now performance.

The modern myth tells us to keep going at all costs. That quitting is failure. That rest is weakness. That pain is proof of progress. But this version of grit confuses endurance with compulsion. It turns persistence into pathology. It rewards builders not for their clarity, but for their capacity to tolerate damage. The longer you hold the weight, the more heroic you're told you are; even if the weight no longer makes sense to carry.

True grit is not blind. It is discerning. It doesn't keep pushing just to prove it can. It knows when to stop. It knows when to adjust. It knows when to rest so that the next move isn't fueled by depletion, but by clarity. The misuse of grit encourages denial of context. It tells the builder to stick to the plan even when the terrain has changed. But wisdom; real grit; adjusts course. It listens. It remains connected to what's real.

This misuse has consequences. It burns people out. It builds brittle organizations. It teaches teams to ignore their signals and to idolize unsustainable behavior. In this model, endurance becomes distortion. Commitment becomes dogma. And the builder, instead of growing in depth, grows in distance; from self, from others, from reality.

To reclaim grit, we must strip it of bravado. We must remember that grit is not the refusal to feel; it is the capacity to stay engaged through discomfort. It is not the will to win; it is the willingness to remain present when winning is no longer guaranteed. Grit is not about how loud you can be while pushing. It's about how quiet you can remain while holding.

Gentle Power: Endurance Without Erosion

Endurance is often mistaken for abrasion; the belief that to last, one must harden. That survival comes from bracing, from thickening, from turning one's self into stone. But the endurance that truly sustains; the kind that moves through time without eroding the builder; is gentle. It is not soft in the sense of fragility. It is soft in the sense of presence. Flexible, rooted, aware.

Gentle power does not announce itself. It doesn't rely on grand gestures or loud victories. Its strength lies in its steadiness. It endures not because it ignores pain, but because it meets pain without resistance. Where force crashes, gentle power flows. Where others tense, it yields; and in that yielding, it persists.

This is not passivity. It is an active discipline. It requires clarity, restraint, and an internal confidence that doesn't need to dominate in order to remain intact. Gentle power is the opposite of resignation; it is the choice to remain open when every instinct screams to close. It is the act of listening in the middle of pressure, of responding instead of reacting, of refusing to become sharp in a world that rewards edge.

Builders who lead with gentle power create different outcomes. Their teams breathe more easily around them. Their structures bend, but do not break. They make fewer decisions from fear, fewer declarations from pride. Their presence transmits not urgency, but gravity. They can hold weight without broadcasting struggle.

This kind of endurance does not erode the builder. It refines them. It doesn't ask for masks or armor. It asks for consistency. Not the consistency of performance; but the consistency of attention, of alignment, of being the same person when things go wrong as when they go right.

Gentle power survives storms not by fighting them, but by understanding them. And through that understanding, it learns to shape the environment rather than be shaped by it.

The Discipline of Staying, Not Pushing

There's a discipline most builders overlook; not because it's hidden, but because it's quiet. It's the discipline of staying. Of remaining present in difficulty without needing to force an outcome. Of refusing to escape discomfort by converting it into urgency. Staying is not inaction. It is active restraint. It is the choice to stay in relationship with a challenge long enough for it to teach, instead of trying to overpower it into submission.

Pushing is easier. It's loud. It gives the illusion of control. It lets the builder feel like progress is being made, even if all that's moving is dust. But staying; staying asks for stillness. For presence. For the courage to hold without demanding that the discomfort resolve itself immediately. Staying is not about tolerating abuse or inertia. It's about honoring process. It's about understanding that some things ripen in silence. That not all progress is visible. That momentum is not always a signal of health.

The builder who learns to stay develops a different kind of intelligence; an ability to distinguish between resistance that must be challenged, and resistance that must be understood. Not every slow moment is a sign to push harder. Some are invitations to listen. Some are warnings that something essential is being missed. Staying opens space for those messages to emerge. Pushing often drowns them out.

This discipline is especially rare in cultures built on velocity. We are conditioned to act, to solve, to resolve. But some tensions are not meant to be resolved. They're meant to be carried. Staying allows us to sit in complexity without rushing to reduce it. It allows us to remain in roles, relationships, and realities long enough to learn what they truly require.

And when movement does come, it comes cleaner. Not from panic. Not from compulsion. But from clarity. From alignment. From the kind of knowing that only reveals itself after we've refused to flee.

The discipline of staying is not dramatic. It won't get you celebrated. But it will get you through. And more importantly, it will grow in you a power deeper than will: the ability to endure without distortion.

Holding Through, Not Holding On

There is a quiet distinction between holding on and holding through; one that defines the difference between endurance and entrapment. Holding on is fear-based. It tightens its grip in resistance to change. It clings to what was, out of attachment, pride, or the illusion of control. It exhausts itself in the name of preservation, refusing to admit when something no longer serves. Holding through, by contrast, is conscious. It steadies itself through discomfort without pretending that permanence is the goal. It holds not to prevent change, but to stay connected through it.

This is a crucial shift for the builder. Many fall into the trap of mistaking attachment for commitment. They believe that the more tightly they hold, the more loyal they are. But in truth, the more we tighten our grip, the less able we are to feel. Holding on narrows awareness. It focuses on survival. It ignores the signals that something may need to evolve; or end. In this state, the builder becomes brittle, reactive, unable to pivot without rupture.

Holding through, instead, is a posture of presence. It is rooted in trust; not in outcomes, but in process. The builder who holds through remains engaged, but not grasping. They allow difficulty to pass through them without becoming defined by it. They are steady without being stubborn. They do not mistake persistence for permanence. And because they are not clutching at what must change, they can endure its unfolding without collapsing.

This difference matters most in long roads; in ventures that test patience, in relationships that evolve, in identities that are shedding old skins. The builder who holds on will try to preserve the form. The builder who holds through will honor the essence. They understand that endurance is not about keeping everything intact. It is about remaining intact as everything changes.

There's a quiet dignity in this. No heroics. No declarations. Just the quiet strength of someone who knows how to remain open in the face of uncertainty; who holds, not to possess, but to accompany.

Rhythm Over Willpower

Willpower is often treated as the highest virtue of the serious builder; a force to summon, a muscle to strengthen, the key to pressing on when things get hard. But willpower is finite. It burns fast. It's reactive by nature, rising to meet moments of strain, then receding in exhaustion. When building for the long arc, willpower alone won't carry you. Rhythm will.

Rhythm is not a surge of effort; it's the disciplined return to a sustainable cadence. It is knowing when to move and when to wait, when to push and when to pull back. It respects cycles; of energy, of clarity, of conditions. Where willpower insists, rhythm listens. Where willpower tries to override limits, rhythm builds around them.

The builder trained only in willpower often confuses collapse with weakness. They interpret rest as retreat, hesitation as doubt. They override fatigue until it becomes injury, override signals until the system breaks. But this isn't endurance; it's erosion. It's an act of violence against one's own structure, justified in the name of grit.

Rhythm is a different kind of mastery. It isn't glamorous. It won't be praised in highlight reels. But it's what allows builders to stay in the work long enough to do it cleanly. Rhythm creates margin. It embeds recovery. It understands that the goal is not intensity; it's continuity.

To live and build in rhythm requires humility. It means letting go of the fantasy that effort can bend time or force timing. It means recognizing that some answers only emerge in the pause. That some truths only rise in stillness. That momentum without rest leads not to progress, but to distortion.

The mature builder aligns their workflow to their internal tides. They work in pulses, not pushes. They create space between chapters, between seasons, between decisions. And because they are not operating at the edge of depletion, they have capacity; creative, emotional, strategic; when it counts.

Willpower may get you through a crisis. Rhythm will carry you through a life.

Endurance That Listens

Endurance is often mistaken for muting; of emotion, of discomfort, of intuition. The prevailing idea is that to endure well, one must silence the inner voice, press forward no matter what, ignore signals that suggest rethinking the path. But true endurance doesn't silence; it listens. Not just to results or outcomes, but to everything in between. It is tuned to the body, to the environment, to the emotional undercurrents that signal when something is shifting beneath the surface.

Listening endurance is subtle. It does not panic at pain, but it pays attention. It does not collapse at confusion, but it pauses. It is less interested in braving through and more committed to staying in dialogue with the moment. This kind of endurance doesn't just survive strain; it learns from it. It adjusts. It reframes. It metabolizes experience in real time.

When endurance is disconnected from listening, it becomes hollow. You can push for years in the wrong direction, carrying a flag that no longer means what it once did. You can become efficient at surviving, but numb to alignment. You can develop an incredible tolerance for discomfort while drifting further and further from purpose.

Endurance that listens is harder. It requires presence. It forces the builder to stop performing invincibility and to start discerning: Is this challenge meaningful or performative? Is this resistance sacred or self-inflicted? Am I enduring something because it is worthy; or because I am afraid to let go?

It also requires that the builder stay in relationship with self and with others. Listening endurance doesn't isolate. It allows for feedback. It absorbs wisdom from those who've walked before. It opens to recalibration without interpreting change as failure.

The builder who learns to endure this way becomes unshakable not because they are rigid, but because they are attuned. Their strength is not the absence of feeling, but the presence of discernment. They last not by outmuscling pain, but by understanding what the pain is trying to say.

Endurance, in its highest form, is not a wall. It is a vessel. It holds; but it breathes.

The Shape of True Resilience

Resilience is not bounce-back energy. It's not toughness, nor is it the ability to pretend nothing happened. True resilience has shape; it bends, it absorbs, it reorganizes. It does not resist impact by denying it. It endures by reshaping around it, integrating the experience rather than bracing against it. The resilient builder doesn't just survive disruption; they metabolize it into deeper wisdom and cleaner structure.

Too often, resilience is treated as return. The ability to return to the same pace, the same mindset, the same form. But that is not resilience; that is repetition. What distinguishes the resilient is their capacity to change shape without losing essence. They can be transformed by crisis without being dismantled by it. They can shift without unraveling.

This shape is not forged in ease. It's sculpted in pressure. But pressure alone isn't enough; it's the response to pressure that matters. Fragile systems resist and shatter. Rigid identities cling and crack. But resilient ones reorient. They slow down when others rush. They narrow focus when others scatter. They don't panic to preserve form. They allow reality to reshape what must be reshaped.

The shape of resilience is also humble. It does not seek applause. It is not loud. It does not feed on attention. It moves beneath the surface. It preserves capacity when others exhaust theirs in performance. It holds energy in reserve, not because of fear, but because of design.

The resilient builder is marked by presence. They do not need to dominate to feel safe. They do not need to win to feel worthy. They build in layers, not in bursts. And because of this, they can take more loss without collapse. They can hold more tension without distortion. They can recover not just quickly, but cleanly.

Resilience is not how fast you bounce; it's how deeply you anchor. It's the shape you take after the world has tested your edges and you remain; changed, yes, but intact where it matters most.

Why the Soft Endures Longer Than the Hard

It's counterintuitive in a world that celebrates hardness; toughness, rigidity, control. But over time, it's softness that endures. Not the kind of softness that collapses, but the kind that yields, absorbs, and adapts. Water carves stone not by force, but by persistence. Trees survive storms not by resisting wind, but by swaying with it. The soft, when rooted, outlasts the hard because it can move without breaking.

Hardness often masquerades as strength. It projects certainty, stability, resolve. But it's brittle. It relies on resistance. And when too much pressure arrives, it snaps. Softness, on the other hand, doesn't need to resist to remain intact. It allows what must pass through to pass. It doesn't take every strike as a threat. It flows around obstruction, not through sheer power, but through patient form.

The builder who learns this gains a new kind of resilience. They stop armoring up for every challenge. They stop over-preparing for battle. They start adapting; not out of weakness, but out of wisdom. They don't fear change because they haven't anchored their identity in fixedness. Their strength isn't in opposition; it's in coherence.

This doesn't mean soft builders are passive. It means their strength is responsive. They know when to move, when to absorb, when to step aside. They don't mistake stubbornness for strategy. They build structures that can evolve. Teams that can listen. Systems that can flex. And because of that, what they build lasts longer; not because it's unyielding, but because it's alive.

In the long game of building, hardness burns out. It protects at first, but isolates in time. Softness grows. It requires humility, emotional fluency, and the discipline to remain open when others shut down. But it also brings durability; of connection, of vision, of presence.

What remains, decades after the noise fades, is not what was hardest, but what was most aligned. Softness is not fragility; it's strategic life. It's the posture of those who intend to stay in the work long after the applause ends.

The Quiet Force That Builds the Long Road

The builders who last are rarely the loudest. They're not chasing headlines, not broadcasting their every move, not addicted to visible proof of progress. They work differently; anchored, disciplined, and often unnoticed. Their power is quiet. Their motion, deliberate. They're building something designed to outlive them, and they know that kind of structure demands more than intensity; it demands longevity. And longevity, in its most refined form, is a quiet force.

This force doesn't surge. It hums. It moves beneath the surface, consistent and attuned. It does not rely on bursts of willpower. It is not driven by drama or performance. It is maintained by rhythm, by values, by a steady return to purpose. The builder who carries this force understands that endurance is not an emergency; it is a way of life.

Quiet force is not absence of strength. It's refinement of it. It's the strength to say no to what is merely urgent. The strength to wait. The strength to hold form when chaos tempts collapse. It's the refusal to abandon nuance in the name of speed. The refusal to sell out truth for traction. The refusal to make the work louder just to be seen.

This quiet force is built over time. It's cultivated in early mornings, in late nights, in the middle space where no one is watching. It is shaped by repetition; how you handle small decisions, how you manage doubt, how you return to alignment after being pulled off course. There is no moment when it announces itself. But one day, others begin to notice that you don't sway like they do. That you're still building while they're still reacting. That what you've made holds even under pressure.

The long road demands this kind of force. Because the noise will come. So will fatigue, betrayal, irrelevance, reinvention. And the builder who endures will not be the one who shouted the longest; but the one who kept working when the lights went out. The one who kept listening when the path grew quiet. The one who stayed when staying no longer felt glamorous.

The long road does not reward noise. It rewards depth. And quiet force is the signature of those who intend not just to begin, but to finish.

Chapter 14

Failing Forward: Collapse as Curriculum

The Myth of Final Failure

Failure, in most cultural narratives, is cast as a conclusion; a final judgment, the closing chapter, the proof that one was never truly worthy of the work. It carries the weight of finality, a verdict wrapped in shame, used to separate the successful from the forgettable. But this idea of failure as final is not only false; it is dangerous. It traps builders in binary thinking: either triumph or collapse, mastery or disgrace. It leaves no room for process, for recalibration, for rebirth.

In reality, failure is rarely final. What ends is a form, not the force behind it. The business may dissolve. The product may miss the mark. The partnership may break. But beneath every collapse, something remains; an instinct, a thread of insight, a deeper integrity now tested. What is lost in appearance can be reclaimed in essence, if the builder knows how to stay present in the aftermath.

The myth of final failure survives because it flatters our fears. It tells us that mistakes are dangerous because they reveal something about us we hoped to keep hidden; that we are fragile, fallible, uncertain. And in response, many try to deny or deflect failure, hoping to outrun its shadow. But the mature builder knows that facing failure directly; naming it, studying it, absorbing what it came to teach; is not defeat. It is the first act of reclaiming authorship.

Finality is rarely real. It is often a posture adopted out of pain, a way to cut short the discomfort of uncertainty. But what looks like the end is usually a beginning in disguise, an unasked-for invitation into a deeper apprenticeship. Builders who take this seriously learn to stop fearing failure as annihilation. They begin to see it as initiation; not into loss, but into clarity.

Failure becomes final only when we refuse to extract its meaning. When we insist that the collapse defines us more than the courage it took to build in the first place. But those who endure long enough to outlive the shame begin to realize something radical: failure does not end the story; it reopens it.

Failure as Mirror, Not Verdict

Failure doesn't arrive to condemn. It arrives to reflect. It holds up a mirror; sometimes gently, often harshly; and shows us what we refused to see while things were moving, while praise was coming, while momentum masked misalignment. It does not create the truth. It reveals it. And in that revelation lies its power.

The builder who treats failure as a verdict misses the point. A verdict closes. It names guilt, assigns blame, hands down a sentence. But failure, when approached with presence, is not sentencing you; it's inviting you. To look closer. To trace the arc of your choices. To examine the foundations that once seemed solid but now show their cracks. The failed launch, the broken team, the lost investor; none of these are final blows. They are reflections of deeper patterns, misjudgments, or blind spots that had been asking for your attention long before things collapsed.

This is not a call to self-flagellation. It's an invitation to precision. Blame is crude. Discernment is sacred. The builder who learns to use failure as a mirror does not spiral into self-doubt or denial. They stand in front of the moment and ask: What is this showing me about my assumptions, my process, my priorities? Not: Am I good enough? But: What was I missing?

The clarity that failure offers is not always immediate. Sometimes it arrives slowly, after the emotion subsides and the ego loosens its grip. But when it comes, it's clean. Failure strips away the excuses. It removes the flattering angles. It leaves only what is real. And if you have the courage to see that; not defensively, not despairingly, but with humility; you leave the mirror with sharper sight than you had before.

Failure does not get the final word. But it does ask for your attention. It will not let you move forward until you have looked long enough to see what it came to show. The immature builder hides from the mirror. The mature one meets its gaze; and walks forward changed.

When What You Built Says 'No'

There is a particular kind of failure that feels more personal than most; the moment when the thing you built, the system you designed, the mission you swore by, begins to resist you. Not because others sabotaged it. Not because the world conspired. But because something within the structure itself starts saying: No. This doesn't work. Not like this. Not anymore.

For builders, this is a destabilizing moment. You pour time, resources, identity into a thing; and then it refuses to cooperate. The offer stops resonating. The team fractures. The model reveals itself to be unsustainable. The momentum that once carried you now drags you. And what makes it hurt is not just the breakdown. It's that it came from something you believed in. Something you authored. It feels like rejection from your own creation.

But this too is a kind of mirror. When what you built says no, it is not betraying you. It is telling the truth. It is speaking what you may have refused to name: that something in your logic, your timing, or your vision is out of step. That the structure has grown beyond its original coherence; or never had it to begin with. It is feedback. And painful as it is, it is also sacred.

This is where many builders double down. They try to overpower the resistance. They add more pressure, more funding, more explanation. They insist that the structure owes them success because of the energy they've invested. But energy doesn't guarantee alignment. Effort doesn't sanctify error. Sometimes what you built has to fall apart because it cannot carry the truth you're now ready to face.

The wisest builders don't panic when their creations push back. They listen. They allow the failure to speak. They let the "no" come through fully; not as defeat, but as information. They ask: What is this refusal revealing? What need was overlooked? What part of me has evolved past this design?

The courage is not in fixing what resists. It's in hearing what it's trying to say.

The Curriculum of Collapse

Collapse is not just an end. It is a classroom. It delivers a curriculum no success could offer; a syllabus written in hindsight, taught through loss, graded not by outcomes but by what you're willing to confront. It doesn't reward speed. It doesn't coddle your ego. It doesn't flatter your previous wins. It strips the enterprise bare and asks: What did you actually understand?

This is the uncomfortable genius of collapse. It forces learning in ways the builder would never choose voluntarily. It teaches discernment by overwhelming your instincts. It teaches humility by removing your titles. It teaches focus by removing your distractions. What felt like chaos becomes, in time, a lesson plan; if you're still listening.

Most builders want to skip the class. They want to move past the wreckage, pivot into the next thing, rebrand and recover. But collapse doesn't certify those who rush through it. It rewards those who remain in the discomfort long enough to see the logic behind the loss. It requires presence. Not the frantic presence of damage control, but the attentive presence of someone who wants to learn. Who asks: What was real? What was wishful thinking? Where did I compromise too much? What did I refuse to feel?

The curriculum is not obvious at first. It unfolds. Often quietly. It's embedded in conversations that sting. In team members who walk. In systems that suddenly reveal their true cost. If you move too fast, you miss it. But if you stay; if you watch the collapse not as a punishment but as a signal; you begin to gather something more valuable than momentum: understanding.

The builder who accepts this curriculum becomes a different kind of builder. One who doesn't chase scale to mask fragility. One who doesn't cling to vision when the terrain has changed. One who can spot a crack before it becomes structural. Because they've studied the anatomy of collapse from the inside. And they've earned their way forward; not by denying the failure, but by mastering its lessons.

The Lessons the Win Can't Teach

There are truths only failure can reveal; truths that victory, with all its glare and applause, is too blinding to illuminate. Success conceals. It flatters your assumptions, masks your blind spots, and rewards even your miscalculations if the timing is lucky. It makes coherence feel optional and inflates confidence beyond what's been tested. And for a time, it works. You're celebrated. You're studied. You become a case study not because you were right, but because things went right.

But collapse is less forgiving. It teaches with sharpness. It leaves no room for illusions. The lessons it brings are humbling, surgical, sometimes brutal; but they're also honest. Failure has no interest in your narrative. It has no need to impress. It does not flatter the ego or let momentum carry you past your mistakes. It stops you. And in that stoppage, it clarifies.

What you learn when you lose is how much of your success was strategy, and how much was noise. You learn whether your team was loyal to the mission or to momentum. Whether your systems were stable or simply lucky. Whether your leadership was anchored in clarity; or camouflaged by growth.

There are insights that cannot emerge while things are working. They require disintegration. They require stillness. They require the absence of applause. Only then do the subtler truths rise; the ones about pace, patience, posture. The ones about how much you contorted yourself to keep something alive. The ones about how much of what you called "vision" was actually fear in disguise.

The win teaches you how to expand. The loss teaches you how to see. And what is seen in failure; if you're willing to face it; becomes the seed of something more refined. Not just a new strategy, but a different relationship to ambition, to risk, to meaning.

The builder who has only known success is often shallow in their wisdom. The builder who has failed, listened, integrated, and returned; builds from a quieter, deeper place. One not rooted in invincibility, but in truth.

Failure Without Shame

There is a version of failure that speaks in data, in signals, in structural feedback. And then there is the version that comes wrapped in shame. Not because the collapse was shameful, but because we were taught that collapse reflects who we are. The narrative becomes personal. Identity fuses with outcome. And what could have been a moment of insight becomes a wound of humiliation.

This is where many builders get stuck; not in the failure itself, but in the shame they attach to it. They avoid analysis because they fear what the postmortem might confirm: that they were foolish, naive, inadequate. They replay moments obsessively, not to learn, but to punish. They hide from others. Or worse, they perform resilience while privately collapsing, afraid that transparency will confirm the judgment they already carry.

But shame clouds learning. It distorts memory. It doesn't clarify; it corrodes. It turns the clean facts of a situation into a fog of self-rejection. And in doing so, it delays growth. The builder who cannot separate self-worth from outcome will never build with freedom. They will hedge every decision. They will create for applause. They will avoid any path with risk; not because the work isn't meaningful, but because failure would feel like proof that they don't belong.

Failure without shame is still painful. But it's clean pain. It hurts without humiliating. It stings without infecting. And because of that, it becomes usable. It can be examined, spoken about, metabolized. It becomes part of the builder's wisdom; not as a warning against future risk, but as a reminder that failure is a function of the work, not a flaw in the person.

To separate failure from shame is not to minimize it. It is to treat it with respect. To look directly at what happened, name it accurately, and extract its meaning; without the static of self-condemnation. This is not emotional detachment. It is maturity. It is the posture of someone who knows that failure is not a verdict on their identity; it is a moment in their education.

The Rebirth of Competence

Collapse humbles the builder, but it also refines them. In the ashes of failure, something unexpected begins to take shape: a deeper, quieter competence. Not the kind polished for investors or marketed on résumés, but the kind forged in silence; after things have fallen, after ego has burned away, after false certainty has been emptied out.

This competence is different. It doesn't swagger. It doesn't seek validation. It comes from having learned the hard way; not just what doesn't work, but how one works. Through failure, the builder begins to understand their tendencies: how they make decisions under pressure, where they ignore tension, when they override instinct, what they mistake for intuition. They gain not just information, but precision.

In success, there is often a distortion. The world reflects back applause that confirms the builder's best assumptions while disguising their worst habits. But in failure, that mirror clears. The work can no longer carry the weight of illusion. The builder sees the seams, the shortcuts, the quiet hesitations that grew into fatal design flaws. And if they're willing to look, they don't just walk away bruised; they walk away calibrated.

This rebirth is not dramatic. It doesn't come with announcements or reinventions. It comes in choices. A cleaner email. A firmer no. A better hire. A slower pitch. A deeper intake of breath before stepping into the next room. It is competence that emerges not from winning, but from enduring. From witnessing the wreckage and deciding, carefully, how to build again without repeating the same fracture lines.

The builder who has failed and learned doesn't crave attention. They crave coherence. They aren't fueled by the desire to prove; they are anchored by the desire to serve more clearly, more honestly, more sustainably. And when they build again, they do so not from ambition, but from understanding.

Competence, once reborn, becomes something sacred. Not a skillset. Not a performance. But a form of presence. A way of moving through the world that has touched the fire and emerged; not unscarred, but aware.

Making the Debris Speak

After failure, what's left is rarely clean. Debris; emotional, operational, relational; scatters in every direction. Plans unfinished. Systems unraveled. Conversations half-buried. The builder, exhausted and disoriented, is left standing in what feels like a ruin with no meaning. And yet, it is precisely in this debris that the most important messages live; if we're willing to listen closely enough.

Most people rush past this part. They want closure, not clarity. They want to sweep up the mess, push it aside, get back to motion. But speed robs them of the deeper lesson. The debris holds information. It shows where the structure failed first. It reveals what no longer belonged. It tells the truth about what was never as strong as it seemed.

To make the debris speak, the builder must resist the urge to romanticize or vilify the past. They must sit with what remains; not as symbols of defeat, but as raw material for understanding. A broken process might reveal a blind spot. A team that dissolved might uncover a misalignment in values. A project that never launched might whisper truths about timing, fear, or identity. These fragments, if examined with care, become signals; not wounds to be hidden, but clues to be followed.

This process is not glamorous. It takes time. It takes humility. And it takes a kind of emotional craftsmanship; the willingness to sort, to ask, to hold fragments without needing them to be whole. But when done with presence, it becomes one of the most powerful forms of strategic intelligence. The builder learns to see not just what broke, but how it broke. And through that lens, they begin to design differently.

The next structure doesn't come from escape. It comes from study. The future is built with the unhurried wisdom that only emerges when we've let the debris speak; and we've listened without flinching.

The Elegance of a Clean Ending

Most builders don't know how to end. They know how to start, how to scale, how to survive; but not how to stop with clarity. They drag what's dying long past its natural closure, mistaking continuation for commitment. They stay loyal to a shape that no longer serves, afraid that letting go will look like failure, or worse; will feel like it.

But there is an elegance in a clean ending. A final act chosen deliberately, not passively surrendered. A moment where the builder steps back; not because they've collapsed, but because they've completed something. Not because it broke, but because it fulfilled its function. The clean ending is not a collapse; it's a decision.

It takes more strength to end something with dignity than to keep it alive out of fear. That is because endings create space. And space, by nature, invites uncertainty. Most would rather clutter the path forward with the remnants of what used to work than face the open air of what comes next. But the mature builder knows that completion is not a threat. It's a form of discipline.

There is no need to romanticize every chapter. Not every ending is profound. Some endings are quiet, unceremonious, necessary. Some closures carry grief. Some carry relief. But all of them; if honored instead of avoided; free up the energy being used to preserve the unsustainable.

The clean ending also teaches humility. It asks the builder to admit: this was as far as this version could go. That isn't failure; it's precision. It's knowing where the form ends and where the formless can begin. It's refusing to disguise stagnation as stability. It's choosing to end cleanly rather than wait for the structure to rot from within.

This kind of ending leaves no residue. No lingering distortion. No resentment baked into the next beginning. It clears the field. It allows for regeneration. It creates a kind of trust in the builder; not just from others, but from within. The trust that says: I know when to move on. I know how to stop without collapse.

Clean endings are rare. But they are the hallmark of serious builders.

The Gift of Having Been Wrong

There's a strange grace in being proven wrong; if you're willing to receive it. Not in the moment of impact, when pride is pierced and assumptions collapse. That part stings. That part humiliates. But in the quiet after the collapse, when the noise dies down and the defensiveness dissolves, there's a clarity that only failure can offer: the realization that being wrong is not an indictment; it's an invitation.

Most builders resist this. We build with conviction. We design with certainty. We defend our ideas because we've tied them to our identity. To be wrong feels like disloyalty to the self we've projected. So we resist, reframe, or rebrand. But the gift of having been wrong is only accessible when we stop trying to reinterpret the fall and start listening to it. When we admit; gently, honestly; that what we thought we knew wasn't complete.

Being wrong is not a character flaw. It's a sign of movement. It means you've outgrown the previous logic. It means your perception is catching up to a deeper truth. It means the world has changed, and you have changed with it. And in that gap between what you insisted and what you now see; there is room to become someone new.

The gift of having been wrong is not just insight. It's humility. It's the softening of the need to be right. The loosening of control. The acceptance that clarity evolves. That your earlier self wasn't a fraud; it was incomplete. And that doesn't make you weak. It makes you trustworthy. People trust those who can update. Who can say, "I missed this," and mean it. Who can rebuild without bitterness and lead without ego.

This is how wisdom is earned. Not through perfection, but through correction. Through the willingness to let being wrong refine your range, not shrink your confidence. Through the discipline of using collapse not to justify retreat; but to prepare for a cleaner re-entry.

Builders who last do not need to always be right. They need to always be learning. And every mistake, every misread, every misstep; if held with clarity; becomes a teacher. One that never shouts, but always shows.

Chapter 15

Rebuilding: The Art of Starting Again Without Bitterness

The Second Beginning

Collapse leaves behind more than debris. It leaves behind silence. Not the silence of rest, but the silence of orientation lost. What once structured your days, your decisions, your sense of forward motion has dissolved, and in its place remains an open, unfamiliar space. This space is often mistaken for emptiness or failure, but it is neither. It is the clearing that follows an ending, and within it lies the possibility of a second beginning.

The second beginning does not arrive with enthusiasm or certainty. It is not animated by the intoxication of novelty or the confidence of inexperience. It does not announce itself as opportunity. Instead, it appears quietly, almost reluctantly, as a question rather than a command: *Will you build again?* This question carries weight precisely because it is no longer theoretical. You now understand what building costs. You remember the long hours, the compromises, the emotional exposure, the moments when conviction wavered and endurance replaced inspiration. You remember how much of yourself was required. And still, the question returns.

This second beginning is not a return to what was. It does not seek restoration, vindication, or correction of the past. It is not an attempt to reclaim status or repair reputation. Those motivations belong to the ego, not to the work. The second beginning is quieter and more deliberate. It emerges from awareness rather than urgency. It accepts that you are no longer the person who first began, and therefore what you build next cannot be shaped by the same posture, pace, or identity.

What distinguishes the second beginning is not optimism, but consent. You are no longer carried forward by momentum or illusion. You choose to step forward with full awareness of risk and consequence. This choice carries a different quality of strength. It is not driven by belief that things will work out, but by commitment to act with integrity regardless of outcome. The second beginning is an act of maturity. It does not promise success; it promises coherence.

Importantly, this beginning does not need witnesses. It does not require permission or affirmation. No external authority will certify that the collapse was meaningful or that you have changed sufficiently to try again. If you wait for validation, the second beginning will never occur. It must be self-authorized. You begin again not because the world is ready, but because you are.

The second beginning also refuses spectacle. It does not announce itself as comeback or reinvention. Those narratives remain tethered to the past. This beginning is oriented toward continuation. The work was never about image or recognition; it was always about alignment with something true. And truth, when it remains alive, inevitably seeks form again.

To begin a second time is not to deny what happened. It is to carry it without letting it dictate posture. The second beginning honors experience without being governed by it. It accepts that you cannot return unchanged, and it does not try. Instead, it allows what comes next to be shaped by depth rather than ambition, by presence rather than proof.

This is not renewal through enthusiasm. It is renewal through clarity. And clarity, once earned, does not shout. It simply moves forward.

What Bitterness Tries to Protect

Bitterness often masquerades as strength. It presents itself as discernment earned through pain, as realism sharpened by disappointment. After collapse, bitterness can feel justified; an emotional armor formed from betrayal, loss, and unmet expectations.

It convinces you that mistrust is wisdom and that distance is maturity. But bitterness is not insight. It is a protective reflex, one that attempts to shield what has already been wounded by hardening around it.

At its core, bitterness is not an expression of anger toward the world; it is a strategy to avoid vulnerability. It emerges when the cost of caring has felt too high, when hope has been exposed and punished. Bitterness says, *Never again.* It promises safety by narrowing engagement, by filtering experience through suspicion, by reducing exposure to disappointment. In this way, bitterness does protect something; but what it protects is not strength. It protects fear.

This fear is subtle. It is not the raw fear of the beginner, uncertain and openly anxious. It is the sophisticated fear of the experienced builder, who knows exactly how much can be lost. This fear does not scream; it calculates. It advises caution, skepticism, emotional restraint. It reframes withdrawal as intelligence. Over time, this posture becomes habitual. The builder believes they are being careful, when in fact they are being constrained.

Bitterness also protects identity. After collapse, the story of being wronged can become a stabilizing narrative. It provides explanation and coherence at a time when coherence feels scarce. But this narrative has a cost. When identity organizes itself around injury, it becomes difficult to imagine building without defensiveness. The builder begins to define themselves by what they will not tolerate, rather than by what they are willing to create. The future is shaped as a reaction to the past, not as an expression of present clarity.

There is also a moral seduction in bitterness. It carries a sense of righteousness; *I see clearly now; I am no longer naive.* This posture can feel like progress, especially when contrasted with earlier innocence. But moral superiority is not the same as wisdom. Wisdom remains open even after pain. It integrates experience without closing the door on possibility. Bitterness closes that door and then calls the closure prudence.

Most importantly, bitterness blocks rebuilding. It limits imagination, restricts trust, and poisons collaboration before it begins. A structure built from bitterness may appear strong, but it will be rigid. It will prioritize control over coherence, safety over service. It will reproduce the very brittleness that led to collapse, only under a different justification. The builder may believe they are protecting themselves, but in truth they are protecting the wound, preserving it as a reference point.

Rebuilding requires something more difficult than bitterness. It requires discernment without cynicism, boundaries without hostility, memory without grievance. This does not mean forgetting what happened or minimizing harm. It means refusing to let injury become the architect of what comes next. The builder must recognize bitterness for what it is: a temporary shelter that becomes a prison if inhabited too long.

What bitterness tries to protect is understandable. But what it protects cannot grow. And rebuilding, by definition, requires growth.

Carrying the Wisdom, Not the Wound

Every collapse leaves behind two inheritances. One is the wound; the emotional residue of loss, betrayal, or failure that lingers in the body and shapes instinctive response. The other is wisdom; the hard-earned understanding of limits, patterns, and truths that were invisible before the fall. Rebuilding depends on learning to separate these two. When the wound is mistaken for wisdom, the future becomes constrained by pain. When wisdom is carried without the wound, the future becomes informed rather than governed by the past.

The wound seeks repetition. It relives moments, replays conversations, and reinforces narratives of harm. It pulls attention backward, not to learn, but to justify withdrawal. Wisdom, by contrast, is quiet and forward-facing. It does not replay events; it distills them. It asks what the experience revealed about timing, structure, character, and self-deception. It extracts principles rather than grievances. Wisdom does not need to stay emotionally activated to remain present. Once integrated, it simply becomes part of how decisions are made.

Carrying the wound forward creates a posture of guardedness. The builder may believe they are being cautious, but the caution is reactive. It anticipates harm everywhere because harm once occurred. This posture limits risk-taking, dulls creativity, and constricts trust. It turns every new opportunity into a test of past injury. Over time, the builder stops responding to what is in front of them and begins responding to what already happened. The present becomes a projection of the past.

Carrying wisdom is different. Wisdom allows the builder to recognize familiar patterns without overidentifying with them. It sharpens discernment without closing the heart. It enables boundaries without hostility. Wisdom remembers that failure often arises not from malice, but from misalignment, immaturity, or illusion. This understanding reduces the need for blame and increases the capacity for clarity. The builder can acknowledge what went wrong without remaining entangled in emotional residue.

To carry wisdom without the wound requires deliberate work. It means allowing grief to complete its cycle rather than hardening into identity. It means telling the story of what happened without reactivating its emotional charge. This is not suppression; it is integration. The experience is honored, not relived. When wisdom is fully integrated, it no longer demands attention. It informs quietly, like a compass rather than an alarm.

There is also humility in this separation. The builder must accept their own role in what occurred; not as an act of self-condemnation, but as a recognition of agency. Wisdom acknowledges misjudgment without collapsing into shame. It understands that clarity often arrives only after consequence. This humility is essential for rebuilding because it prevents the builder from projecting unresolved blame onto new contexts and relationships.

The difference between carrying the wound and carrying the wisdom becomes visible in posture. One is tense, defensive, vigilant. The other is grounded, selective, attentive. One narrows possibility; the other refines it. Rebuilding cannot occur from a posture of reactivity. It requires presence.

To begin again with wisdom rather than wounds is not to deny pain. It is to refuse to let pain dictate architecture. What comes next deserves to be shaped by understanding, not by injury.

Starting Small Without Shame

After collapse, ambition often carries a residue of embarrassment. The builder remembers what once existed; the scale, the visibility, the sense of momentum; and feels the contrast acutely. To start again from a smaller place can feel like regression, as though beginning modestly is an admission of failure rather than a strategic choice. Shame enters quietly here, not as humiliation, but as a subtle pressure to skip steps, to accelerate prematurely, to rebuild size before rebuilding coherence. This pressure is dangerous. It tempts the builder to repeat the very errors that led to collapse.

Starting small is not a concession; it is a discipline. It reflects an understanding that strength is not measured by scale, but by alignment. The second beginning does not need to impress. It needs to be sound. Smallness allows for attentiveness. It permits careful construction, honest feedback, and real-time correction. Large structures amplify flaws; small structures reveal them early. The builder who accepts small beginnings creates space for integrity to form before complexity arrives.

Shame distorts this process by framing smallness as inadequacy. It whispers comparisons; *You used to be further along; others are moving faster; this should be easier by now.* These comparisons are irrelevant. They arise from an outdated identity, one that measured worth through expansion rather than coherence. The builder must recognize that the metric has changed. This is not the first ascent; it is a return informed by depth. The starting line is not behind; it is simply different.

There is also freedom in starting small. Without the weight of expectation or the pressure of visibility, the builder can experiment without spectacle. Mistakes are less costly. Adjustments are easier. Learning happens faster because ego is no longer defending an image. The work becomes quieter, more precise, more honest. What emerges is not the adrenaline of growth, but the steadiness of construction done well.

Starting small also restores agency. Large systems often trap builders in maintenance mode, reacting to demands rather than shaping direction. Small beginnings return control to the hands of the builder. Decisions are made deliberately. Values are embedded consciously. Culture is shaped through behavior rather than policy. This foundation becomes the reference point for any future growth, ensuring that expansion, when it comes, amplifies strength rather than magnifying weakness.

Most importantly, starting small without shame requires a redefinition of dignity. Dignity is not found in how much is built, but in how it is built. A modest structure formed with clarity and care carries more integrity than an impressive one erected in haste. The builder who understands this no longer rushes to prove relevance. They focus instead on building something that can be trusted; by themselves first, and then by others.

The second beginning does not demand grand gestures. It demands correctness of scale. Starting small is not an act of retreat; it is an act of precision.

The Discipline of Clean Slate Thinking

Rebuilding tempts the mind to carry forward old frameworks, familiar strategies, and inherited assumptions. After all, they once worked; or appeared to. But the second beginning demands a more exacting discipline: clean slate thinking. This does not mean forgetting experience or discarding hard-earned insight. It means refusing to let previous structures dictate the shape of what comes next. Clean slate thinking clears the mental residue that causes builders to rebuild replicas of what failed, only with better intentions and tighter controls.

The danger of rebuilding without a clean slate is subtle. The builder believes they are being prudent by applying lessons learned, but those lessons may be entangled with outdated identities, obsolete contexts, or compensatory behaviors formed under pressure. What feels like wisdom can become constraint. Old assumptions quietly determine scale, pace, hierarchy, and strategy before the new work has had a chance to declare its own needs. The result is a structure that looks new but behaves old.

Clean slate thinking begins with suspension. The builder pauses long enough to question what they believe is necessary. Must it be this big? Must it move this fast? Must it be structured this way? Must it involve the same roles, markets, or partners? These questions are not theoretical; they are architectural. They prevent the premature hardening of form. They allow the work to reveal itself rather than be imposed upon.

This discipline also requires restraint. There is comfort in familiarity, even when familiarity failed. Clean slate thinking asks the builder to tolerate not knowing for longer than feels comfortable. It resists the urge to fill uncertainty with premature decisions. This restraint creates space for intuition to recalibrate, for priorities to emerge organically, and for alignment to precede execution. It replaces certainty with attentiveness.

Importantly, a clean slate is not empty. It is prepared. The builder brings forward principles, not prescriptions. Values, not blueprints. Awareness, not attachment. These elements act as guides rather than constraints. They allow the new structure to be informed by experience without being governed by it. The builder becomes responsive rather than reactive.

Clean slate thinking also restores creativity. When old narratives loosen their grip, imagination returns. Possibilities widen. The builder can explore forms of contribution that were previously dismissed as impractical or insufficiently ambitious. This creativity is grounded, not grandiose. It seeks coherence rather than spectacle. It asks not, *What would impress?* but, *What would endure?*

Rebuilding demands this discipline because the second beginning is not an iteration; it is a reorientation. The work ahead deserves to be shaped by present clarity, not past momentum. Clean slate thinking honors experience while refusing to let experience become a cage.

To rebuild well, the builder must clear the ground completely; not to forget what stood there before, but to ensure that what rises next is not built on invisible ruins.

Trusting the Process Again

One of the quiet casualties of collapse is trust; not trust in others first, but trust in the process itself. After failure, effort can begin to feel naïve. Patience can feel like exposure. Faith in gradual construction can feel irresponsible. The builder may still believe in discipline, skill, and intention, yet doubt that these are enough. Something inside has learned that doing things "the right way" does not guarantee protection. This doubt lingers beneath the surface, shaping behavior long after the collapse has passed.

To rebuild, trust must be restored; not as blind optimism, but as informed commitment. Trusting the process again does not mean believing that outcomes will be favorable. It means believing that coherence matters even when outcomes are uncertain. It is the decision to act in alignment without demanding reassurance. The builder accepts that no structure is immune to disruption, but also that integrity of process remains the only reliable foundation for endurance.

Distrust of the process often shows up as urgency. The builder pushes prematurely, compresses timelines, and over-controls execution in an attempt to outpace uncertainty. These behaviors feel protective, but they undermine the very stability the builder seeks. When pace accelerates without grounding, fragility increases. Trusting the process requires slowing down enough to let structure form properly. It requires patience not as delay, but as precision.

There is also grief beneath the distrust. The builder may mourn the belief that effort alone was sufficient, that good intentions ensured continuity. This grief must be acknowledged rather than bypassed. Only then can trust return in a more realistic form; one that understands risk without being governed by fear. Trust matures. It becomes quieter, less idealistic, more resilient.

Trusting the process again also means allowing incremental progress to matter. After collapse, small gains can feel insignificant compared to what was lost. The builder may dismiss them as inconsequential. But rebuilding happens through accumulation, not leaps. Each aligned action restores confidence in the process itself.

Over time, this confidence compounds. Not because success is guaranteed, but because integrity has been practiced consistently.

This trust also extends inward. The builder must trust their own capacity to respond to difficulty without unraveling. The second beginning tests this trust repeatedly. Setbacks will occur. Delays will surface. Ambiguity will persist longer than expected. Trusting the process means staying present through these moments without reverting to old defensive patterns. It means believing that steadiness, once cultivated, can be maintained.

Rebuilding is not an act of force; it is an act of continuity. Trusting the process again is the decision to engage fully without illusion. It is the recognition that while outcomes remain uncertain, the manner of building remains within one's control. And that control, exercised with clarity and care, is enough to begin again.

Rebuilding Without Needing to Prove

After collapse, the impulse to prove returns quickly. It dresses itself as motivation, as resolve, as the determination to show that the failure did not define you. This impulse is understandable. When identity has been shaken, proof offers a way to stabilize it. But rebuilding in order to prove something; to others or to yourself; quietly distorts the work. It reintroduces urgency where patience is required and performance where presence is needed. What begins as resolve becomes pressure, and pressure reshapes architecture.

The need to prove is tethered to an audience, real or imagined. It assumes judgment and responds with display. The builder measures progress not by coherence, but by visibility. Success becomes something that must be seen in order to count. This orientation pulls attention outward, away from the integrity of the structure itself. Decisions become reactive. Pace accelerates. Subtle compromises are justified as necessary signals of momentum. The work begins to carry the weight of narrative rather than purpose.

Rebuilding without needing to prove requires a different posture. It asks the builder to sever the connection between worth and outcome. The work does not exist to vindicate the past or silence critics. It exists because it is aligned with something true and worth serving. This alignment must be sufficient. When it is not, the builder will unconsciously ask the structure to compensate for unresolved identity wounds. No enterprise can carry that burden without distortion.

There is also a quieter form of proving that operates internally. The builder may feel the need to prove resilience, competence, or relevance to themselves. This internal audience can be even more demanding than the external one. It insists on progress as reassurance. It grows impatient with ambiguity. It pressures the builder to perform certainty rather than tolerate not knowing. Rebuilding under this pressure reproduces the same fragility that collapse revealed.

Letting go of the need to prove does not mean abandoning standards. On the contrary, it allows standards to become cleaner. Without performance anxiety, decisions can be made on their actual merit. Timelines can be shaped by readiness rather than optics. Growth can be paced according to capacity rather than expectation. The builder begins to work from sufficiency rather than deficit.

This posture also restores dignity to the process. The work is no longer a defense or a rebuttal. It is an offering. It does not argue for the builder's value; it expresses it through care, coherence, and consistency. Over time, this quiet integrity speaks more clearly than any display of success ever could.

Rebuilding without needing to prove is an act of maturity. It signals that the builder has learned what collapse was meant to teach: that validation is unstable ground, and that only alignment sustains. When proof is no longer required, the work can finally be honest.

Letting the New Be New

One of the most subtle obstacles to rebuilding is the tendency to compare what is emerging with what once existed. The builder watches the new take shape and instinctively measures it against the old; its scale, its speed, its promise. This comparison is corrosive. It binds the future to a past that no longer exists and prevents the new from developing according to its own nature. To rebuild well, the builder must allow the new to be new, unburdened by expectations formed in a different season.

The second beginning cannot be judged by first-beginning standards. The conditions are different. The builder is different. The purpose may be clearer, narrower, or quieter. What once required expansion may now require depth. What once demanded visibility may now demand discretion. When the builder insists that the new mirror the old, they impose an identity that no longer fits. The structure resists, tension increases, and frustration follows. The work begins to feel misaligned, not because it is wrong, but because it is being asked to become something it is not.

Letting the new be new requires relinquishing nostalgia. Nostalgia romanticizes the past, filtering out its costs and magnifying its highs. It tempts the builder to recreate moments rather than build meaning. This backward gaze drains energy from the present and clouds judgment. The second beginning does not benefit from reenactment; it benefits from attention. The builder must stay with what is actually unfolding, not what they wish would return.

There is also fear beneath comparison. If the new remains distinct, it may never replicate the validation or recognition the old once provided. Letting it be new means accepting uncertainty about how it will be received, how far it will go, and what form success will take. This uncertainty is uncomfortable, but it is honest. It frees the builder from chasing replication and allows the work to evolve organically.

When the new is allowed to be new, creativity reopens. Possibilities expand beyond previously accepted constraints. The builder can explore forms of contribution that were once dismissed as insufficient or impractical. The work becomes responsive rather than derivative. It grows according to present clarity rather than inherited expectation.

Rebuilding is not an exercise in restoration. It is an act of emergence. The new does not owe the old continuity. It owes only coherence. Letting the new be new is the builder's way of honoring that truth.

The Quiet Confidence of Returning

The confidence that accompanies rebuilding is unlike the confidence of beginnings. It is not energized by certainty or fueled by ambition. It does not announce itself. It settles. This quiet confidence arises not from belief that things will succeed, but from trust in one's capacity to remain steady regardless of outcome. It is the confidence of someone who has endured collapse and discovered that survival did not depend on illusion.

This confidence is often mistaken for caution or reserve. In reality, it is rooted in self-knowledge. The builder understands their limits more clearly. They recognize the signs of misalignment earlier. They are less seduced by momentum and less intimidated by uncertainty. This clarity reduces noise. Decisions become cleaner. Effort becomes more focused. The work progresses without the urgency that once masqueraded as drive.

Returning with quiet confidence also changes how the builder relates to others. There is less need to persuade, impress, or defend. The builder speaks more plainly and listens more carefully. Collaboration becomes easier because ego is less invested in control. Boundaries are firmer because they are no longer reactive. This steadiness creates trust. Others sense that the builder is not trying to extract validation or secure position. They are simply doing the work.

Importantly, this confidence does not eliminate doubt. Doubt still appears, but it no longer destabilizes. It is treated as information rather than threat. The builder can question direction without collapsing into paralysis. They can adjust course without interpreting adjustment as failure. This flexibility strengthens resilience. The work becomes adaptive rather than brittle.

The quiet confidence of returning is not visible to everyone. It does not translate immediately into recognition or applause. But it is felt; by those who work alongside the builder, by those who engage with the structure, by those who sense coherence without spectacle. Over time, this confidence accumulates. It becomes a signature of presence rather than performance.

To return with quiet confidence is to accept that rebuilding is not about reclaiming status. It is about resuming alignment. The builder moves forward not because they are certain, but because they are ready.

Not Redemption; Continuation

Rebuilding is often framed as redemption; a chance to correct the past, to make things right, to restore what was lost. This framing is seductive, but it misplaces the work. Redemption looks backward; rebuilding must look forward. When the builder seeks redemption, they anchor the future to the past, asking the new to justify what came before. This burden distorts intention and reintroduces pressure where clarity is needed.

What is required instead is continuation. The work did not end with collapse; it paused. The form dissolved, but the impulse to create, to serve, to build with integrity remained alive. Rebuilding is not an act of atonement. It is an act of fidelity; to the deeper current that motivated the work in the first place. This current does not demand justification. It simply seeks expression.

Continuation reframes failure. Collapse becomes part of the arc, not its negation. It informs rather than defines. The builder does not need to prove that the past was worthwhile; its worth is evident in the wisdom it produced. The future does not need to redeem the past; it needs to be shaped by what the past revealed. This distinction releases the builder from narrative obligation. The work can proceed without carrying symbolic weight.

In continuation, the builder no longer seeks closure through success. They accept that some questions will remain unanswered, some losses unrecovered. This acceptance creates space for presence. The builder is no longer trying to finish a story; they are participating in an ongoing one. Each step becomes sufficient in itself.

This posture restores simplicity. The work is no longer burdened with meaning beyond its immediate purpose. It exists to be done well, to be aligned, to be honest. Over time, this simplicity produces depth. The structure grows not because it must, but because it can. It endures not because it redeems, but because it belongs.

Rebuilding, then, is not a return to glory or a correction of error. It is the continuation of a discipline. The builder begins again not to erase what happened, but to carry forward what remains true. And what remains true is enough to begin.

Chapter 16

Radical Stillness: The Antidote to Burnout

The Noise That Burns Us

Burnout is often framed as a failure of stamina. The assumption is that the builder simply did not manage energy well enough, did not optimize rest, or did not pace themselves correctly. But this explanation misses the deeper cause. Burnout is not the result of working too much. It is the result of being immersed for too long in unrelenting noise without refuge or orientation. The modern builder does not merely work in a fast world; they live inside a continuous assault on attention.

Noise today is not limited to sound. It is informational, emotional, and psychological. It arrives through constant updates, endless communication, performance metrics, market commentary, social comparison, and the expectation of perpetual responsiveness. Every signal demands engagement. Every delay feels consequential. Over time, this environment trains the builder's nervous system to remain in a state of low-grade alarm. The body never fully settles. The mind never fully clears. Action becomes reflexive rather than intentional.

In this state, motion is mistaken for momentum. Reaction is mistaken for relevance. Urgency is mistaken for importance. The builder remains busy but loses orientation. Decisions are made quickly but without depth. Days are full but strangely unproductive. Progress feels constant, yet direction becomes increasingly vague. The work continues, but its meaning thins.

What makes this noise especially corrosive is that it has no memory. It does not care what was decided yesterday or what matters long-term. It rewards immediacy, not coherence. The builder who remains submerged in this environment gradually loses the ability to distinguish between what is essential and what is merely loud. Attention fractures. Perspective collapses. The work begins to feel simultaneously overwhelming and hollow.

Burnout emerges slowly in this context. It does not announce itself as collapse. It appears as dullness, irritability, and a quiet sense of depletion. The builder still functions, still produces, still responds. But something central has disengaged. Satisfaction disappears. Completion brings no relief. Praise feels distant. Fatigue lingers even after rest. This is not exhaustion of the body alone; it is erosion of meaning.

The danger of this state is that it feels normal. Noise becomes the baseline. Stillness begins to feel foreign, even threatening. Silence is interpreted as absence rather than restoration. The builder becomes disconnected not only from rest, but from themselves. And without that internal reference point, work loses its grounding.

Burnout is not cured by efficiency, delegation, or even time off if the noise remains uninterrupted. What is required is not escape, but interruption. A deliberate return to stillness; not as a reward, but as a structural necessity. Stillness is the antidote precisely because it restores what noise dissolves: clarity, orientation, and the capacity to choose rather than react.

Stillness as a Skill, Not a Mood

Stillness is commonly misunderstood as a feeling; something that arrives when conditions are favorable, when pressure eases, or when life momentarily allows space. In this framing, stillness becomes passive and circumstantial, dependent on external calm. For the entrepreneur, this makes stillness unreliable and rare. The work is never truly finished. Demands do not resolve themselves. If stillness requires quiet surroundings or emotional ease, it will almost never occur. This misunderstanding keeps builders in perpetual motion, waiting for a calm that never comes.

In reality, stillness is not a mood; it is a skill. Like any skill, it must be practiced deliberately and under imperfect conditions. It is the capacity to settle attention even when pressure remains, to pause internal reactivity even while external demands persist. Stillness does not require the absence of noise; it requires the ability to step out of its grip. This distinction is critical. Without it, stillness becomes a luxury rather than a discipline.

Developing stillness as a skill involves training the nervous system to tolerate non-action. Many builders are deeply uncomfortable with pauses because their sense of value has become intertwined with output. Stillness feels like loss of control, loss of relevance, or loss of momentum. The body responds with restlessness. The mind searches for stimulation. This discomfort is not a flaw; it is evidence of conditioning. The builder has learned to equate movement with safety. Stillness threatens that equation.

Practiced skillfully, stillness interrupts this pattern. It teaches the builder that nothing collapses when action stops briefly. Systems do not fail. Identity does not evaporate. The world continues. This realization gradually restores internal autonomy. The builder learns that they can choose when to act rather than being compelled by urgency. This choice is the foundation of sustainable leadership.

Stillness as a skill also refines perception. When the impulse to react is suspended, subtler information becomes available. Patterns emerge. Priorities clarify. Decisions that felt urgent lose their force, while matters that were previously overlooked gain weight. This is not mysticism; it is neurological. Reduced stimulation allows the brain to integrate information rather than merely process it. Insight becomes possible because attention is no longer fragmented.

Importantly, skillful stillness is not withdrawal from responsibility. It is preparation for it. Builders who cultivate stillness act with greater precision because their actions are informed by clarity rather than compulsion. They intervene less often, but more effectively. They speak less, but with more weight. Over time, this changes the entire rhythm of work. Effort becomes intentional. Energy is conserved. Burnout loses its grip.

Stillness, practiced as a skill, becomes portable. It can be accessed in meetings, during conflict, in moments of uncertainty. It no longer depends on retreat or isolation. It becomes an internal posture; one that stabilizes the builder regardless of circumstance. This posture is not passive. It is the ground from which deliberate action emerges.

The entrepreneur who learns stillness as a skill does not slow down indiscriminately. They slow down precisely. And precision, not speed, is what sustains.

The Lie of Momentum

Momentum is one of the most celebrated concepts in modern entrepreneurship. It is spoken of as though it were an intrinsic good; something to be protected at all costs, something that once achieved must never be interrupted. Builders are taught to fear losing momentum more than making poor decisions, to prioritize forward motion even when direction is unclear. This belief is deeply ingrained, and it is profoundly misleading. Momentum, when unexamined, becomes one of the primary accelerants of burnout.

The lie of momentum is that motion itself creates safety. As long as things are moving, the builder feels protected from stagnation, irrelevance, or failure. Action becomes a form of reassurance. The enterprise appears alive because it is busy. But motion without orientation does not produce strength; it produces drift. Momentum can carry a structure far from its center before anyone realizes it has lost alignment. By the time the problem becomes visible, the cost of correction is immense.

Unchecked momentum also suppresses reflection. When speed is rewarded, questioning feels dangerous. Pausing to reassess is interpreted as hesitation. Stillness is framed as weakness. The builder internalizes this logic and begins to equate slowing down with falling behind. Over time, this creates a culture where activity is constant but understanding is shallow. Decisions pile up without integration. Complexity increases without coherence. The enterprise moves faster while seeing less.

Momentum also erodes consent. Early in the building process, action is chosen deliberately. Later, momentum takes over and action becomes compulsory. The builder no longer asks whether a particular initiative is necessary or aligned; they ask only whether it maintains motion. This shift is subtle but consequential. When consent disappears, burnout becomes inevitable. The body and mind resist what they no longer choose. Fatigue becomes chronic because effort is no longer voluntary.

The most dangerous aspect of momentum is that it disguises avoidance. Continuous action can prevent the builder from confronting uncomfortable truths; misalignment, fatigue, diminishing returns, or unresolved conflict. As long as things keep moving, these issues remain in the background. Stillness would bring them forward, which is precisely why it is resisted. Momentum becomes a defense mechanism rather than a strategy.

Breaking the spell of momentum requires courage. The builder must be willing to interrupt motion without immediate justification. They must tolerate the anxiety that arises when speed slows and noise diminishes. This interruption does not signal collapse. It signals recalibration. Only when momentum is paused can direction be reassessed and intention restored.

True strength is not found in endless motion. It is found in the capacity to stop deliberately. The builder who can halt momentum without panic regains authorship of the work. Action once again becomes a choice rather than a compulsion. And in that return to choice, burnout loses its momentum as well.

The Entrepreneur's Fear of Inactivity

Inactivity is one of the entrepreneur's deepest, least examined fears. It is rarely named directly. Instead, it appears as restlessness, impatience, and the compulsion to stay busy even when activity no longer serves the work. Stillness feels risky because it threatens the identity that has been built around usefulness and output. When action stops, the builder is forced to confront a quieter question: *Who am I when I am not producing?*

This fear is reinforced by cultural narratives that equate value with visibility and effort with worth. The entrepreneur learns early that presence must be justified through motion. Silence becomes suspect. Pauses feel like exposure. Inactivity is interpreted not as space, but as vulnerability. The builder fears that if they stop, something will be lost; momentum, relevance, control, or credibility. These fears persist even when evidence suggests otherwise.

At a physiological level, this fear is not abstract. Prolonged engagement with urgency trains the nervous system to associate stillness with threat. The body remains prepared for action, scanning for stimuli, resisting rest. When activity ceases, the system does not immediately relax; it escalates. Thoughts race. Discomfort surfaces. The builder interprets this activation as proof that stopping is dangerous, rather than as a sign of long-standing overstimulation. Stillness feels wrong because the body has forgotten how to settle.

This fear also conceals grief. Inactivity creates space for emotions that have been deferred; disappointment, doubt, exhaustion, and loss. Constant action keeps these emotions at bay. To stop is to allow them entry. The builder may unconsciously prefer fatigue to feeling, because fatigue at least feels productive. Stillness offers no such disguise. It demands honesty.

Yet this fear is based on a false assumption: that inactivity equals abandonment of responsibility. In reality, stillness is often the most responsible act available. It prevents unnecessary action, reduces error, and restores perspective. The builder who cannot tolerate inactivity becomes reactive, making decisions to relieve discomfort rather than to serve the work. Over time, this reactivity undermines leadership and accelerates burnout.

Learning to tolerate inactivity is therefore not indulgent; it is essential. It requires reframing stillness not as absence of work, but as a different mode of engagement. The builder is not disengaged; they are recalibrating. They are allowing the system; internal and external; to settle enough to reveal what is actually needed.

The fear of inactivity fades only through practice. Each deliberate pause teaches the builder that nothing essential collapses in the absence of immediate action. Trust returns gradually. The body relearns that stillness is not danger. The mind relearns that clarity does not emerge from force.

In overcoming this fear, the entrepreneur regains sovereignty over their time and energy. Action resumes not from compulsion, but from choice. And choice, once restored, is the beginning of sustainable leadership.

The Nervous System of the Builder

Burnout is often discussed in strategic or psychological terms, but its roots are physiological. The builder's nervous system carries the cumulative impact of sustained urgency, prolonged stress, and unbroken stimulation. Over time, this system adapts by remaining activated even when threat is absent. What begins as responsiveness becomes hypervigilance. The body forgets how to downshift. Rest no longer restores because the nervous system no longer recognizes safety.

In this state, the builder lives in a constant readiness for action. Muscles remain subtly tense. Breathing becomes shallow. Attention narrows. The mind scans for problems even in moments meant for recovery. This chronic activation distorts perception. Neutral events feel pressing. Minor setbacks feel destabilizing. The builder becomes less tolerant of ambiguity and more reactive under pressure. None of this is a failure of character. It is the predictable result of operating for too long without interruption.

Stillness directly addresses this physiological condition. When practiced deliberately, it signals safety to the nervous system. It allows the body to complete stress cycles that were previously left unresolved. Over time, this reduces baseline tension and restores capacity for regulation. The builder becomes less reactive not through discipline alone, but through biological recalibration. Clarity returns because the system is no longer flooded with false urgency.

Understanding the nervous system also reframes self-judgment. Builders often criticize themselves for irritability, exhaustion, or diminished creativity, interpreting these as personal shortcomings. In reality, these are signals of overload. Without addressing the underlying physiological state, no amount of mindset adjustment will suffice. The body must be included in the work of rebuilding resilience.

Leadership quality is inseparable from nervous system regulation. A dysregulated leader transmits instability to the entire organization. Their urgency spreads. Their reactivity shapes culture. Conversely, a regulated leader becomes a stabilizing force. Their presence lowers ambient stress. Their decisions carry weight without aggression. Stillness, practiced consistently, becomes contagious. It alters the emotional climate of the enterprise.

Reclaiming the nervous system is therefore not a personal luxury. It is an ethical responsibility. The builder who restores their own regulation creates conditions in which others can function without chronic strain. Burnout recedes not because demands vanish, but because the system is no longer perpetually braced against them.

Stillness restores the builder's nervous system to its proper role; not as an alarm that never stops ringing, but as an instrument capable of discernment, recovery, and sustained engagement.

Stillness as Strategic Power

Stillness is often framed as withdrawal from power, as though influence requires constant assertion and visibility. In entrepreneurial culture, power is associated with decisiveness, speed, and control. Stillness appears passive by comparison, even indulgent. This perception is inaccurate. Stillness, when practiced deliberately, is not the absence of power; it is the consolidation of it. It is the condition that allows power to be exercised with precision rather than force.

Strategic power depends on perspective. Without distance, perspective collapses. The builder immersed in constant activity loses the ability to see systems clearly. They respond to surface signals rather than underlying patterns. Stillness restores elevation. It creates the space necessary to observe without immediately intervening. From this vantage point, the builder can distinguish between what is urgent and what is merely noisy, between what requires action and what will resolve on its own. This discernment is a strategic advantage.

Stillness also concentrates authority. Leaders who act continuously dilute their influence. Every decision becomes one among many. Urgency flattens hierarchy because everything feels equally important. In contrast, leaders who pause act less frequently, but with greater impact. Their interventions carry weight because they are selective. The organization learns to listen when they speak. Stillness refines timing, and timing amplifies power.

There is also a psychological dimension to this power. Stillness interrupts reactive loops. When the builder does not respond immediately, emotional escalation dissipates. Conflicts de-escalate. Impulsive decisions lose momentum. This restraint is not avoidance; it is control exercised inwardly before being applied outwardly. The builder who can govern their own impulses governs the system more effectively than one who reacts reflexively.

Strategic stillness also protects long-term objectives. In fast-moving environments, short-term pressures often override foundational priorities. Stillness creates space to remember what the enterprise is actually building toward. It allows values to reassert themselves amid competing demands. This alignment prevents drift and preserves coherence over time. Power exercised without alignment becomes destructive; power grounded in stillness becomes sustaining.

Importantly, stillness does not remove the need for action. It refines it. Action that emerges from stillness is quieter, more deliberate, and more durable. It requires less correction because it is better timed. Over time, this reduces friction throughout the organization. Energy is conserved. Burnout recedes. Effectiveness increases.

Stillness is strategic power precisely because it is rare. In a world addicted to motion, the builder who can pause without panic gains leverage. They see what others miss. They choose where others react. And in doing so, they build not just faster, but wiser.

Interrupting the Loop: When to Stop, and Why

Burnout does not arrive suddenly. It is the product of loops; patterns of behavior, thought, and response that repeat without examination. The builder wakes, engages, reacts, resolves, and repeats. Each cycle reinforces the next. Urgency begets urgency. Responsiveness becomes reflex. Over time, the loop tightens. There is less space between stimulus and action, less room for reflection, less capacity to choose differently. The builder remains active but increasingly constrained.

Interrupting this loop is not intuitive. The loop feels necessary, even virtuous. Stopping can feel irresponsible, as though disengagement itself poses risk. The builder fears that pausing will allow problems to multiply or opportunities to vanish. This fear is reinforced by short-term feedback: when the builder responds immediately, tension decreases. When they delay, discomfort rises. The loop teaches the builder that motion is relief and stillness is threat.

But this relief is temporary. Each completed cycle resets the conditions for the next, often at a higher level of intensity. Problems recur. Demands escalate. The builder becomes indispensable not because they are uniquely effective, but because the system has been conditioned to depend on their constant intervention. This dependency accelerates burnout. The loop sustains itself by consuming the builder's attention.

Interrupting the loop requires a deliberate refusal to respond automatically. The builder must learn to identify moments when action is habitual rather than necessary. This identification often occurs through discomfort; irritation, fatigue, or the sense of repetition without progress. These signals are not weaknesses; they are diagnostic. They indicate that the loop has replaced intention.

Stopping at these moments is not abandonment. It is recalibration. The builder pauses not to escape responsibility, but to restore authorship. By creating space between stimulus and response, they reintroduce choice. This space allows alternative actions to emerge: delegation instead of intervention, clarification instead of escalation, patience instead of force.

The timing of the interruption matters. Waiting until exhaustion ensures collapse. Interrupting earlier preserves capacity. The builder must therefore cultivate sensitivity to early signals rather than dramatic symptoms. When decisions begin to feel automatic, when urgency feels constant, when rest no longer restores, the loop is already in motion. Stillness at these moments is preventive, not reactive.

Why stop? Because continuation without interruption erodes clarity. Because loops do not self-correct. Because systems adapt to what is tolerated. When the builder consistently interrupts unsustainable patterns, the organization recalibrates. New rhythms emerge. Responsibility redistributes. Pressure diffuses.

Interrupting the loop is an act of leadership. It demonstrates that not every demand dictates action and not every moment requires response. Over time, this interruption reshapes culture. The enterprise learns to function without constant acceleration. Burnout loses its inevitability.

Stopping, when done deliberately, is not retreat. It is structural correction.

Making Room for the Unforced

One of the quiet casualties of chronic urgency is the unforced. When every moment is scheduled, optimized, and accounted for, nothing is allowed to arise naturally. The builder moves from task to task with efficiency, but creativity, insight, and genuine connection diminish. These elements cannot be commanded. They require space. Making room for the unforced is therefore not an indulgence; it is a prerequisite for depth.

The unforced emerges when pressure eases. Not when work stops entirely, but when it ceases to be driven by compulsion. In these moments, the mind is no longer preoccupied with execution alone. It begins to wander productively. Associations form. Intuition surfaces. Solutions appear that could not be reached through direct effort.

This phenomenon is well documented, yet consistently ignored. Builders continue to demand results through force, overlooking the fact that many of the most valuable insights arrive indirectly.

Stillness creates the conditions for the unforced by removing constant demand. It signals that not every outcome must be engineered immediately. This signal allows deeper cognitive processes to engage. Problems reorganize themselves. Priorities reorder naturally. What once felt complex becomes simpler, not through analysis, but through integration. The builder does not solve the problem; the problem resolves itself into clarity.

There is also a relational dimension to the unforced. Conversations become more honest when not rushed. Collaboration deepens when space exists for listening rather than performance. Trust strengthens when people are not constantly pressed for output. These qualities cannot be mandated through policy. They arise when the environment permits them. Stillness alters the environment in subtle but decisive ways.

Making room for the unforced requires restraint. The builder must resist the urge to fill every silence with instruction or intervention. They must tolerate ambiguity without rushing to closure. This restraint feels counterintuitive, especially for those accustomed to leading through action. But it is precisely this restraint that allows the system to reveal what it needs next.

The unforced is not passive. It is responsive. It does not negate discipline; it complements it. Structured stillness creates a container in which spontaneity can occur without chaos. The builder remains attentive, not disengaged. They observe rather than impose. Over time, this posture yields more coherent outcomes with less expenditure of energy.

In making room for the unforced, the builder restores balance. Effort and ease coexist. Control loosens just enough for insight to enter. Burnout recedes because the work no longer depends solely on exertion. It is supported by the quiet intelligence that emerges when pressure gives way to space.

The Return of Clarity Through Silence

Clarity does not arrive through accumulation. It emerges through subtraction. When inputs multiply without pause, the mind becomes crowded, and discernment deteriorates. The builder continues to process information, but integration stops. Everything feels equally pressing because nothing has been allowed to settle. Silence restores clarity not by providing answers, but by removing interference.

Silence is not the absence of thought; it is the absence of compulsion. In silence, the mind is no longer forced to respond. Attention stabilizes. What matters rises naturally to the surface, while what does not recede without effort. This process cannot be rushed. It unfolds only when stimulation is sufficiently reduced for the system to recalibrate. The builder does not manufacture clarity; they allow it to return.

This return often surprises. Issues that seemed complex resolve themselves. Decisions that felt heavy lighten. Some problems dissolve entirely once they are no longer reinforced by constant attention. Silence reveals that much of what felt urgent was sustained by noise rather than necessity. The builder regains the ability to distinguish between signal and distraction.

Silence also reconnects the builder with internal reference points that were drowned out by activity. Intuition, often dismissed as unreliable, reasserts itself as a form of pattern recognition grounded in experience. Values become felt rather than merely articulated. The builder remembers not just what they are doing, but why. This remembrance anchors decision-making in meaning rather than reaction.

Importantly, silence does not eliminate uncertainty. It reframes it. Uncertainty becomes information rather than threat. The builder can sit with not knowing without rushing toward premature resolution. This tolerance allows better questions to emerge, which in turn lead to better structures. Clarity becomes durable because it is not forced into existence.

The return of clarity through silence changes how the builder engages with the world. They speak less, but with greater precision. They decide less often, but more effectively. Their presence carries weight because it is not diluted by constant output. Others sense this clarity and respond accordingly. Leadership becomes steadier, less reactive, more trustworthy.

Silence is not withdrawal from responsibility. It is a return to it. When clarity returns, action follows naturally, aligned with what actually matters rather than what merely demands attention. Burnout recedes not because effort disappears, but because effort is finally directed with purpose.

Stillness Not as Escape, But as Structure

Stillness is often approached as a temporary refuge; a place to retreat when exhaustion becomes unavoidable. In this framing, it exists outside the real work, something to be visited briefly before returning to the demands that caused the strain. This approach ensures that burnout repeats. When stillness is treated as escape, it remains optional, fragile, and easily abandoned. For stillness to serve as an antidote to burnout, it must become structural.

Structural stillness is embedded, not appended. It is designed into the rhythms of work, decision-making, and leadership rather than added as a corrective measure. It shapes when action occurs, how often intervention is required, and how attention is distributed. Stillness becomes part of the architecture of the enterprise and the posture of the builder. It is no longer reactive; it is preventative.

This requires intentional design. Time for non-action must be protected with the same seriousness as time for execution. Silence must be treated as a resource rather than a void. Leaders must model restraint rather than constant availability. When stillness is visible at the top, it legitimizes pause throughout the organization. The culture learns that clarity is valued as much as speed.

Structural stillness also establishes boundaries. It limits unnecessary communication, interrupts habitual urgency, and creates space between stimulus and response. These boundaries reduce cognitive load and prevent chronic activation. The builder is no longer required to absorb every signal. They choose which inputs deserve attention. This selectivity restores sovereignty over time and energy.

Importantly, stillness as structure does not weaken performance. It strengthens it. Decisions improve. Errors decrease. Relationships stabilize. The enterprise becomes less dependent on heroic effort and more reliant on coherent systems. Burnout loses its leverage because the environment no longer demands perpetual exertion.

When stillness is integrated structurally, it ceases to feel radical. It becomes normal. Action and rest find equilibrium. Momentum becomes intentional rather than compulsive. The builder operates from presence rather than pressure. This is not a retreat from ambition; it is its maturation.

Stillness, when treated as structure, is not an escape from the work. It is what allows the work to continue without consuming those who carry it.

Chapter 17

Flow States: How to Work Like Water

The Nature of Flow

Flow is not a peak state, a motivational surge, or a productivity trick. It is not something engineered through stimulants, pressure, or willpower. Flow is a condition of alignment; between attention and task, effort and timing, inner rhythm and outer movement. When it is present, work no longer feels imposed. Action unfolds without resistance, and intensity arises without strain. The builder is neither pushing nor withholding. They are participating.

This alignment produces a distinctive quality of experience. Self-consciousness recedes. The constant internal commentary that evaluates, compares, and corrects grows quiet. Time changes texture. Hours compress or expand without friction. The builder does not feel absent, but absorbed. There is no sense of performance, no split between observer and actor. The work proceeds, and the builder proceeds with it, as part of the same motion.

What distinguishes flow from ordinary focus is not concentration alone, but unity. Focus can still be effortful. It can involve tension, self-monitoring, and the sense of holding oneself to task. Flow dissolves that holding. The builder is no longer managing their attention; attention is carried naturally by the work itself. This does not make the work easier. It makes it cleaner. Energy that would have been spent on resistance becomes available for execution.

Flow is often misunderstood because it is described through outcomes rather than structure. People speak of it as speed, output, or excellence. These may accompany flow, but they are not its essence. Flow is about depth, not volume. It is about coherence, not intensity for its own sake. In flow, the builder is fully engaged, yet not compressed by urgency. The work matters, but it does not demand self-violence.

There is also something impersonal about true flow. The builder does not feel like the origin of the work, nor its owner. Ideas arise without clear authorship. Decisions seem obvious in retrospect, though they were not calculated step by step. This can feel mysterious, but it is not mystical. It is what happens when interference is removed and skill is allowed to operate without obstruction.

Flow is sacred not because it is dramatic, but because it is honest. It reveals what the builder is capable of when ego, fear, and distraction step aside. It is harmony in motion; work done in accordance with its own nature, rather than forced into shape. And because it cannot be faked or sustained through effort alone, it remains one of the clearest indicators of alignment between the builder and the work.

Where Resistance Comes From

Resistance is often mistaken for difficulty inherent in the work itself. Builders assume that if something feels heavy, stalled, or frustrating, the task must be wrong, ill-timed, or beyond their capacity. In reality, resistance rarely originates in the work. It arises from interference; internal conditions that disrupt alignment between attention, effort, and intention. Flow disappears not because the stream dries up, but because something has been placed in its path.

The most common source of resistance is ego. Ego insists on authorship, recognition, and control. It monitors performance constantly, asking whether the work is impressive enough, fast enough, visible enough. This self-surveillance fractures attention. Part of the builder is working; another part is watching the work, evaluating it in real time. This split creates friction. The builder is no longer immersed; they are managing an image. Flow cannot occur under observation.

Distraction compounds this interference. Modern environments fragment attention through constant input; messages, notifications, updates, and comparisons. Even when these inputs are ignored, their presence pulls on awareness. The mind remains partially oriented elsewhere, anticipating interruption. This partial engagement prevents depth. Flow requires continuity. When attention is repeatedly broken, the work never gathers enough coherence to carry the builder forward.

Force is another common source of resistance. When the builder pushes beyond capacity, ignores rhythm, or attempts to override fatigue, effort becomes abrasive. Progress may continue temporarily, but friction increases. The work feels strained. Errors multiply. Creativity narrows. Force attempts to compensate for misalignment through intensity, but intensity without alignment only deepens resistance. Flow recedes because the system is being coerced rather than invited.

Fear also plays a role. Fear of failure, fear of inadequacy, fear of wasted time; all generate tension that constricts attention. The builder becomes outcome-focused, preoccupied with whether the work will succeed rather than how it is unfolding. This future orientation pulls energy away from the present task. Flow requires presence. Fear pulls the builder elsewhere.

Resistance, then, is diagnostic. It signals not that the builder should abandon the work, but that conditions are misaligned. Something extraneous has entered the channel; ego, distraction, force, or fear. Removing resistance does not require greater effort. It requires subtraction. When interference is reduced, flow often returns on its own.

Understanding the sources of resistance shifts the builder's approach. Instead of pushing harder, they pause. Instead of judging the work, they examine their posture toward it. Flow is restored not by conquest, but by clearing the path.

The Conditions That Invite Flow

Flow cannot be commanded. It arrives when conditions are right, not when demanded. Builders who chase it directly often push it further away, mistaking intensity for alignment. The more reliable approach is indirect: creating environments, rhythms, and boundaries that reduce interference and allow immersion to occur naturally. Flow is invited, not forced.

Simplicity is the first condition. Flow requires a narrow field of attention. When tasks are overcomplicated, poorly defined, or burdened with excess objectives, attention fragments. The builder expends energy clarifying rather than creating. Simplicity does not mean triviality; it means clarity of purpose. The work must be defined tightly enough that the builder knows exactly what they are doing and why. Ambiguity dissipates flow before it begins.

Boundaries are equally essential. Flow depends on continuity, and continuity requires protection. Interruptions; whether external or self-imposed; fracture immersion. The builder must therefore establish firm boundaries around time, space, and access. This is not rigidity; it is respect for the conditions under which depth becomes possible. Without boundaries, attention remains porous, and flow cannot stabilize.

Rhythm provides the temporal structure that flow inhabits. The builder who ignores natural cycles of energy and fatigue undermines their own capacity for immersion. Flow arises more readily when work is aligned with periods of heightened clarity and alertness. This alignment cannot be optimized universally; it must be observed and honored individually. Rhythm transforms effort from brute force into timing.

Immersion is the final condition. Flow requires sufficient duration for attention to consolidate. Short bursts rarely suffice. The builder must remain with the work long enough for surface concerns to fall away. Early discomfort is common; the mind resists settling. If the builder persists without forcing, a threshold is crossed. Engagement deepens. The work begins to carry attention rather than demand it.

These conditions; simplicity, boundaries, rhythm, immersion; do not guarantee flow. They remove obstacles to it. When present consistently, they create an environment in which flow becomes more likely, more frequent, and more sustainable. The builder stops chasing the state and instead tends the conditions that allow it to appear.

Flow rewards preparation, not urgency. It favors those who shape
their environment with care and patience. When conditions are right,
alignment follows.

Intensity Without Tension

Intensity is often conflated with strain. Builders assume that working
with full power requires compression, urgency, and force. Muscles
tighten. Breathing shortens. Attention narrows into effort. This
posture produces output, but it also generates resistance. Over time,
it exhausts the system and fractures alignment. Flow offers a
different model; one in which intensity is sustained without tension.

In flow, effort is present, but it is distributed rather than concentrated.
The builder is fully engaged, yet not braced against the work.
Energy moves through the task rather than being pushed into it.
This distinction is subtle but critical. Tension arises when the builder
attempts to control outcome, timing, or perception. Intensity arises
when attention is fully committed to the process itself. One constricts;
the other mobilizes.

The body reveals this difference clearly. Under tension, movement
becomes rigid. Small adjustments feel costly. Errors provoke
irritation. Under intensity without tension, movement remains fluid.
Corrections happen naturally. Feedback is absorbed without
disruption. The builder remains responsive rather than defensive.
This physical ease is not laziness; it is efficiency at a systemic level.

Psychologically, intensity without tension requires relinquishing self-
monitoring. The builder stops checking whether they are doing well
and commits to doing the work well. Evaluation is deferred.
Presence replaces performance. This shift frees cognitive resources
previously spent on internal commentary. The mind becomes
quieter, not empty. Focus sharpens because it is no longer divided.

This mode of working also preserves endurance. Tension consumes
energy rapidly because it maintains unnecessary activation.
Intensity without tension draws from deeper reserves. It can be

sustained longer without depletion because it respects the body's mechanics and the mind's need for coherence. Burnout is avoided not by reducing engagement, but by removing friction.

Learning this distinction takes practice. Many builders are habituated to strain and mistake it for seriousness. Letting go of tension can feel like letting go of commitment. In reality, it is a refinement of commitment. The builder remains fully invested, but no longer self-opposed.

Flow depends on this refinement. Without it, intensity collapses into force. With it, effort becomes elegant. The work moves forward with power that does not exhaust itself, and alignment is preserved even at high levels of engagement.

The Builder's Channel

In moments of flow, builders often describe a shift in authorship. The work no longer feels manufactured through effort alone; it feels as though it is moving through them rather than being produced by them. Ideas arrive without strain. Decisions feel obvious in hindsight. The builder is active, yet not exerting control in the usual sense. This experience can be disorienting, especially for those accustomed to identifying closely with output. But it reveals an important truth: flow depends on becoming a channel rather than a controller.

Being a channel does not imply passivity or surrender of responsibility. Skill, preparation, and discipline remain essential. What changes is the relationship between the builder and the work. Instead of imposing form, the builder allows form to emerge. Attention follows the task rather than directing it. This shift reduces friction because the builder is no longer fighting the material, the timing, or themselves.

Control introduces resistance when it becomes excessive. The builder attempts to manage every variable, anticipate every outcome, and correct every deviation. This vigilance fractures attention and tightens posture. Flow recedes because the system is overconstrained. By contrast, channeling requires trust; not in outcome, but in process. The builder trusts their preparation enough to step aside and let the work unfold.

This trust is cultivated through repetition. As competence increases, the need for conscious oversight decreases. The builder recognizes patterns intuitively. Judgment operates in the background rather than the foreground. This does not eliminate error, but it reduces overcorrection. The work retains momentum because it is not constantly interrupted by self-doubt.

There is also humility in becoming a channel. The builder acknowledges that the work is not an extension of ego, but an expression of alignment. Credit becomes secondary. The focus shifts from ownership to stewardship. This humility further reduces resistance because it removes the pressure to perform. The builder is present, not proving.

Flow thrives in this posture because it allows coherence to operate across levels; physical, cognitive, and emotional. The builder is no longer split between doing and watching. Action and awareness converge. The work feels directed because it is no longer obstructed by interference.

To build as a channel is not to diminish agency. It is to refine it. The builder remains responsible for preparation, boundaries, and commitment. Within those structures, they allow the current to carry the work forward. This is not loss of control; it is mastery expressed as trust.

Flow as Devotion

Flow is often treated as a personal reward; an enjoyable state that makes work feel easier or more satisfying. This framing reduces it to indulgence, something earned after sufficient effort or luck. In truth, flow is not a benefit granted to the builder; it is a form of offering made by the builder. It arises when attention is given fully, without reservation or self-interest. In this sense, flow is devotional.

Devotion here does not imply ritual or belief. It refers to the quality of presence brought to the work. When the builder commits attention completely, without bargaining for recognition or outcome, the work becomes the focus rather than the self. This devotion removes the friction created by egoic negotiation. The builder is no longer asking what the work will provide in return. They are simply doing it well.

This posture changes the emotional texture of effort. Work no longer feels transactional. It becomes an act of care. The builder attends to detail not to impress, but because the work deserves it. Time spent in this mode feels meaningful regardless of external result. Satisfaction arises from fidelity to the task rather than from applause or advancement.

Flow deepens under this posture because devotion stabilizes attention. When the builder is not monitoring reward, attention remains uninterrupted. The mind does not wander toward future validation or past comparison. Presence consolidates. Intensity becomes steady rather than spiking. The work benefits from this steadiness through improved coherence and depth.

There is also an ethical dimension to flow as devotion. When builders work in this way, they respect the people who will be affected by the outcome. Products, systems, and decisions shaped in flow tend to carry care within them. They feel considered rather than rushed. This quality is perceptible. It builds trust and longevity.

Devotion also protects against burnout. When work is approached as offering rather than extraction, energy circulates differently. The builder gives, but is not drained in the same way because the giving is aligned. Effort feels purposeful rather than consuming. Recovery becomes easier because the work did not require self-violence.

Flow as devotion reframes excellence. It is no longer about outperforming others or maximizing output. It is about honoring the work through presence. In this framing, flow is not a perk. It is the natural result of showing up fully, without agenda, and allowing alignment to do its quiet work.

Interruptions and Recovery

Flow is fragile not because it is rare, but because modern work environments are hostile to continuity. Interruptions are inevitable. Messages arrive. Decisions intrude. Fatigue surfaces. The mistake builders make is assuming that once flow is broken, it must be abandoned or rebuilt from scratch. This assumption turns interruption into collapse. In reality, flow is resilient when recovery is understood as part of the practice.

Interruptions disrupt flow primarily by fragmenting attention. The builder is pulled out of immersion and forced to reorient repeatedly. Each reorientation carries a cognitive cost. When interruptions are treated as failures, frustration compounds this cost, making return increasingly difficult. The builder expends energy lamenting the loss of flow rather than restoring the conditions that allow it to re-emerge.

Recovery begins with acceptance. Interruptions do not negate alignment; they interrupt it temporarily. The builder must resist the urge to judge the disruption or rush back into intensity. Instead, they pause briefly to reset posture. This pause is not procrastination; it is recalibration. It allows attention to settle before re-engagement. Without it, the builder returns fragmented, carrying residue from the interruption into the work.

Effective recovery also depends on containment. Builders who allow interruptions to sprawl; checking multiple channels, addressing unrelated tasks; extend the disruption unnecessarily. Recovery improves when interruptions are bounded tightly. Address what must be addressed, then disengage cleanly. This containment preserves mental continuity and reduces the effort required to re-enter flow.

There is also a physiological component to recovery. Brief movement, intentional breathing, or a moment of stillness can signal the nervous system to reset. These actions are not distractions; they are transitions. They mark the boundary between interruption and return. Over time, these rituals condition the body to move back into immersion more readily.

Importantly, recovery requires patience. Flow rarely resumes instantly. The builder must remain with the work long enough for attention to consolidate again. Early resistance is normal. If the builder interprets this resistance as failure, they abandon the attempt prematurely. If they persist without force, alignment often returns.

Interruptions are not the enemy of flow. Poor recovery is. When builders learn to return without collapse, flow becomes more durable. It bends without breaking. And this resilience is what allows deep work to coexist with the realities of modern enterprise.

The Ritual of Entrance

Flow does not begin at the moment work starts. It begins at the moment the builder crosses a threshold. Without a clear transition into depth, attention drags fragments of prior activity with it; unfinished conversations, lingering decisions, residual urgency. These fragments prevent immersion. The builder may be working, but they are not yet *with* the work. The ritual of entrance exists to mark this transition deliberately.

Ritual here does not imply ceremony or rigidity. It refers to a consistent sequence that signals to the mind and body that a different mode of engagement is beginning. This sequence creates predictability. Over time, predictability reduces resistance. The nervous system learns that depth is approaching and prepares accordingly. Without such preparation, the builder relies on willpower to force focus, which increases friction and shortens endurance.

An effective ritual of entrance is simple and repeatable. It may involve clearing the physical workspace, closing communication channels, or taking a brief moment of stillness. What matters is not the content of the ritual, but its consistency. Repetition builds association. The builder no longer needs to convince themselves to focus; the ritual initiates the shift automatically.

This transition also establishes intention. Before immersion, the builder clarifies what the session is for. Not a long list of tasks, but a single, well-defined aim. This clarity prevents attention from splintering once work begins. The builder enters flow with orientation rather than improvisation. The work has a container.

The ritual of entrance also serves as a boundary. It separates deep work from the surrounding noise of obligation and responsiveness. By marking this boundary explicitly, the builder protects immersion from casual intrusion. Others learn when access is limited. More importantly, the builder learns to respect their own depth. Flow becomes something entered deliberately, not stumbled into by accident.

Over time, this ritual shortens the distance between starting and immersion. What once took long effortful minutes begins to happen more naturally. The builder arrives more fully, more quickly. Flow becomes less rare not because it is chased, but because the path to it has been made clear.

The ritual of entrance is not about control. It is about invitation. It creates the conditions under which alignment can occur, and then it steps aside.

Letting the Current Lead

Flow changes the builder's relationship to momentum. Instead of generating motion through effort, the builder begins to sense an existing current within the work. This current has its own direction, pace, and intensity. When the builder aligns with it, progress feels supported rather than forced. Letting the current lead does not mean surrendering agency; it means shifting from domination to cooperation.

Many builders are conditioned to impose rhythm on their day. They schedule tasks according to external expectations rather than internal readiness. This imposition often creates resistance. Flow, by contrast, emerges when the builder listens for where energy naturally wants to go. Some tasks invite depth early; others require incubation. When the builder honors this variability, effort becomes more efficient because it is better timed.

Letting the current lead also requires humility. The builder must accept that not all progress is linear or immediately visible. There are moments when insight needs to gestate, when action must wait for clarity. Forcing movement during these moments disrupts flow. Allowing the current to guide timing preserves alignment. The builder remains attentive, not idle.

This approach does not eliminate planning. It refines it. Structure provides the channel; responsiveness determines how the water moves within it. The builder sets boundaries and intentions, then observes how the work unfolds. Adjustments are made in response to feedback rather than impulse. This responsiveness sustains momentum without coercion.

There is also a psychological release in letting the current lead. The builder no longer carries the full burden of propulsion. They participate rather than propel. This reduces anxiety and preserves energy. The work becomes a collaboration between preparation and emergence.

When the builder works with the current, resistance decreases. Decisions feel timely. Execution feels clean. The day unfolds with coherence rather than fragmentation. Flow is not something achieved; it is something joined.

Letting the current lead is not passivity. It is attentiveness practiced at a high level. It requires sensitivity, restraint, and trust. And when mastered, it allows work to move with a grace that effort alone cannot produce.

Beyond Control: The Grace of Flow

At its deepest level, flow requires the builder to relinquish a particular illusion: the belief that excellence is produced through control. Control promises predictability. It reassures the builder that outcomes can be secured through sufficient oversight, pressure, and intervention. But this promise is incomplete. Control can manage process, but it cannot generate coherence. Flow appears only when control gives way to something more refined; trust shaped by preparation.

Beyond control does not mean beyond discipline. Discipline remains the foundation. Skill, structure, and boundaries are all prerequisites. What changes is the builder's relationship to them. Instead of gripping these elements tightly, the builder allows them to operate quietly in the background. Attention is no longer consumed by management. It is freed for participation. This is where grace enters; not as ease, but as effort aligned so precisely that resistance dissolves.

Grace in work is often misinterpreted as luck or talent. In reality, it is the visible result of surrender at the right moment. The builder has done the necessary work to prepare, then steps out of the way enough for the work to move. Decisions are made without strain. Adjustments occur without defensiveness. The builder is fully responsible, yet not burdened by self-conscious control.

This surrender is not dramatic. It is subtle and continuous. The builder notices when effort begins to harden into force and relaxes just enough to restore flow. They recognize when interference is returning and remove it. Over time, this sensitivity becomes intuitive. Flow is not something entered and exited consciously; it becomes the default mode of engagement when alignment is maintained.

Beyond control also transforms mastery. Mastery is no longer defined by domination over the task, but by intimacy with it. The builder understands the work so well that intervention becomes minimal. Like water finding its path, the work adapts to contours rather than breaking against them. This adaptability is strength expressed as responsiveness.

In this state, the boundary between builder and work thins. Effort feels purposeful rather than extractive. Time spent feels complete rather than draining. The builder is not diminished by giving attention; they are sustained by it. Burnout loses its hold because the work no longer requires self-opposition.

Flow, then, is not an achievement to be claimed. It is a grace that appears when preparation meets humility. When control relaxes without collapsing, when effort aligns without strain, when presence replaces performance, work becomes what it was always meant to be: a moving harmony between intention and action.

This is how water works. And this is how enduring builders learn to work as well.

Chapter 18

Non-Attachment to Outcomes: Mastery Through Surrender

The Paradox of Purpose and Surrender

To build without purpose is to drift. Effort disperses, energy leaks, and work loses coherence. Purpose provides orientation; it answers the question of *why this work exists at all*. Yet purpose, when clung to too tightly, becomes a source of distortion. The builder begins to defend it, force it, and preserve it beyond its natural lifespan. What once guided the work now constrains it. The paradox at the heart of enduring creation is this: purpose must be held firmly enough to guide action, yet lightly enough to allow reality to respond.

Surrender is often misunderstood as resignation, as though releasing attachment to outcomes requires diminishing ambition or commitment. In truth, surrender refines ambition. It separates devotion from possession. The builder commits fully to the work; time, attention, rigor, and care; while refusing to bind identity or worth to how the work is received. This refusal is not detachment in the cold sense. It is non-attachment in the disciplined sense: engagement without entanglement.

Caring deeply without clinging tightly is a learned posture. It does not arise naturally, especially for builders accustomed to measuring themselves through results. The instinct to equate outcome with value is strong. When a project succeeds, identity expands; when it fails, identity contracts. This volatility destabilizes the builder and introduces pressure into every decision. Purpose becomes anxious. The work begins to carry the weight of self-justification rather than service.

Non-attachment restores balance. The builder remains serious, invested, and awake in the process, but does not collapse when circumstances shift. They understand that structures serve for seasons. Markets change. Audiences move. Timing intervenes. None of this invalidates the integrity of the work itself. Purpose is not proven by permanence; it is expressed through alignment while the work exists.

This posture allows the builder to endure volatility without bitterness. When outcomes disappoint, surrender prevents contraction. When outcomes exceed expectation, surrender prevents inflation. In both cases, clarity is preserved. The builder continues to act from center rather than reaction. This steadiness is not passive; it is sovereign.

The paradox resolves itself in practice. Purpose provides direction; surrender preserves freedom. One without the other leads either to drift or suffocation. Held together, they allow the builder to move decisively without becoming rigid, to care intensely without becoming captive. This balance is not philosophical decoration. It is structural. It determines whether the work remains alive or calcifies under the weight of expectation.

Purpose guides the hands. Surrender frees them.

Outcome Addiction

The modern builder is trained to measure worth through results. Metrics dominate language, evaluation, and identity. Progress is tracked numerically. Success is quantified, compared, displayed. Over time, this orientation hardens into dependence. Outcomes cease to be feedback and become currency. The builder does not simply want results; they need them to stabilize self-perception. This dependency is subtle, socially reinforced, and deeply corrosive.

Outcome addiction narrows attention. When results become the primary reference point, the builder begins to optimize for appearance rather than integrity. Decisions are shaped by what will register externally rather than what will endure structurally. Short-term gains are privileged over long-term coherence. The work bends toward what can be measured quickly, not what must be cultivated patiently. Clarity erodes because the builder is no longer asking what is right, only what will count.

This addiction also distorts effort. The builder oscillates between overexertion and collapse, driven by the pressure to produce visible wins. Rest feels undeserved unless justified by success. Reflection feels indulgent if it does not yield immediate output. Failure becomes intolerable because it threatens identity rather than simply informing strategy. In this state, the builder is no longer serving the work; the work is serving the builder's need for validation.

Outcome addiction introduces volatility into the system. Emotional stability rises and falls with external response. Praise inflates. Silence destabilizes. Criticism wounds disproportionately. The builder's nervous system becomes entangled with feedback loops they do not control. Burnout accelerates because effort is no longer grounded in purpose but in the pursuit of reassurance. The work becomes extractive rather than expressive.

There is also a strategic cost. Builders addicted to outcomes become less adaptable. They resist necessary pivots because change threatens momentum. They defend failing initiatives because abandonment feels like personal loss. They miss subtle signals because they are focused on dashboards rather than dynamics. In trying to secure results, they lose responsiveness. The system becomes rigid.

Breaking outcome addiction does not mean abandoning standards or ambition. It means relocating value from result to alignment. Outcomes remain relevant, but they no longer define worth. They inform decisions without dictating posture. The builder learns to assess work by coherence, not applause. This shift restores agency. Action becomes intentional again rather than compulsive.

Non-attachment is the antidote to outcome addiction because it restores freedom. The builder can act fully without bargaining for affirmation. They can risk honestly without protecting ego. They can fail without collapse and succeed without inflation. In this freedom, clarity returns. And clarity, not fixation, is what produces enduring results over time.

The Illusion of Control Revisited

Control is one of the builder's most persistent fantasies. It promises predictability in an uncertain world and offers the comfort of believing that effort, intelligence, and vigilance can secure outcomes. This belief is reinforced early, when small systems respond directly to individual action. Over time, however, complexity increases. Markets shift, people change, timing intervenes, and variables multiply beyond any single person's reach. Yet the impulse to control remains, often intensifying precisely when control is least possible.

The illusion of control reasserts itself most strongly around outcomes. The builder assumes that if they plan carefully enough, monitor closely enough, and intervene quickly enough, results can be guaranteed. When outcomes deviate, the response is often to tighten grip rather than reassess posture. More oversight is applied. More pressure is exerted. More energy is spent managing perception. This escalation does not restore control; it amplifies tension. The system grows rigid under strain.

What the builder can truly govern is limited, but significant. They can govern intention: the clarity of why the work exists. They can govern process: the integrity of how decisions are made, how people are treated, how effort is applied. They can govern rhythm: the pace at which work unfolds and the boundaries that protect sustainability. These domains are within reach and require discipline. Outcomes are not.

Outcomes emerge from the interaction of countless factors, many of which remain invisible or uncontrollable. Timing alone can determine success or failure independent of quality. Audience readiness, cultural context, economic conditions, and chance all exert influence. To pretend otherwise is not confidence; it is denial. When builders accept this reality, they do not become passive. They become precise. They stop expending energy on what cannot be commanded and concentrate it where it matters.

Revisiting the illusion of control reveals its emotional cost. Control-seeking binds the builder's nervous system to constant vigilance. It creates anxiety because the world refuses to comply fully. It fuels frustration because effort does not always correlate with reward. Surrender interrupts this cycle. It allows the builder to engage fully while releasing the demand for certainty. This release is not weakness. It is realism applied with courage.

When control loosens, attention sharpens. The builder becomes more responsive, not less responsible. They observe conditions rather than impose assumptions. They adjust intelligently rather than react defensively. The work benefits from this adaptability because it remains alive to context rather than locked into expectation.

The illusion of control fades not through philosophy, but through practice. Each time the builder releases outcome fixation and recommits to process, the system stabilizes. Mastery shifts from domination to stewardship. And in that shift, endurance replaces anxiety as the foundation of serious work.

Attachment as Tension in the System

Attachment to outcomes introduces tension long before results appear. It tightens posture, narrows perception, and compresses time. The builder begins to lean toward a future that has not yet arrived, pulling effort forward in anticipation. This forward-leaning stance may feel like commitment, but it subtly distorts the system. Energy is no longer applied evenly; it is strained. The work becomes heavier because it is carrying expectation in addition to purpose.

This tension shows up first in decision-making. When the builder is attached to a specific result, alternatives are filtered out prematurely. Options that do not lead directly toward the desired outcome are dismissed, even if they might offer resilience or clarity. The builder becomes less curious and more defensive. Feedback is interpreted as threat rather than information. Adaptation slows because change endangers the imagined future.

Attachment also alters pace. Urgency increases because the builder wants to arrive. Timelines compress artificially. Rest is deferred. Reflection is postponed. The present moment is treated as a hurdle rather than a place of construction. Over time, this accelerates burnout. The builder is always arriving and never inhabiting. Effort continues, but satisfaction recedes because the work is never allowed to be enough where it is.

At a physiological level, attachment manifests as chronic activation. The nervous system remains engaged beyond necessity, anticipating success or failure. This sustained tension reduces recovery capacity and increases irritability. The builder may interpret this as passion or intensity, but the body experiences it as strain. Burnout does not require overwork alone; it requires unresolved tension carried forward repeatedly.

Attachment also creates fragility. When identity is bound to outcome, any deviation threatens coherence. Setbacks feel personal. Delays feel destabilizing. Even success can be disruptive, creating pressure to replicate or exceed. The system oscillates because it has lost a stable center. The builder is pulled by expectation rather than anchored by intention.

Releasing attachment does not reduce care. It redistributes it. Care returns to the process, where it can be applied constructively. Attention settles into the present task. Decisions become cleaner because they are no longer distorted by fear of loss or hunger for validation. The system relaxes, not into passivity, but into responsiveness.

When attachment loosens, tension dissipates. Energy flows more evenly. The builder can move forward without dragging the future behind them. Burnout loses momentum because effort is no longer self-opposed. What remains is seriousness without strain; a posture that allows the work to endure.

The Builder's True Responsibility

When outcomes are released, responsibility does not disappear; it clarifies. Non-attachment does not absolve the builder of rigor. It refines where rigor belongs. The builder's true responsibility is not to guarantee results, but to steward the conditions under which results may emerge with integrity. This distinction is foundational. Confusing the two leads either to control obsession or to abdication. Mastery lives in between.

The builder is responsible for intention. This means knowing why the work exists and refusing to dilute that purpose for convenience, approval, or speed. Intention provides orientation when outcomes fluctuate. It anchors decision-making during uncertainty. Without clear intention, surrender becomes drift. With it, surrender becomes disciplined openness.

The builder is also responsible for process. How decisions are made, how people are treated, how resources are allocated, how conflict is handled; these elements define the moral and structural quality of the enterprise. Process is where integrity is practiced daily. Outcomes may vary, but process compounds. Over time, it shapes culture, trust, and resilience. Neglecting process in favor of results produces short-lived success and long-term erosion.

Rhythm is another core responsibility. The builder must set and protect a pace that allows the work to remain alive. This includes honoring limits, building rest into cycles, and resisting unnecessary acceleration. Rhythm is not softness; it is sustainability engineered. Without it, even well-intended efforts exhaust themselves. With it, endurance becomes possible.

Finally, the builder is responsible for presence. Attention is a finite resource, and where it is placed determines what grows. Presence means engaging fully with the work at hand rather than scattering focus across imagined futures. It means listening before acting and observing before intervening. Presence is the ground on which all other responsibilities rest.

What the builder is not responsible for is reception. They cannot govern timing, interpretation, or external response. Attempting to do so distorts effort and introduces anxiety. Releasing this burden allows the builder to direct energy where it can actually make a difference.

When responsibility is properly located, surrender no longer feels like loss. It feels like accuracy. The builder stops carrying weight that does not belong to them and reclaims authority where it does. This redistribution of effort restores clarity, reduces strain, and strengthens the system from within.

Clarity of Intention, Freedom from Expectation

Clarity of intention and freedom from expectation are often mistaken as opposing forces. Builders assume that to release expectation is to weaken resolve, and that to maintain intention requires gripping a specific future. This misunderstanding leads to either rigidity or drift. In reality, these two qualities are complementary. Intention provides direction; freedom from expectation preserves responsiveness. Together, they form the foundation of sovereign creation.

Clarity of intention answers a narrow but decisive question: *What am I here to do?* It does not concern itself with how the work will be received or how far it will go. It identifies the core contribution being made and commits to executing it with integrity. This clarity stabilizes effort. When challenges arise, the builder does not panic or overcorrect. They return to intention as reference. The work remains oriented even when outcomes are uncertain.

Expectation, by contrast, reaches forward and demands a particular return. It imagines validation, success, or permanence and begins to act in service of that imagined future. This forward pull distorts judgment. The builder starts shaping decisions around hoped-for reactions rather than present truth. Freedom from expectation severs this pull. It allows the builder to remain rooted in the current moment, responding to what is real rather than what is desired.

When intention is clear and expectation is released, effort becomes clean. The builder works fully without bargaining. They do not rush to secure results or protect against disappointment. This posture reduces anxiety because the future is no longer being managed emotionally. Attention remains available for execution. The system relaxes into coherence.

This combination also enhances adaptability. Without expectation, the builder can adjust course without interpreting change as failure.

Without intention, adjustment becomes aimless. Together, they allow intelligent evolution. The work stays alive because it is neither frozen by attachment nor diluted by indecision.

Freedom from expectation also protects stamina. When builders are attached to outcomes, every delay feels costly. When expectation is released, time regains neutrality. The builder can move at the pace required by the work rather than the pace demanded by imagined reward. Burnout recedes because effort is no longer strained by anticipation.

Clarity of intention does not fluctuate with circumstances. Freedom from expectation absorbs fluctuation without damage. In this balance, the builder regains sovereignty. They act decisively without clinging, and care deeply without being consumed. This is not detachment from the work. It is fidelity to it.

What Gets Built in the Absence of Clinging

When attachment loosens, the character of what is built changes. Structures formed without clinging are not weaker or less ambitious; they are cleaner. They reflect the actual needs of the moment rather than the builder's imagined future. Without the pressure to arrive at a predetermined result, design becomes responsive. The work evolves in dialogue with reality instead of being imposed upon it.

In the absence of clinging, unexpected outcomes emerge. These outcomes are often quieter than those the builder initially envisioned, but they carry greater integrity. They fit the context more precisely. They endure because they were allowed to form according to conditions rather than expectations. The builder may not have planned them, but they recognize their rightness once they appear.

Purer structures also emerge because compromise decreases. Attachment encourages shortcuts when results are delayed. Without attachment, there is less incentive to dilute standards for the sake of progress. Decisions are made on their actual merit. The work is shaped by coherence rather than urgency. Over time, this discipline compounds. The structure gains trust, internally and externally, because it behaves consistently.

Emergent design thrives in this environment. Instead of forcing scale, the builder allows scale to arise where it is warranted. Instead of expanding uniformly, the work develops depth where it is strongest. This selectivity produces resilience. The enterprise grows organically rather than symmetrically, responding to signals rather than projections.

There is also an emotional shift. Without clinging, the builder experiences less anxiety around direction. The work no longer feels like a referendum on worth. This freedom restores curiosity. The builder can explore possibilities without fear of being wrong. Learning accelerates because experimentation is no longer penalized by ego.

What gets built without clinging often surprises the builder. It may not resemble the original vision, yet it carries the original intention more faithfully than any forced outcome could. This is the quiet reward of surrender: not loss of ambition, but the emergence of something more aligned than ambition alone could produce.

Failure and the Gift of the Unintended

Failure is most instructive when it is no longer defended against. As long as the builder clings to outcome, failure is experienced as rupture; something to be avoided, explained away, or redeemed as quickly as possible. In this posture, its lessons remain obscured. Ego rushes to recover position, and the work moves on unchanged. When attachment loosens, failure is no longer an enemy. It becomes a signal; one that reveals information unavailable under conditions of success.

The unintended is often dismissed as error. Builders focus on what did not work rather than what unexpectedly appeared. Yet when outcomes are not tightly gripped, the unintended becomes visible as a parallel result rather than a deviation. New capacities emerge.

Hidden constraints surface. Assumptions are exposed. These revelations do not arrive gently, but they arrive accurately. They show the builder what the system is actually capable of sustaining, not what was imagined.

Failure also clarifies timing. Some efforts fail not because they lack merit, but because conditions are not ready. Without attachment, the builder can recognize this distinction without shame. The work may be sound, but premature. Or the form may be wrong, while the underlying intention remains valid. This discernment is only possible when ego is not demanding immediate validation.

There is a structural gift in failure when it is met without clinging. It removes excess. Illusions dissolve. What remains is simpler, truer, and more workable. The builder is forced to rebuild from what actually functions rather than from what was hoped would function. This pruning strengthens the system. It reduces fragility by aligning ambition with reality.

Emotionally, failure without attachment is still felt, but it is not catastrophic. Disappointment does not metastasize into self-rejection. Grief completes its cycle rather than calcifying into bitterness. The builder can mourn what was lost without turning loss into identity. This emotional mobility preserves stamina and prevents burnout.

The gift of the unintended is that it reorients the builder toward discovery rather than defense. What emerges may not match the original goal, but it often carries deeper coherence. Many enduring structures arise not from fulfilled plans, but from attentive response to what appeared when plans fell apart.

Failure, when met without clinging, does not end the work. It refines it.

The Discipline of Emotional Non-Interference

Non-attachment is often mistaken for emotional distance, as though surrender requires numbing or suppression. This misunderstanding leads builders to harden themselves in the name of discipline, creating emotional rigidity rather than freedom. True non-attachment does not deny feeling; it regulates interference. Emotional non-interference means allowing emotions to arise fully without permitting them to hijack perception, decision-making, or identity.

Emotions are information. They register alignment and misalignment, effort and strain, resonance and resistance. When builders attempt to suppress emotion, they lose access to this data. When they indulge emotion, they become governed by it. Emotional non-interference occupies the narrow space between these extremes. The builder feels disappointment without collapsing into discouragement. They feel excitement without rushing into overextension. They feel fear without retreating into control.

This discipline is developed through observation rather than management. The builder notices emotional responses as they appear and allows them to move without assigning authority. Emotions are acknowledged but not consulted as decision-makers. This separation restores clarity. The builder remains responsive without becoming reactive. Over time, emotional charge diminishes because it is no longer reinforced through resistance or indulgence.

Emotional interference is one of the primary drivers of burnout. When feelings are resisted, tension accumulates. When feelings dominate, volatility increases. Both exhaust the system. Non-interference allows emotional energy to pass through without stagnation. The nervous system stabilizes. Attention remains available for the work itself.

This discipline also preserves relationships. Builders who act from emotional interference tend to overcorrect, withdraw, or escalate unnecessarily. When emotions are allowed without interference, communication becomes cleaner. Boundaries are set without hostility. Feedback is received without defensiveness. The system benefits from this emotional hygiene.

Emotional non-interference does not eliminate passion. It refines it. Passion becomes sustained rather than erratic. Care remains deep, but it no longer destabilizes the builder. The work is engaged fully, yet the builder remains sovereign.

This discipline is not passive. It requires attentiveness and restraint. But its rewards are structural. When emotions inform rather than command, clarity endures and stamina increases.

Surrender as Strategic Edge

Surrender is often portrayed as the opposite of strategy; as though letting go weakens leverage and reduces effectiveness. In reality, surrender sharpens strategic capacity by removing distortion. When the builder is no longer entangled with outcome, perception clears. Energy is no longer divided between execution and self-protection. Attention becomes precise. This precision is the strategic edge.

Non-attachment improves timing. Builders who cling to results push prematurely or hesitate defensively. Those who surrender can wait without anxiety and act without hesitation. They recognize when conditions are not ready and do not force movement. They also recognize when alignment appears and move decisively. This responsiveness cannot be simulated through planning alone. It emerges from presence unburdened by expectation.

Surrender also preserves stamina. When effort is no longer strained by emotional bargaining, energy circulates more efficiently. The builder can sustain high engagement without depletion because they are not fighting reality. They work with conditions rather than against them. Over time, this endurance compounds into consistency, which is far more powerful than sporadic intensity.

There is a competitive dimension to this edge, though it rarely looks like competition. Builders who surrender outperform those who cling because their systems remain adaptable. They pivot without panic. They release failing initiatives without shame. They invest where coherence appears rather than where ego insists. This adaptability allows them to survive volatility that exhausts others.

Surrender also enhances judgment. Without the need to defend identity or justify past decisions, the builder can see clearly. Mistakes are corrected earlier. Signals are read accurately. Strategy becomes lighter because it is no longer burdened with narrative maintenance. The work moves forward cleanly.

Ultimately, surrender redefines mastery. Mastery is no longer measured by dominance over outcome, but by fidelity to process. The builder acts fully, releases cleanly, and remains available for what emerges next. This availability is strength. It allows the work to evolve without consuming the one who carries it.

Surrender is not retreat. It is the most efficient use of effort available. By letting go of what cannot be governed, the builder gains authority where it matters most. And in that redistribution of control, endurance, clarity, and precision converge.

Chapter 19

The Entrepreneur as Gardener: Tending What You Cannot Force

Seeds, Not Schematics

Builders are trained to think in schematics. They draw plans, define milestones, and expect materials to obey intention. This mindset works well with inert structures. Walls rise when pressure is applied. Systems respond predictably when inputs are controlled. But living systems do not behave this way. Enterprises, teams, ideas, and cultures grow rather than assemble. They respond to conditions, not commands. The mature entrepreneur eventually learns that building something alive requires a different starting point. Not schematics, but seeds.

A seed contains potential, not certainty. It carries within it the entire architecture of what may emerge, yet offers no guarantee regarding timing, scale, or form. Its intelligence is latent. It responds to soil, season, and care rather than instruction. To work with seeds is to accept uncertainty at the outset. It is to begin without the reassurance of visibility. This is not poor planning; it is a more demanding form of it.

Seeds require trust in process. They demand patience before evidence. The entrepreneur accustomed to immediate feedback often finds this uncomfortable. Early stages feel unproductive because progress is hidden. Roots develop underground. Nothing appears to be happening. The temptation to intervene prematurely is strong. But interference at this stage is destructive. A seed cannot be forced open without being ruined. Growth unfolds according to its own internal logic.

This distinction reshapes how serious builders approach innovation. Instead of obsessing over execution plans before life has even appeared, they focus on conditions. They ask whether the environment can sustain what is being planted. They pay attention to readiness rather than projection. They stop mistaking control for competence. This shift does not reduce ambition. It refines it.

Working with seeds also requires humility. The entrepreneur relinquishes the fantasy of authorship over every detail. They accept that emergence will involve surprise. The final form may differ from the initial idea. This is not failure; it is fidelity to life. Structures that endure often do so precisely because they were allowed to evolve rather than being frozen at inception.

Beginning with seeds rather than schematics is an act of disciplined restraint. It acknowledges that some forms of intelligence operate beyond conscious design. The entrepreneur still works, tends, and commits fully. But they no longer confuse effort with domination. They collaborate with growth rather than attempting to command it.

This is the gardener's posture. And it marks the transition from mechanical building to living stewardship.

The Illusion of Control in Growth

Growth tempts the entrepreneur into believing it can be directed with the same precision as execution. When early indicators respond positively, confidence escalates into assumption. Metrics rise. Engagement increases. Demand appears predictable. The builder begins to believe that growth is something to be managed through pressure and planning alone. This belief is understandable; it is also incomplete. Growth, unlike construction, does not submit fully to control. It responds to conditions, not coercion.

The illusion of control in growth emerges when correlation is mistaken for causation. The builder observes that certain actions preceded expansion and assumes repetition will guarantee continuation. But living systems are not linear. What worked in one phase may fail in another. Context shifts. Capacity changes. External variables intervene. When growth is forced to comply with outdated assumptions, strain appears. Quality degrades. Culture thins. The system begins to resist.

Control-driven growth often accelerates fragility. The builder pushes scale without reinforcing roots. Expansion outruns integration. Decisions multiply faster than understanding. The enterprise looks larger, but becomes less resilient. Like a plant stretched toward light without sufficient support, it grows tall and weak. Collapse becomes a matter of timing rather than possibility.

This illusion also distorts leadership behavior. The builder intervenes more frequently, monitoring outcomes obsessively and correcting deviations prematurely. Teams lose autonomy. Initiative narrows. Learning slows because mistakes are not allowed to complete their instructional arc. Growth becomes brittle because it depends on constant oversight rather than internal coherence.

Letting go of control in growth does not mean abandoning responsibility. It means relocating it. The builder focuses on strengthening conditions rather than manipulating outcomes. They invest in culture, clarity, and rhythm. They ensure that systems can absorb expansion rather than merely display it. Growth is allowed to emerge where capacity exists and slow where it does not.

When control loosens, growth often becomes more sustainable. It may proceed unevenly, but it carries depth. The enterprise develops internal intelligence, adapting to pressure without requiring constant intervention. This adaptability is not accidental; it is the result of stewardship rather than force.

The gardener understands this intuitively. Growth cannot be commanded. It can only be invited. And what is invited patiently tends to endure longer than what is imposed aggressively.

Watering Without Pulling

When growth begins to appear, the urge to accelerate it becomes nearly irresistible. The entrepreneur sees movement and wants confirmation. They want proof that the effort is working, that the direction is correct, that momentum will continue. This urge expresses itself as pulling; checking too often, intervening too quickly, scaling before stabilization. What feels like attentiveness is often anxiety disguised as management. In living systems, this behavior is counterproductive. Growth cannot be pulled forward without damage.

Watering is care applied without demand. It is consistent, patient, and proportionate. It responds to need rather than expectation. Pulling, by contrast, is care distorted by urgency. It attempts to extract visible progress rather than support internal development. In enterprises, pulling shows up as premature launches, excessive measurement, constant pivots, and pressure for immediate returns. These actions disturb the root system before it has established resilience.

The difficulty is that watering offers little immediate reassurance. Its effects are cumulative and often invisible at first. The builder must trust that what is being tended will respond in its own time. This trust is not passive. It requires discipline to continue providing resources, clarity, and protection without demanding proof at every step. Watering is an act of faith grounded in observation, not in fantasy.

Pulling often damages what it seeks to confirm. Teams become reactive rather than thoughtful. Products are shaped by feedback before they have coherence. Culture adapts to pressure rather than purpose. The enterprise appears busy, but its internal strength diminishes. Like a plant pulled from the soil to check its roots, the system is repeatedly destabilized in the name of reassurance.

Learning to water without pulling requires restraint. The builder must tolerate uncertainty and delay. They must distinguish between signals that require intervention and those that simply require time. This discernment develops through experience and humility. It involves stepping back enough to let processes complete their cycles.

When watering replaces pulling, growth becomes steadier. The system develops confidence in itself. Feedback loops mature. The builder's role shifts from constant adjustment to attentive support. Over time, this posture produces structures that can sustain expansion without collapse.

Watering is not inaction. It is care without coercion. And in living systems, that difference determines whether growth strengthens or fractures under its own weight.

Soil, Season, Sunlight: What You Cannot Manufacture

Every living system depends on conditions that cannot be engineered on demand. Soil quality, seasonal timing, and exposure to light are not variables the gardener controls directly. They are realities to be read, respected, and worked within. Entrepreneurs often resist this truth. Accustomed to shaping outcomes through effort and intelligence, they search for substitutes; capital instead of soil, speed instead of season, visibility instead of sunlight. These substitutions work briefly, then fail.

Soil represents the underlying environment in which the enterprise grows. It includes culture, trust, shared language, and the emotional climate of the team. Poor soil cannot be compensated for with better strategy. No amount of execution can override a toxic environment. Ideas struggle to take root. Talent withers. Energy dissipates. Improving soil is slow, unglamorous work. It involves repairing trust, clarifying values, and removing contaminants that have accumulated over time. This work rarely produces immediate results, but without it, nothing else holds.

Season refers to timing; both internal and external. Markets have seasons. People have seasons. The builder has seasons of capacity and clarity. Ignoring season leads to misalignment. Launches fail not because they are flawed, but because the ground is not ready. Expansion strains because the organization has not yet integrated its previous phase. Pushing against season exhausts resources and breeds frustration. Working with season requires patience and humility. It demands the ability to wait without disengaging.

Sunlight represents exposure and attention. Too little and growth stagnates; too much and it scorches. Entrepreneurs often mistake visibility for validation and overexpose early structures to scrutiny.

Ideas are forced into public evaluation before they have strength. Feedback overwhelms formation. Conversely, some builders withhold exposure too long, starving the work of the energy it needs to mature. Discernment is required to know when and how much attention to allow.

None of these conditions can be manufactured directly. They can only be cultivated indirectly. The builder improves soil through care, season through timing, and sunlight through calibrated exposure. Attempts to bypass these realities produce brittle growth that collapses under pressure.

The gardener's wisdom lies in acceptance. Not resignation, but realism. Growth is not accelerated by denying conditions; it is sustained by aligning with them. When the builder learns to work within what cannot be forced, effort becomes more effective, not less. The system grows at a pace it can survive.

Pruning: Letting Go for Greater Growth

Growth without pruning leads to congestion. Energy disperses across too many branches, none of which receive enough nourishment to mature fully. In enterprises, this shows up as bloated offerings, overlapping initiatives, and diluted focus. The builder assumes that addition equals progress and hesitates to remove what is already in motion. But living systems do not strengthen through accumulation alone. They strengthen through selective release.

Pruning is an act of discernment, not destruction. It removes what diverts energy from the core and redirects nourishment toward what can bear fruit. This requires clarity about what the enterprise exists to serve. Without that clarity, pruning feels arbitrary or punitive. With it, pruning becomes precise. The builder does not cut indiscriminately; they remove what no longer aligns, even if it once did.

Emotionally, pruning is difficult because it confronts attachment. The builder may have invested time, identity, or reputation in what must be released. Letting go can feel like admitting error or wasting effort. This interpretation is misleading. What is pruned contributed to the system's learning. Its value is not erased by its removal. Pruning honors growth by preventing stagnation.

There is also a timing element. Pruning too early stunts development; pruning too late exhausts resources. The gardener learns to read signals rather than rely on fixed schedules. In enterprises, these signals appear as diminishing returns, increasing friction, or loss of coherence. When effort increases but vitality declines, pruning is often required.

Effective pruning strengthens resilience. It reduces complexity, clarifies direction, and restores energy. Teams regain focus. Decision-making accelerates. The enterprise breathes more easily because it is no longer sustaining unnecessary weight. Growth that follows pruning is often more robust because it is supported by clearer structure.

Pruning is not retreat. It is preparation. By releasing what weakens the whole, the builder creates space for healthier expansion. What remains grows stronger because it is no longer competing for limited resources. This is how living systems maintain vitality over time.

Letting go, when done deliberately, is an act of care.

Compost and Return: Using Waste as Fertilizer

In living systems, nothing is truly wasted. What decays becomes nourishment. What collapses returns as material for future growth. Entrepreneurs often resist this cycle. They treat failure, excess, and abandonment as loss rather than transformation. This resistance compounds pain and obscures value. Composting, by contrast, requires patience and perspective. It asks the builder to allow what is finished to break down fully before reusing its substance.

Compost is not repurposing in haste. It is decomposition allowed to complete its work. Ideas that failed, strategies that exhausted themselves, relationships that no longer serve; all contain nutrients, but only after their form has dissolved. Premature reuse preserves contamination. Lessons are distorted when they are extracted defensively. True composting requires distance. The builder must step back long enough for emotion, justification, and narrative to settle.

When composting is done well, the system gains depth. Patterns become visible. Repeated mistakes reveal structural flaws rather than isolated errors. Excess clarifies where boundaries were missing. Waste identifies misalignment more clearly than success ever could. These insights enrich the soil of the next iteration. The builder does not repeat the past because the past has been integrated rather than avoided.

This process also restores dignity to what ended. Failed initiatives are no longer treated as embarrassments to be buried. They are acknowledged as contributors to learning. Teams regain trust when endings are handled with respect rather than denial. Culture strengthens because honesty replaces spin. The enterprise becomes capable of metabolizing experience rather than accumulating scar tissue.

Composting also requires restraint. Not everything must be salvaged. Some material simply nourishes indirectly. The builder resists the urge to extract immediate utility and allows meaning to emerge gradually. This patience pays dividends. The next growth cycle benefits from richer soil, fewer toxins, and clearer boundaries.

Return is inevitable. What is not composted returns as unresolved pattern. What is composted returns as strength. The gardener understands that decay is not the opposite of growth; it is its prerequisite. The entrepreneur who learns this cycle builds enterprises capable of renewal rather than repetition.

Waste, when honored properly, becomes fertilizer.

Invasive Weeds: Distractions Masquerading as Opportunities

Not everything that grows belongs. In living systems, invasive weeds often appear vigorous and opportunistic, spreading quickly and consuming resources. They mimic vitality while undermining health. In enterprises, these weeds take the form of distractions disguised as opportunity; projects that promise expansion but dilute focus, partnerships that add visibility but erode coherence, innovations that excite but misalign. Left unchecked, they crowd out what actually sustains growth.

These distractions are seductive because they arrive with momentum. They flatter ambition and appeal to fear of missing out. The builder is tempted to say yes because saying no feels like contraction. But growth that depends on constant addition loses discernment. Energy disperses. The enterprise becomes reactive, responding to whatever appears rather than tending what matters. Over time, the core weakens because it is competing for resources with elements that do not belong.

Invasive weeds often thrive in poorly defined systems. When purpose is vague and boundaries are porous, almost anything can justify entry. The builder mistakes openness for adaptability. In reality, adaptability requires a strong center. Without it, the system cannot distinguish nourishment from depletion. Every opportunity feels equally urgent, and decision-making becomes opportunistic rather than intentional.

Removing invasive weeds is uncomfortable because it involves reversal. The builder must acknowledge that something once welcomed no longer serves. This acknowledgment can feel like failure or inconsistency. In truth, it is evidence of maturation. As the system clarifies, discernment sharpens. What once seemed promising is revealed as misaligned. Removal restores balance.

Effective weeding is proactive rather than reactive. The builder regularly assesses where energy is going and what it is producing. They look for signs of crowding; overextended teams, diluted messaging, diminishing returns. When these signs appear, removal is decisive. Delay allows roots to deepen, making extraction more costly.

Clearing distractions restores vitality. Resources return to what matters. The enterprise regains coherence. Growth becomes intentional again. Like a well-tended garden, the system breathes because space has been reclaimed.

Discernment, not accumulation, determines what thrives.

Weathering: Endurance Over Ideal Conditions

Entrepreneurs often design for ideal conditions. Plans assume cooperation, stability, and favorable timing. When reality diverges; as it inevitably does; frustration follows. The builder waits for circumstances to improve before re-engaging fully, believing that progress depends on optimization of external variables. This belief misreads how living systems survive. Endurance is not built through ideal conditions; it is forged through weathering.

Weathering refers to the system's capacity to remain intact under fluctuation. Wind, drought, excess rain, and sudden cold do not signal failure; they test resilience. Enterprises exposed only to favorable conditions grow soft. They perform well when protected, but fracture under pressure. Systems that endure have learned to absorb stress without collapsing. They bend, adapt, and recover because they were shaped in imperfect environments.

For the builder, weathering requires a shift in posture. Instead of waiting for clarity before acting, they act with clarity amid uncertainty. Instead of designing for permanence, they design for adaptability. This does not mean abandoning standards. It means acknowledging that volatility is not an interruption of the work; it is the context in which the work exists.

Weathering also recalibrates expectation. The builder learns to measure progress by continuity rather than comfort. Survival through difficulty becomes success in its own right. Momentum is redefined as persistence rather than acceleration. This reframing protects morale and preserves stamina. The system remains engaged even when conditions are unfavorable.

At an organizational level, weathering distributes strength. Teams learn to problem-solve rather than wait for instruction. Redundancies develop naturally. Knowledge spreads because no single pathway can be relied upon exclusively. This decentralization increases resilience. The enterprise becomes less dependent on perfect execution and more capable of recovery.

Weathering teaches humility. It reminds the builder that control is partial and that endurance matters more than dominance. Those who endure through unfavorable seasons emerge with deeper coherence and greater credibility. Their structures carry the imprint of having survived.

Ideal conditions are temporary. Endurance is cumulative. The entrepreneur who designs for weather rather than fantasy builds systems that last.

Harvest Without Attachment

Harvest is the moment most builders anticipate, yet it is also where distortion often re-enters. After long periods of tending, waiting, and weathering, results finally become visible. Revenue arrives. Recognition follows. Impact can be measured. At this stage, attachment easily resurfaces. The builder wants the harvest to confirm worth, justify effort, and secure the future. When this happens, the harvest is burdened with meaning it cannot sustain.

Harvest without attachment requires restraint. The builder receives what the season offers without demanding more than what has ripened. They do not pull prematurely, nor do they hoard excessively. They understand that harvest is not culmination, but transition. What is gathered will be distributed, reinvested, or allowed to rest. The cycle continues regardless of satisfaction or disappointment.

Attachment at harvest introduces imbalance. Success tempts overexpansion. The builder assumes favorable conditions will persist and accelerates growth beyond capacity. Alternatively, fear of loss leads to clinging; overprotection of gains, resistance to change, reluctance to reinvest. Both responses distort rhythm. The system tightens when it should circulate. Vitality diminishes because energy is trapped rather than moved.

Harvest without attachment preserves clarity. The builder evaluates outcomes soberly, neither inflating nor dismissing them. Success is acknowledged without becoming identity. Failure is noted without becoming verdict. This neutrality allows learning to continue. Patterns are observed accurately because emotion is not distorting interpretation.

There is also generosity in unattached harvest. The builder recognizes that value is meant to move. Resources are shared appropriately. Credit is distributed. The system nourishes its contributors rather than centralizing reward. This circulation strengthens trust and prepares the ground for future cycles.

Unattached harvest honors effort without idolizing outcome. It respects the work without freezing it in place. The builder remains grateful but not dependent. Satisfaction arises from having tended well, not from having arrived permanently.

When harvest is met this way, it completes the cycle cleanly. Nothing is clung to. Nothing is wasted. The system remains alive and ready for what comes next.

Stewardship Over Ownership

The final discipline of the gardener is remembering what does not belong to them. Ownership implies control, entitlement, and permanence. Stewardship implies care, responsibility, and transience. Entrepreneurs are often encouraged to see themselves as owners; of ideas, systems, cultures, outcomes. This framing inflates authority and distorts judgment. What is owned must be defended. What is stewarded must be tended.

Stewardship reframes the builder's role. The enterprise is not an extension of ego or a monument to identity. It is a living system temporarily entrusted to the builder's care. This trust carries obligation without possession. Decisions are made in service of health rather than dominance. Short-term gain is weighed against long-term vitality. The builder asks not what they can extract, but what the system requires to remain alive.

This posture reduces anxiety because it releases the burden of permanence. The builder no longer needs to secure legacy through control. They accept that all systems evolve beyond their originators. Teams change. Markets shift. Leadership transitions. Stewardship prepares for this reality rather than resisting it. Structures are designed to function without constant oversight. Knowledge is shared rather than hoarded. Authority is distributed where possible.

Stewardship also sharpens ethics. When the builder understands themselves as a caretaker rather than an owner, decisions affecting people, resources, and communities are approached with greater care. Impact is considered beyond immediate benefit. Harm is taken seriously because it affects something entrusted, not possessed. This ethical clarity strengthens credibility and trust.

There is humility in stewardship. The builder acknowledges that their role is significant but not central. The work does not exist to validate them. It exists to serve a purpose larger than individual ambition. This humility does not weaken leadership; it stabilizes it. Others sense when power is exercised in service rather than self-interest.

Choosing stewardship over ownership completes the gardener's arc. It aligns with seeds rather than schematics, watering rather than pulling, pruning rather than hoarding. The builder becomes a participant in cycles they do not control but can influence through care.

In this posture, endurance becomes possible. The work continues, changes, and eventually passes on. The builder steps back without bitterness because nothing was ever owned. It was tended, faithfully, for as long as it was theirs to tend.

Chapter 20

Seasons of Withdrawal: Restoring to Rebuild

The Necessity of Retreat

Withdrawal is not an interruption of serious work; it is one of its essential structures. Builders who never step back confuse persistence with wisdom and endurance with strain. Over time, this confusion exacts a cost. Vision narrows. Judgment hardens. The work continues, but it loses depth. Retreat exists to prevent this erosion. It restores perspective before damage becomes visible.

The necessity of retreat lies in the nature of sustained creation. No system, human or otherwise, can remain in continuous output without degradation. Muscles require rest to strengthen. Land requires fallow seasons to recover fertility. Attention requires silence to regain clarity. Builders are not exempt from these laws. Ignoring them does not produce superiority; it produces fragility.

Retreat is often mischaracterized as disengagement. In truth, it is a shift in mode rather than a cessation of effort. The builder steps out of execution and into observation. They pause action not to abandon responsibility, but to realign it. This pause allows accumulated signals to register. Patterns become visible. What was previously obscured by motion comes into focus.

Modern systems rarely encourage this pause. The environment rewards availability, responsiveness, and constant production. Silence is misread as absence. Rest is framed as indulgence. In such conditions, retreat must be chosen deliberately. It cannot be outsourced to circumstance or postponed until exhaustion enforces it. Builders who wait for permission to withdraw rarely receive it. By then, the cost is higher and the recovery longer.

What the builder restores through retreat is not merely energy, but orientation. Distance from the work reveals whether effort remains aligned with purpose or has drifted into habit. The builder remembers why the work matters and whether it still serves. This remembrance protects against building structures that demand sacrifice without meaning.

Retreat also preserves the builder's integrity. Without it, identity fuses with output. The builder becomes consumed by the act of building and loses the ability to witness it. Withdrawal reestablishes separation. The builder remembers they are not the work, but its steward. This distinction is subtle but decisive. It prevents collapse when structures change or seasons end.

The necessity of retreat is therefore structural, not optional. It ensures that what is built remains coherent and that the one building remains whole. Without retreat, the work continues until something breaks. With retreat, the work pauses long enough to endure.

Cycles, Not Straight Lines

Builders are taught to imagine progress as a straight line. Effort leads to results; results lead to expansion; expansion leads to stability. This model simplifies planning and flatters ambition, but it misrepresents how living systems actually develop. Growth does not proceed continuously forward. It moves in cycles; periods of activity followed by consolidation, exertion followed by withdrawal, visibility followed by obscurity. Ignoring these cycles does not eliminate them; it only ensures they will assert themselves through breakdown rather than design.

Cycles govern everything that endures. Seasons alternate. Tides advance and retreat. Breathing expands and contracts. When builders attempt to operate outside these rhythms, they create tension. The system is pushed beyond its capacity to integrate change. Progress appears rapid, but coherence lags behind. Over time, this imbalance accumulates as fragility. What looks like momentum becomes overextension.

Understanding cycles changes how retreat is perceived. Withdrawal is no longer failure or hesitation. It is the natural counterpart to exertion. Periods of consolidation allow gains to stabilize. Lessons are integrated. Structures harden enough to bear additional weight. Without this consolidation, expansion remains superficial. The enterprise grows in size but not in strength.

Linear thinking also distorts emotional expectations. Builders become frustrated when effort does not produce immediate advancement. They interpret plateaus as stagnation rather than integration. This impatience drives unnecessary action, which disrupts the very processes needed for maturation. Cyclical thinking restores patience. It recognizes that apparent stillness often masks internal reorganization.

In cyclical systems, timing matters more than force. Pushing during a contraction phase wastes energy and creates resistance. Withdrawing during an expansion phase misses opportunity. The builder's task is not to eliminate cycles, but to read them accurately. This reading requires attentiveness rather than intensity. It rewards those who can pause without panic and act without compulsion.

Retreat fits naturally into this framework. It marks the inward arc of the cycle, where energy turns from expression to assimilation. What was learned is digested. What was built is tested internally. The system prepares for its next outward movement. When retreat is honored as part of the cycle, return becomes cleaner and more effective.

Cycles, not straight lines, produce endurance. Builders who align with this reality conserve energy, reduce burnout, and build structures capable of renewing themselves. Retreat becomes an intelligent response to rhythm rather than a reaction to crisis.

Recognizing the Signs of Exhaustion

Exhaustion rarely arrives without warning. Long before collapse, the system signals distress. These signals are subtle at first and easily dismissed, especially by builders accustomed to pushing through discomfort. Fatigue is reframed as dedication. Irritability is justified as pressure. Loss of curiosity is mistaken for focus. Over time, these misinterpretations accumulate, and the builder crosses from exertion into depletion without noticing the threshold.

One of the earliest signs of exhaustion is narrowing. Attention contracts. The builder becomes less receptive to nuance and more reliant on familiar patterns. Decisions are made quickly but without depth. New information feels intrusive rather than informative. This narrowing is not efficiency; it is conservation under strain. The system is reducing complexity because it lacks the energy to integrate it.

Another signal is emotional flattening. Success no longer brings satisfaction, and setbacks feel disproportionately heavy. The builder continues to function, but engagement thins. Work becomes transactional rather than meaningful. This detachment is often rationalized as professionalism, but it is actually a sign that inner resources are being preserved by disengaging emotionally.

Physical indicators follow. Sleep loses its restorative quality. Minor stressors provoke outsized reactions. The body remains activated even during rest. These symptoms are not separate from the work; they are expressions of how the work is being carried. When the nervous system remains in a state of readiness for too long, recovery becomes incomplete. Energy is spent faster than it can be replenished.

Exhaustion also alters perception of time. The future feels compressed and urgent. There is little tolerance for delay or reflection. The builder feels compelled to act immediately, not because action is required, but because stillness feels intolerable. This urgency is a sign that retreat is overdue. The system is attempting to resolve imbalance through motion rather than restoration.

Recognizing these signs requires honesty. Builders often pride themselves on resilience and interpret warning signals as challenges to overcome. In reality, these signals are invitations to withdraw before damage occurs. Ignoring them does not demonstrate strength; it demonstrates disconnection. Retreat taken at this stage preserves capacity. Retreat delayed becomes recovery from collapse.

The disciplined builder learns to read exhaustion early. They do not wait for breakdown to justify withdrawal. They respect the signals as intelligence rather than weakness. In doing so, they protect both the work and themselves from unnecessary erosion.

Invisible Growth: What Happens Underground

Not all growth announces itself. Some of the most consequential development occurs beyond visibility, beneath the surface, where progress cannot be measured or displayed. Retreat creates the conditions for this invisible growth. When outward motion slows or stops, internal processes accelerate. Integration replaces expansion. What was scattered begins to organize itself quietly.

During withdrawal, the builder's attention turns inward. Experiences are digested rather than accumulated. Lessons that were registered intellectually during active phases settle into understanding. Patterns become clearer because they are no longer obscured by urgency. This internal reorganization cannot occur while the system is in constant output. Motion interrupts digestion. Stillness completes it.

Invisible growth also occurs at the structural level. Ideas incubate. Assumptions soften. New connections form without conscious effort. What appears as inactivity from the outside is often a period of intense internal alignment. The builder may feel unproductive, yet foundations are being strengthened. When activity resumes, it does so with greater coherence because underlying contradictions have been resolved.

This underground work is uncomfortable for those conditioned to equate value with visibility. Without external markers of progress, the builder may doubt the legitimacy of withdrawal. Anxiety arises: *Am I falling behind? Am I wasting time?* These doubts are predictable. They reflect cultural bias rather than reality. Living systems require unseen phases to remain healthy. Roots grow in darkness. Soil restores itself unseen.

Invisible growth also repairs trust. Distance from execution allows emotional residue to dissipate. Frustrations lose intensity. Conflicts soften. The builder returns with greater neutrality, able to engage without reactivity. This emotional reset is not incidental; it is structural. Without it, unresolved tension contaminates future effort.

What happens underground determines what can happen above. Builders who skip this phase return quickly, but unchanged. They repeat patterns because nothing internal has shifted. Builders who allow invisible growth to complete its cycle return fewer times, but differently. Their actions carry new clarity because the work has been metabolized.

Retreat protects this invisible phase from interruption. It gives growth the privacy it requires. What emerges later will appear sudden, but it was not spontaneous. It was prepared quietly, out of sight, where force could not reach it.

Strategic Pause vs. Burnout Collapse

There is a critical difference between choosing to pause and being forced to stop. A strategic pause is deliberate, measured, and timely. Burnout collapse is abrupt, disorganizing, and costly. Both involve cessation of forward motion, but their consequences diverge sharply. One preserves capacity; the other depletes it further. Understanding this distinction allows the builder to intervene early, when withdrawal remains an act of agency rather than necessity.

A strategic pause occurs while resources are still available. Energy is low, but not exhausted. Clarity is strained, but not lost. The builder senses misalignment and responds before damage accumulates. This pause creates space to reassess direction, restore rhythm, and recalibrate effort. Because it is taken voluntarily, it carries dignity. The builder remains in relationship with the work rather than being expelled from it.

Burnout collapse, by contrast, arrives after signals have been ignored too long. The system fails abruptly. Cognitive function declines. Emotional regulation fractures. The builder may experience aversion to the work itself, not because the work is wrong, but because it has become associated with prolonged strain. Recovery from collapse takes longer because it involves repair, not just rest. Trust in one's capacity must be rebuilt alongside energy.

The strategic pause prevents this outcome by honoring limits early. It treats withdrawal as maintenance rather than repair. Just as machinery is serviced before failure, the builder steps back while systems remain intact. This foresight protects morale, preserves relationships, and maintains continuity. The work can be resumed without resentment because it was not allowed to become toxic.

There is also a psychological distinction. In a strategic pause, the builder remains oriented. They are still in dialogue with the work, observing it from a distance. In burnout collapse, orientation is lost. The builder feels overwhelmed and disconnected. Decisions are deferred not by choice, but by incapacity. This disorientation compounds anxiety and delays recovery.

Choosing a strategic pause requires courage. It means resisting external pressure to continue and internal pressure to prove resilience. It requires trust that stepping back will not erase progress. In reality, it often protects progress from being undone by exhaustion-driven mistakes.

The disciplined builder learns to pause early and deliberately. They understand that withdrawal taken by design preserves strength, while withdrawal enforced by collapse exacts a far greater cost. Strategic pause is not an interruption of the work; it is a continuation of it by other means.

The Inner Renovation: What Only Withdrawal Can Do

Some forms of change cannot occur in motion. They require quiet, distance, and the suspension of immediate demands. Withdrawal creates the conditions for this inner renovation. When the builder steps out of constant engagement, deeper layers of orientation are exposed. Assumptions loosen. Identity softens. The internal architecture that governs how work is approached begins to reorganize itself.

Inner renovation differs from surface adjustment. It is not about optimizing habits or refining strategy. It is about recalibrating relationship; to effort, to ambition, to responsibility. These shifts cannot be forced through analysis alone. They emerge when the builder is no longer performing a role or maintaining momentum. In retreat, the builder is relieved of the need to act, allowing deeper questions to surface without interruption.

This renovation often begins with discomfort. Without the structure of daily execution, unresolved tensions appear. Doubts that were postponed by activity demand attention. This exposure can feel destabilizing, which is why many builders avoid withdrawal. Yet this discomfort is diagnostic. It reveals where alignment has drifted and where renewal is needed. Suppressing it through continued action only postpones repair.

Withdrawal also restores discernment. Away from constant feedback, the builder can distinguish between what genuinely matters and what merely occupied attention. Noise loses its authority. Priorities reorder themselves naturally. Decisions that felt complex simplify. This clarity does not come from effort; it comes from space.

There is also an ethical dimension to inner renovation. Builders who never withdraw risk becoming hardened, instrumentalizing people and process in the name of progress. Distance reintroduces perspective. The builder remembers the human cost of decisions and the purpose beyond metrics. This remembrance realigns leadership with stewardship.

Inner renovation cannot be scheduled precisely. It unfolds at its own pace. The builder's task is to protect the conditions long enough for it to complete. Rushing return interrupts the process, leaving the renovation half-finished. When allowed to complete, the builder returns with a different posture. Effort feels cleaner. Boundaries are firmer. Engagement is renewed without compulsion.

Withdrawal is the workshop where this renovation occurs. It does work that action cannot. And without it, rebuilding remains superficial.

Letting the Field Lie Fallow

Agricultural wisdom recognizes the necessity of fallow periods. Land that is cultivated continuously loses fertility, regardless of how skillfully it is worked. Nutrients are depleted. Structure erodes. Yield declines. Letting a field lie fallow is not neglect; it is renewal through restraint. The same principle applies to builders. Continuous output without periods of non-use exhausts internal resources and degrades the quality of creation.

Allowing the field to lie fallow means resisting the impulse to fill every moment with productive activity. It requires accepting that value can be preserved through absence as much as through effort. For builders accustomed to equating motion with worth, this is uncomfortable. Inactivity feels like risk. Yet without fallow time, even the most disciplined systems degrade.

During fallow periods, unseen processes restore capacity. Soil structure repairs itself. Microorganisms regenerate. Balance returns. For the builder, fallow time allows emotional residue to dissipate and cognitive bandwidth to recover. The mind stops rehearsing problems and begins to reset. This reset is not passive. It prepares the ground for future planting by restoring receptivity.

Fallow time also protects against compulsion. When the builder is constantly engaged, action becomes habitual. Effort continues even when it no longer serves. Withdrawal interrupts this habit, allowing intention to be reasserted. The builder can choose again rather than simply continue.

Importantly, fallow periods must be protected from optimization. Attempting to make rest productive undermines its function. Reflection, planning, and learning may arise naturally, but they should not be imposed. The field recovers precisely because it is not being extracted from. The builder recovers when they stop demanding output from themselves.

Letting the field lie fallow is a commitment to future vitality. It acknowledges that productivity has a cost and that replenishment requires time. Builders who honor fallow periods return with greater clarity and renewed capacity. Those who do not eventually face enforced fallow through exhaustion or disillusionment.

Rest is not the opposite of work. It is part of its cycle.

Rest as Part of the Rhythm, Not a Reward

Rest is often framed as compensation; something earned after sufficient effort, granted once milestones are reached or exhaustion becomes undeniable. This framing distorts its function. When rest is treated as a reward, it is postponed indefinitely. There is always more to do, another threshold to cross, another urgency to address. Over time, rest disappears from the rhythm of work and reappears only as collapse. This is not discipline; it is neglect.

In living systems, rest is not conditional. It is rhythmic. Activity and recovery alternate as a matter of design. Muscles rebuild during rest, not exertion. Attention resets during silence, not stimulation. Creativity renews itself in space, not pressure. When builders remove rest from the rhythm and attach it to performance, they undermine the very capacities they rely on.

Rest as rhythm requires intentional placement. It is scheduled not because the builder is tired, but because the cycle demands it. This placement removes moral judgment from rest. The builder no longer asks whether they deserve to pause. They recognize that pause is part of the work's architecture. This recognition reduces guilt and prevents overexertion driven by self-justification.

When rest is integrated rhythmically, it becomes preventative rather than reparative. Energy is replenished before depletion becomes severe. Perspective is restored before distortion hardens. The builder remains available to the work without being consumed by it. Over time, this consistency produces greater output with less strain, not because effort increases, but because friction decreases.

There is also a cultural impact. Builders who model rest as rhythm legitimize it for others. Teams learn that sustainability matters. Performance becomes steadier. Burnout loses its inevitability. The system no longer depends on heroics, but on coherence.

Rest is not the opposite of seriousness. It is one of its expressions. When builders integrate rest into rhythm, they demonstrate respect for the work's longevity and for their own capacity to carry it. Reward-based rest collapses under pressure. Rhythmic rest endures.

Signals of Readiness to Return

Return should never be driven by impatience or guilt. When withdrawal has done its work, readiness announces itself quietly through shifts in posture rather than spikes in motivation. The builder does not feel compelled to re-enter; they feel available. This distinction matters. Compulsion recreates the conditions that required retreat in the first place. Availability signals that restoration has occurred.

One of the clearest signals of readiness is the return of curiosity. During exhaustion, curiosity contracts. Questions feel burdensome. Exploration feels risky. As renewal takes place, interest resurfaces naturally. The builder begins to wonder again; not anxiously, but attentively. Possibilities appear without urgency. This curiosity indicates that cognitive and emotional bandwidth has been restored.

Another signal is neutrality toward the work. Strong aversion or intense craving both suggest unfinished withdrawal. Readiness appears as steadiness. The builder can think about returning without dread and without inflation. The work is neither escape nor salvation. It is simply work again; meaningful, but not consuming. This neutrality preserves sovereignty.

Clarity is another marker. Decisions that felt tangled begin to resolve themselves without force. Priorities reorder quietly. The builder no longer needs to rehearse arguments internally. Direction emerges with less effort. This clarity is not absolute certainty, but sufficient orientation to act without strain.

Physiologically, readiness shows up as regulation. Sleep restores. The body settles more quickly after stimulation. Stressors provoke proportionate responses rather than cascading reactions. These changes indicate that the nervous system has recalibrated enough to support engagement without immediate depletion.

Perhaps most importantly, readiness includes acceptance of change. The builder no longer expects to return as they were. They recognize that withdrawal has altered perspective. Old rhythms may no longer fit. This acceptance prevents repetition. Return becomes an act of renewal rather than resumption.

Signals of readiness are not dramatic. They are subtle and cumulative. The disciplined builder learns to trust them rather than override them. When return is timed to readiness rather than pressure, engagement begins cleanly. The work is met with steadiness, not compensation.

Coming Back Different: Re-entering Without Repeating

Return marks the most delicate moment in the cycle of withdrawal. The builder re-enters the work not to restore what was, but to engage what remains with a changed posture. This difference is essential. Without it, withdrawal becomes temporary relief rather than transformation. Re-entry without repetition requires intention, restraint, and memory; memory not of exhaustion, but of what it revealed.

The temptation on return is to compensate. The builder feels renewed and wants to make up for lost time. Momentum is reclaimed too quickly. Old patterns reassert themselves under the banner of productivity. This rush undoes the work of withdrawal.

Coming back different means resisting this impulse. The builder moves deliberately, allowing new rhythms to stabilize before scaling effort.

Difference is expressed first through boundaries. The builder re-enters with clearer limits around time, availability, and scope. These limits are not defensive; they are structural. They protect the conditions that made renewal possible. Without them, the system reverts to extraction. With them, engagement remains sustainable.

Re-entry also reflects recalibrated values. Decisions are made with greater selectivity. Some initiatives are declined without justification. Others are reshaped to fit new constraints. The builder no longer tries to recover everything. They focus on what aligns with the renewed center that emerged during withdrawal.

There is humility in this return. The builder accepts that certain ambitions may no longer be appropriate. Others may need to be redefined. This acceptance prevents resentment. The work is approached with care rather than conquest. Authority becomes quieter. Presence deepens.

Coming back different also means honoring the cycle. The builder recognizes that withdrawal will be required again. This recognition changes how effort is applied. There is less urgency to extract value from every moment. Progress is measured by continuity rather than acceleration. The system is designed with exit points, pauses, and fallow periods built in.

Re-entry without repetition completes the arc of withdrawal. The builder does not escape the work; they return to it transformed. What resumes is not the same rhythm, not the same posture, not the same relationship. The work continues, but it does so under a different governance; one shaped by restraint, clarity, and respect for cycles.

In this way, withdrawal restores not only capacity, but wisdom. And wisdom, once integrated, changes how building unfolds forever.

Chapter 21

Business as Lifework, Not Escape

The Fantasy of the Exit

Nearly every entrepreneur carries, at some point, the fantasy of the exit. It appears as a promise of relief: the moment when responsibility lifts, scrutiny ends, and the weight of constant decision-making dissolves. The exit is imagined as stillness earned, as a final proof that the effort meant something. This fantasy is rarely examined closely. When it is, its true nature becomes clear. It is not a vision of freedom. It is a vision of escape.

The desire to exit often arises not from success, but from fatigue. The builder feels worn down by the accumulation of pressure and begins to imagine a future where the work no longer asks anything of them. In this imagination, the business is treated as a burden to be shed rather than a structure to be lived within. The exit becomes a psychological finish line where meaning is expected to resolve itself automatically.

This expectation is misplaced. Those who reach an exit without having developed a deeper relationship to the work frequently discover an unexpected emptiness afterward. Without the daily demands of building, unresolved questions surface. Identity, previously stabilized by effort, loses its anchor. The builder confronts themselves without the buffering effect of motion. If becoming was postponed in favor of achievement, the exit offers no shelter from that delay.

There is nothing inherently wrong with selling, closing, or stepping away. Harvest and transition are natural phases of any cycle. The problem emerges when business is used as a temporary anesthetic, a way to stay busy enough to avoid interior reckoning. In this case, the exit is burdened with impossible expectations. It is asked to deliver peace that was never cultivated during the building itself.

Freedom built on running does not endure. If the primary function of the enterprise is to provide an escape route, every milestone will feel hollow. Growth will feel like entrapment rather than expansion. The builder will experience success as pressure, not fulfillment, because the work was never designed to be inhabited. It was designed to be left.

Lifework operates differently. It is not a vehicle for departure, but a place of formation. It shapes ethics, patience, endurance, and clarity over time. Even when it ends, it leaves the builder more coherent than when it began. The question is not whether one exits, but whether the work was lived inside deeply enough that leaving does not feel like abandonment of self.

The fantasy of the exit dissolves when the builder stops asking when the work will end and begins asking who they are becoming through it. Only then does business shift from escape to lifework.

The Myth of Arrival

Closely related to the fantasy of the exit is the myth of arrival. This myth suggests that there is a definitive point at which the builder reaches stability, fulfillment, and certainty, after which struggle recedes and effort becomes effortless. Arrival is imagined as a plateau where questions are resolved, identity is secured, and the work finally rests. This belief is seductive because it promises closure. It is also inaccurate.

In practice, arrival is always provisional. Each achievement reveals new complexity. Each resolution opens new questions. Stability is temporary, not because of failure, but because life and work are dynamic systems. Builders who expect arrival interpret this dynamism as disappointment. They assume something is wrong when satisfaction does not last. This assumption generates restlessness. The builder keeps moving the finish line, hoping the next milestone will finally deliver permanence.

The myth of arrival distorts motivation. Instead of engaging the work for its own sake, the builder endures it in anticipation of a future state. The present becomes instrumental. Effort is tolerated rather than inhabited. When arrival fails to materialize, frustration accumulates. The builder feels misled, as though the work broke a promise it never made.

This myth also encourages premature conclusions. Builders who believe in arrival rush to declare success, lock identity, and freeze systems. They resist change because it threatens the illusion of having arrived. In doing so, they undermine adaptability. The work becomes brittle because it is asked to preserve a static identity rather than continue evolving.

Recognizing the myth of arrival changes posture. The builder stops asking when the work will be finished and starts attending to how it is shaping them now. Progress is no longer measured by distance from a starting point, but by depth of engagement. Satisfaction becomes cyclical rather than cumulative. There are seasons of fulfillment and seasons of difficulty, each with their own function.

This recognition also reduces anxiety. If arrival is not expected, then fluctuation is no longer failure. The builder can rest within motion, knowing that uncertainty is not a flaw to be corrected but a condition to be navigated. The work remains alive because it is not forced to conclude itself.

Lifework does not culminate in arrival. It unfolds. Meaning emerges through continuity rather than completion. When the builder releases the myth of arrival, they recover the capacity to be present, serious, and grounded in each phase of the work without waiting for it to finally end.

The Difference Between Work and Lifework

Work is activity directed toward outcome. It is task-oriented, bounded, and often transactional. It answers specific needs and concludes when those needs are met. There is nothing inherently inferior about work in this sense. Societies depend on it. Enterprises require it. But work alone does not account for the deeper relationship some builders develop with what they are creating. That relationship belongs to a different category entirely. It is lifework.

Lifework is not defined by scale, permanence, or recognition. It is defined by continuity of engagement and depth of formation. While work asks what must be done, lifework asks who the builder must become to do it well. The distinction is subtle but decisive. In lifework, the builder is shaped by the structure they are shaping. Skills accumulate, but so do discernment, patience, and ethical clarity. The work becomes a long conversation rather than a sequence of transactions.

This difference alters how effort is experienced. In ordinary work, difficulty is something to be minimized or endured until reward arrives. In lifework, difficulty is instructional. Friction is not immediately eliminated because it often signals where growth is required. The builder does not seek struggle, but neither do they rush to bypass it. They remain present long enough to learn what the work is demanding of them internally.

Lifework also reframes success. Instead of asking whether the work paid off, the builder asks whether it deepened alignment. Outcomes still matter, but they are not the sole measure of value. A project may end, pivot, or fail and still contribute meaningfully to lifework if it refined judgment or strengthened integrity. In this way, lifework accumulates even when specific efforts conclude.

There is also a temporal shift. Work often belongs to a season. Lifework spans seasons. It evolves across roles, ventures, and contexts, carrying a consistent orientation even as forms change. The builder may step away from one enterprise and into another, yet the lifework continues uninterrupted because it is not attached to a single structure. It is attached to a way of engaging reality.

Understanding this difference frees the builder from confusion. They no longer expect every task to be meaningful, nor do they dismiss meaningful work because it lacks immediate payoff. They recognize which efforts are instrumental and which are formative. This discernment prevents burnout by allowing energy to be allocated appropriately.

Work completes. Lifework continues. When the builder recognizes which they are engaged in, they stop waiting for meaning to arrive later and begin participating in it now.

When Building Becomes a Mirror

Over time, sustained building reveals patterns that have little to do with strategy and everything to do with the builder. Reactions repeat. Conflicts echo. Certain challenges arise with suspicious consistency. At this stage, the work ceases to be merely external. It becomes a mirror. What is unresolved internally begins to express itself structurally. How the builder relates to pressure, authority, risk, and limitation is reflected back through the enterprise.

This mirroring is unavoidable in lifework. Short-term projects may conceal it, but long engagement exposes it. Builders who avoid reflection often blame circumstances or people when friction appears. They assume the problem lies outside. In reality, persistent patterns signal internal postures that have not yet evolved. The work is not malfunctioning; it is responding accurately.

The mirror can be uncomfortable. It reveals impatience disguised as urgency, control masquerading as leadership, or fear rationalized as prudence. These traits may have once served the builder well. In early phases, intensity and control can drive progress. Over time, however, they become liabilities. The work stalls or strains because the builder has not adapted internally to the scale and complexity they have created.

When building becomes a mirror, resistance intensifies if the builder refuses to look. More force is applied. More systems are added. More people are managed. These interventions treat symptoms rather than cause. The pattern persists because its origin remains unaddressed. Progress slows not due to lack of effort, but due to misalignment between the builder's inner posture and the work's current demands.

Engaging the mirror requires humility. The builder must be willing to ask what the work is teaching them about themselves. This inquiry is not self-criticism. It is responsibility taken at the correct level. As the builder adjusts internally, external friction often resolves without additional intervention. Decisions become cleaner. Relationships stabilize. Structures regain coherence.

This mirroring also deepens meaning. The work becomes a site of formation rather than mere production. Challenges are no longer obstacles to bypass, but invitations to mature. The builder grows alongside the enterprise rather than standing apart from it. This parallel development is one of lifework's defining qualities.

When building becomes a mirror, escape is no longer possible. The work will continue to reflect what is present until it is addressed. This is not punishment. It is precision. Lifework reveals what the builder is ready to see.

Why "Freedom" Is a Byproduct, Not a Goal

Freedom is one of the most frequently cited motivations for building a business. It is imagined as autonomy over time, relief from constraint, and release from obligation. Builders pursue ownership in the hope that it will loosen the grip of necessity. Yet when freedom is treated as the goal, it rarely materializes. Instead, it recedes. The builder exchanges one set of constraints for another, often heavier and more complex than before.

This happens because freedom cannot be engineered directly. When it is pursued as an outcome, decisions become distorted. Builders optimize for optionality rather than coherence. They avoid commitments that might deepen responsibility. They keep structures loose to preserve future escape. Ironically, this avoidance produces fragility. Systems lack depth. Trust remains provisional. The builder stays busy managing risk rather than inhabiting the work.

True freedom emerges indirectly. It appears when the builder commits deeply enough that effort becomes fluent rather than forced.

Structure stabilizes. Rhythm settles. Decision-making simplifies because values are clear and consistently applied. In this environment, autonomy grows naturally. The builder gains freedom of movement not by avoiding responsibility, but by integrating it fully.

Freedom also depends on competence and trust. Builders who have not yet developed mastery remain constrained by oversight and correction. Their attention is constantly pulled back into control. As skill deepens and judgment stabilizes, intervention becomes less necessary. The system can operate without constant supervision. Freedom appears as a consequence of reliability, not as a reward for ambition.

There is also an internal dimension. Builders who seek freedom often seek relief from internal pressure rather than external constraint. They want the noise to stop. But noise does not disappear with success; it disappears with clarity. When intention is stable and identity is not bound to outcome, pressure decreases. The builder feels free even while carrying responsibility. This freedom is resilient because it is not dependent on circumstance.

Lifework reframes freedom entirely. It is no longer an endpoint to reach, but a quality of engagement that emerges over time. The builder stops asking how to escape and starts asking how to inhabit the work well. In doing so, they discover that freedom was never something to chase. It was something to cultivate through fidelity, depth, and patience.

The Discipline of Staying

Staying is rarely celebrated. In a culture that rewards speed, novelty, and visible advancement, remaining with the same work can appear unimaginative or complacent. Builders are encouraged to pivot quickly, rebrand frequently, and abandon what becomes difficult. Yet lifework is shaped less by clever exits than by the discipline of staying. Staying is not stagnation; it is commitment expressed over time.

The discipline of staying reveals itself when initial momentum fades. Early stages are often fueled by excitement and possibility. Later stages require patience, repetition, and refinement. The work becomes less dramatic and more exacting. It asks for consistency rather than inspiration. Many builders misinterpret this transition as loss of alignment and seek novelty to restore stimulation. In doing so, they abandon depth just as it becomes available.

Staying does not mean refusing change. It means remaining in relationship with the work long enough to allow it to mature. Builders who stay learn the difference between discomfort that signals growth and discomfort that signals misalignment. This discernment develops only through proximity. Distance makes everything seem either intolerable or idealized. Staying clarifies.

There is also an ethical dimension to staying. Commitments made to people, communities, and systems deepen over time. Leaving prematurely can fracture trust and externalize costs. Staying allows responsibility to be carried through cycles rather than transferred when it becomes inconvenient. This continuity builds credibility. Others sense when leadership is durable rather than opportunistic.

Staying shapes character. Repetition exposes habits. Long engagement surfaces impatience, control, and avoidance that short projects conceal. As these traits are confronted, the builder evolves. The work becomes formative rather than extractive. This formation cannot be accelerated. It requires time spent within constraints rather than fleeing them.

The discipline of staying does not deny rest or withdrawal. It incorporates them. Staying means returning after retreat, not escaping permanently. It means recommitting with greater clarity rather than abandoning at the first sign of fatigue. Over time, this rhythm builds trust between the builder and the work itself.

Lifework is sustained not by constant reinvention, but by the willingness to remain present through unglamorous phases. Staying allows substance to replace spectacle. What endures is rarely what was chased. It is what was stayed with long enough to become real.

Shaping the Self Through Structure

Every structure imposes form. Schedules constrain time. Systems channel attention. Roles shape behavior. Builders often believe they are designing structures solely to achieve external outcomes. In reality, these structures are simultaneously shaping the builder. How one organizes work, distributes authority, and responds to pressure gradually forms character. Lifework recognizes this reciprocity and engages it deliberately.

When structure is treated as purely instrumental, its formative power goes unexamined. The builder adapts unconsciously. Habits harden. Reactions become default. Over time, the structure trains impatience or patience, reactivity or restraint, clarity or confusion. The builder may achieve results while becoming misaligned internally. This misalignment eventually surfaces as dissatisfaction or burnout, even in the presence of success.

Intentional structure works differently. The builder designs systems not only to produce outcomes, but to cultivate qualities they wish to embody. Rhythm is chosen to support steadiness rather than urgency. Boundaries are established to protect presence rather than maximize availability. Decision-making frameworks are shaped to encourage reflection rather than impulse. In this way, structure becomes a teacher.

This approach requires foresight. The builder must ask what kind of person this work is shaping them into. Not in abstraction, but in daily practice. Are they becoming more attentive or more scattered? More grounded or more anxious? These shifts are not moral judgments; they are indicators. Structure reveals its effects through lived experience.

Over time, this alignment between structure and self deepens coherence. The builder no longer feels divided between who they are and what the work demands. Effort feels integrated rather than conflicting. Decisions carry less internal friction because they are made from within a system that supports the builder's values.

Lifework embraces this shaping process. It treats external design as an opportunity for internal formation. The builder does not seek neutrality from the work; they accept that it will change them and choose how. This choice transforms building into a practice rather than a performance.

Structure always shapes the self. The only question is whether this shaping is accidental or intentional.

Success as Fidelity, Not Finish

Success is commonly framed as arrival at a destination. A target is met, a valuation achieved, a milestone crossed. In this framing, success concludes effort and justifies what preceded it. Lifework rejects this definition. When work is lived inside over time, success is no longer a finish line. It is fidelity sustained across changing conditions.

Fidelity refers to consistency of alignment. The builder remains true to purpose, standards, and care even as circumstances shift. Decisions are not optimized solely for advantage, but measured against integrity. This does not guarantee comfort or recognition. It guarantees coherence. The work remains honest to what it claims to be. In lifework, this honesty matters more than spectacle.

This understanding of success alters how achievement is experienced. Milestones are acknowledged, but they do not terminate engagement. The builder does not collapse into celebration or disengage into complacency. Nor do they escalate compulsively in search of the next proof. They continue. The work is met again, with the same seriousness and presence as before. Success becomes continuity rather than culmination.

Fidelity also reframes failure. When success is defined by finish, failure feels definitive. When success is defined by fidelity, failure becomes contextual. A project may end unsuccessfully and still represent success if it was carried with care, clarity, and responsibility. The builder evaluates themselves not by external verdict, but by whether they honored the work while it was theirs to carry.

This posture protects against burnout. Builders who chase finishes exhaust themselves trying to secure finality in a system that does not offer it. Builders who practice fidelity distribute effort more evenly. They remain engaged without urgency to conclude. Satisfaction comes from staying aligned rather than arriving somewhere permanent.

Success as fidelity also deepens trust. Others sense when leadership is consistent rather than opportunistic. The enterprise gains credibility because it behaves predictably at the level of values, even when strategy evolves. This trust compounds over time and becomes one of the most durable forms of capital available.

In lifework, success is not declared. It is practiced. Each decision either reinforces alignment or erodes it. Fidelity is renewed daily, not celebrated once. And through this renewal, the work remains alive long after any single milestone fades.

Sustaining Passion Without Needing Drama

Passion is often confused with intensity. Builders learn to associate engagement with urgency, sacrifice, and emotional volatility. When these elements fade, they assume passion has been lost. In reality, what has disappeared is drama. True passion does not require constant crisis to remain alive. It is quieter, steadier, and far more durable.

Drama feeds on contrast. It creates spikes of excitement and valleys of exhaustion. While this cycle can feel energizing in the short term, it is unsustainable. Over time, the nervous system becomes dependent on stimulation to feel engaged. When stability emerges, boredom follows. The builder misreads this calm as loss of purpose and seeks disruption to restore feeling. This pattern undermines lifework by substituting sensation for substance.

Sustained passion operates differently. It is rooted in care rather than adrenaline. The builder remains interested even when the work is repetitive, because attention has shifted from novelty to refinement. Small improvements matter. Nuance becomes engaging. The work deepens instead of escalating. This form of passion does not announce itself loudly, but it endures because it is not consuming itself for effect.

Maintaining this steadiness requires regulation. The builder must resist the temptation to manufacture urgency when none exists. They allow periods of calm without interpreting them as decline. They trust that engagement can exist without emotional extremes. This trust stabilizes effort and prevents burnout driven by self-induced crises.

There is also maturity in this posture. Early passion often seeks validation. Later passion seeks coherence. The builder no longer needs to feel constantly inspired to remain committed. They show up because the work matters, not because it excites them every day. This reliability strengthens both the builder and the enterprise.

Sustained passion also improves judgment. Without emotional swings, decisions are less reactive. The builder can assess situations without distortion and respond proportionately. Energy is conserved and applied where it matters most. Over time, this measured engagement produces greater impact than dramatic exertion ever could.

Lifework does not demand constant fire. It requires a steady flame. When passion is freed from drama, it becomes something the builder can carry for decades rather than burn through in years.

Letting the Work Change You

Lifework is not a static expression of who the builder already is. It is a process that reshapes the builder over time. Those who attempt to protect themselves from this influence keep the work superficial. They extract results without allowing formation. Over long horizons, this resistance shows. The work stagnates because the builder has refused to evolve alongside it.

Letting the work change you requires openness without passivity. The builder remains discerning, but receptive. They notice how prolonged engagement alters perception, values, and tolerance. What once felt urgent may lose its grip. What once seemed insignificant may gain weight. These shifts are not betrayals of identity; they are refinements of it.

Change often arrives through friction. The work confronts the builder with limits; of patience, control, certainty. Each confrontation presents a choice: reinforce existing defenses or adapt. Builders who treat these moments as inconveniences miss their formative power. Builders who engage them thoughtfully develop depth. Over time, their leadership becomes quieter, more precise, and less reactive.

This transformation also affects ambition. Early ambition often seeks proof. Later ambition seeks alignment. The builder becomes less interested in conquering terrain and more interested in stewarding coherence. Success is pursued, but not at the expense of integrity. The work becomes a place of practice rather than performance.

Letting the work change you also restores humility. Long engagement reveals how little remains fixed. Context shifts. What once worked fails. New realities demand new responses. The builder learns to adapt without self-rejection. Identity becomes less rigid and more resilient. This flexibility supports longevity.

In the end, lifework offers a rare exchange. The builder gives attention, effort, and care. In return, the work offers formation. It teaches discernment, patience, and restraint; qualities that cannot be acquired through theory alone. This exchange only occurs when the builder allows it.

Business as lifework is not about building something that lasts forever. It is about becoming someone who can stay present, ethical, and alive across changing seasons. When the work is allowed to shape the builder, both endure longer than either could alone.

Chapter 22

Integration of Self and Structure

No More Split Selves: The End of the Double Life

Many founders operate under a quiet but corrosive assumption: that it is possible to live one way internally and build another way externally. They believe they can hold personal values privately while suspending them in leadership. That inner coherence can be deferred while the enterprise demands speed, pressure, and compromise. This assumption rarely announces itself openly, yet it governs countless decisions. Over time, it becomes unsustainable.

The split self shows up as contradiction. The founder believes in clarity but tolerates chaos. Values depth but rewards urgency. Seeks freedom while constructing systems that imprison attention. These contradictions do not remain internal. They leak into structure. Strategy becomes inconsistent. Culture feels unstable. The business begins to oscillate between opposing impulses because its origin point is unresolved.

At first, the split may feel manageable. Performance compensates for dissonance. Results create momentum. But as the enterprise grows, the cost of fragmentation increases. Decisions require more energy because there is no unified reference point. The founder begins performing leadership rather than inhabiting it. Stress accumulates not because the work is hard, but because it is being carried from an inauthentic posture.

Eventually, the double life demands resolution. The business becomes either a mechanism for integration or an engine of erosion. If the founder refuses alignment, the structure amplifies internal conflict. Teams feel it. Systems reflect it. The work becomes heavier than it needs to be because it is compensating for a divided center.

Ending the split is not an act of idealism. It is infrastructural. When the founder's inner life and leadership posture align, decisions simplify. Boundaries become clearer. Culture stabilizes because it no longer receives mixed signals. The business gains coherence not through tighter control, but through consistency of being.

Integration does not require perfection. It requires honesty. The founder must stop asking who they need to be perceived as and start leading from who they actually are. When this shift occurs, leadership becomes less performative and more grounded. The work no longer demands armor. Presence replaces persona.

A business built from a whole founder does not fracture under pressure as easily. Its systems carry the same logic internally and externally. This coherence is felt immediately, even if it is difficult to articulate. The end of the double life marks the beginning of structural integrity. What is built from wholeness does not require constant justification. It stands on its own.

Founders Shape Culture More Than They Know

Culture is often treated as a downstream artifact; something that emerges from policies, incentives, or stated values. Founders draft mission statements, publish principles, and assume that culture will follow accordingly. In reality, culture forms long before it is named. It is shaped less by what leaders declare and more by how they inhabit pressure, make tradeoffs, and respond when values are tested. The founder's inner posture becomes the template others unconsciously follow.

Every unresolved pattern in a founder expresses itself structurally. If the founder avoids conflict, ambiguity will persist in decision-making. If they equate worth with output, urgency will dominate rhythm. If they tolerate misalignment privately, inconsistency will spread publicly. These patterns do not require instruction. They transmit through tone, timing, and omission. Teams learn what matters not by listening to speeches, but by observing what is rewarded, what is ignored, and what is endured.

Founders often underestimate this influence because it is indirect. They assume culture is shaped through management layers, not personal presence. Yet presence is precisely where culture takes form. How the founder listens sets the standard for dialogue. How they handle mistakes defines psychological safety. How they treat boundaries determines whether burnout is normalized or prevented. These signals accumulate into norms long before they are codified.

This influence intensifies as organizations scale. Early teams absorb the founder's habits and pass them on without interpretation. What began as a personal workaround becomes institutional behavior. If the founder operates from internal tension or contradiction, the organization inherits that tension. The system begins to work harder than necessary because it is compensating for ambiguity at the source.

Alignment at the founder level simplifies culture dramatically. When values are lived rather than announced, fewer rules are required. Decisions decentralize naturally because judgment is shared. Trust increases because behavior is predictable. The organization does not need constant correction because it has absorbed a consistent logic of action.

This does not mean founders must become exemplary or polished. It means they must become congruent. Self-awareness matters more than self-mastery. A founder who acknowledges limits openly creates more stability than one who performs certainty while remaining internally fragmented. Honesty establishes coherence. Pretense undermines it.

Culture is not something founders manage from a distance. It is something they transmit continuously, whether they intend to or not. Recognizing this responsibility reframes leadership. The work begins not with slogans, but with alignment. When founders take responsibility for their inner posture, culture becomes an extension of integrity rather than a corrective effort.

Personal Values as Operational Logic

Values are often treated as abstract ideals; statements to inspire rather than principles to govern. In practice, every business already operates on values, whether articulated or not. These values appear in how decisions are made under constraint, which tradeoffs are accepted, and what behavior is tolerated when pressure rises. The question is not whether values exist, but whether they are conscious, coherent, and aligned with the founder's inner life.

When personal values remain private, operational logic fills the vacuum. Speed becomes the default value. Convenience overrides care. Short-term advantage displaces long-term coherence. These outcomes are not the result of malice; they emerge from unexamined assumptions. The system behaves according to what is easiest to execute, not what is most aligned. Over time, this divergence produces tension. The founder feels disconnected from the enterprise they created.

Integrating values into operations requires translation. Values must move from belief into behavior, from intention into design. This translation is precise work. If clarity is valued, decision rights must be defined. If respect is central, feedback systems must protect dignity. If sustainability matters, pace must be regulated. Values that cannot be traced into structure are decorative. They offer comfort but no guidance.

Personal values become most visible when they conflict with efficiency. Choosing integrity over speed, care over scale, or coherence over opportunism reveals what truly governs the system. These moments define culture more than any declaration. Teams learn what values mean by watching how inconvenience is handled. When founders act consistently with their stated values under pressure, trust solidifies.

This integration also simplifies leadership. When values serve as operational logic, decisions require less deliberation. The founder does not weigh every option equally; they filter choices through a stable framework. This stability reduces cognitive load and prevents reactive decision-making. The system gains momentum not through acceleration, but through alignment.

Values integration does not eliminate conflict. It clarifies it. Tradeoffs become explicit rather than hidden. Disagreement is framed around shared principles rather than personal preference. This clarity strengthens dialogue and preserves respect even when consensus is not immediate.

When personal values shape operations, the enterprise begins to reflect the founder's deeper commitments. Work feels less alien because it follows a recognizable logic. The builder no longer has to compartmentalize identity to function. The business becomes an extension of inner order rather than a departure from it.

The Myth of Objectivity in Leadership

Leaders are often encouraged to strive for objectivity, as though decisions could be made from a neutral position untouched by history, temperament, or values. This aspiration sounds responsible, but it is misleading. No leader operates from a blank slate. Every judgment is filtered through perception, experience, and internal orientation. Pretending otherwise does not eliminate bias; it obscures it.

The myth of objectivity becomes particularly dangerous when it is used to avoid self-examination. Leaders invoke data, process, or "best practices" to mask unacknowledged preferences or fears. Decisions are framed as inevitable rather than chosen. Responsibility is displaced onto systems rather than owned personally. This posture erodes trust because teams sense the incongruence between stated neutrality and lived impact.

True leadership clarity does not come from denying subjectivity. It comes from integrating it consciously. Leaders who understand their own tendencies; toward control, avoidance, optimism, or caution; can compensate intelligently. They seek perspective where their blind spots are known. They do not claim objectivity; they practice accountability.

This integration improves decision quality. When leaders acknowledge how values and temperament influence judgment, they can use data as input rather than justification. Evidence informs rather than conceals. Dialogue becomes more honest because assumptions are surfaced rather than hidden. Disagreement becomes constructive because it addresses differences in orientation rather than arguing over false neutrality.

The myth of objectivity also reinforces separation between self and structure. Leaders attempt to design systems that are "purely rational" while ignoring the emotional and ethical currents that inevitably shape behavior. These systems often fail because they are brittle. They do not account for human variance. They demand compliance rather than engagement.

Integrated leadership designs with subjectivity in mind. It recognizes that every system will express the inner state of those who lead it. Rather than denying this reality, the leader works to align inner orientation with external design. Systems become more adaptive because they are built with an understanding of human complexity rather than against it.

Objectivity, in the strict sense, is unattainable. Integrity is not. Leaders who accept this distinction stop performing neutrality and start practicing coherence. Their decisions carry weight not because they are detached, but because they are accountable, transparent, and aligned with a clear internal compass.

Integrating Vision with Infrastructure

Vision without infrastructure remains aspirational. Infrastructure without vision becomes mechanical. Many enterprises suffer because these two elements develop out of sync. Founders articulate expansive visions while relying on ad hoc systems to execute them. Alternatively, they build sophisticated structures that optimize efficiency while gradually losing sight of purpose. In both cases, misalignment produces friction and eventual fatigue.

Integrating vision with infrastructure requires translating intention into form. Vision clarifies *why* the work exists and *what* it seeks to serve. Infrastructure determines *how* that service is delivered repeatedly and reliably. When these elements align, systems reinforce meaning rather than dilute it. Work feels coherent because daily actions echo long-term intent.

This integration begins with honesty about capacity. Vision must be constrained enough to be carried by the available structure. When vision outruns infrastructure, pressure accumulates. Teams are asked to compensate with effort what systems cannot support. Conversely, when infrastructure outpaces vision, the organization becomes efficient but hollow. Activity increases while significance diminishes.

Effective integration is iterative. Vision evolves as infrastructure reveals its limits. Systems are adjusted as understanding deepens. The founder remains engaged in this dialogue rather than delegating it entirely. Vision is not something delivered once and preserved; it is refined through lived execution.

Infrastructure also expresses values. How decisions are routed, how feedback flows, and how resources are allocated communicate priorities more clearly than vision statements. When infrastructure contradicts vision, confusion spreads. Teams lose confidence because they are asked to act in ways that conflict with stated purpose. Alignment restores trust by making intention visible in operation.

Integrating vision and infrastructure reduces reliance on heroics. When systems embody purpose, individuals do not need to compensate through overexertion. The work sustains itself because meaning is built into its mechanics. This sustainability becomes a competitive advantage. Enterprises with aligned infrastructure adapt more easily because change does not require reinterpreting identity at every turn.

For the founder, this integration resolves internal tension. They no longer feel pulled between ideals and execution. The business reflects their thinking at multiple levels simultaneously. Vision is no longer something defended verbally; it is experienced through structure.

Integration does not guarantee success. It guarantees coherence. And coherence is the condition that allows endurance.

When Inner Chaos Becomes External Confusion

Disorder within a founder rarely remains contained. It expresses itself outwardly through inconsistency, misalignment, and reactive decision-making. When internal priorities are unclear or conflicting, the enterprise mirrors that state. Strategies shift abruptly. Messaging fragments. Teams receive mixed signals about what matters. What appears as organizational confusion often originates as unresolved inner tension.

This transfer is subtle. Founders may believe they are shielding others from uncertainty by making decisions quickly or maintaining a confident front. In reality, unprocessed doubt leaks through behavior. Decisions are reversed without explanation. Initiatives begin without clear completion criteria. Boundaries are enforced unevenly. The system struggles not because it lacks intelligence, but because it is responding to incoherent leadership signals.

Inner chaos also amplifies stress. When the founder is internally unsettled, every external variable feels destabilizing. Minor disruptions provoke disproportionate responses. Urgency replaces discernment. The organization becomes reactive because its reference point is unstable. Over time, this reactivity erodes trust. Teams stop anticipating direction and start waiting for correction.

Attempts to solve external confusion solely through process often fail. More meetings, frameworks, and controls are introduced, but the underlying inconsistency remains. These additions increase complexity without resolving the source. The system becomes heavier and less responsive. Frustration grows because effort does not produce clarity.

Restoring coherence requires addressing the origin. Founders must confront their own unresolved tensions; competing ambitions, unexamined fears, conflicting values. This work cannot be delegated.

Until internal alignment improves, external order will remain fragile. Once clarity is restored internally, many external issues resolve with minimal intervention.

This does not mean leaders must eliminate all uncertainty. It means they must distinguish between uncertainty they can hold responsibly and confusion that arises from avoidance. Transparency about what is known and unknown stabilizes systems. Pretending certainty where none exists destabilizes them.

When inner order improves, leadership signals become consistent. Decisions align over time. Communication simplifies. The organization regains confidence because it is no longer compensating for hidden volatility. External confusion recedes as a natural consequence of internal integration.

Integrity Is the Invisible Architecture

Integrity is often discussed as a moral quality, something admirable but abstract. In practice, integrity functions as architecture. It determines whether structures hold under pressure, whether systems behave predictably, and whether trust can accumulate over time. This architecture is invisible, yet its effects are unmistakable. Enterprises with integrity feel stable even when conditions are volatile. Those without it require constant reinforcement to prevent collapse.

Integrity emerges when internal commitments match external behavior. Leaders do what they say, not occasionally, but consistently. Policies align with practice. Promises are made carefully and kept deliberately. This consistency reduces friction because people do not have to second-guess intent. The system becomes easier to operate because it behaves reliably.

Without integrity, structures become brittle. Rules are enforced selectively. Exceptions proliferate. Short-term expedience overrides long-term coherence. These deviations may seem minor individually, but they accumulate. Over time, the system loses credibility. People stop trusting process and begin navigating around it. Informal power replaces formal structure. Chaos increases not because of rebellion, but because predictability has been lost.

Integrity also governs pacing. Leaders who lack it often oscillate between overcommitment and withdrawal. They promise more than they can sustain, then retreat abruptly when overwhelmed. This volatility destabilizes teams and erodes morale. Integrity stabilizes rhythm by aligning capacity with commitment. The organization learns to trust timing because it reflects reality rather than aspiration.

As invisible architecture, integrity supports complexity. Systems can scale when their foundational logic remains intact. Decision-making can decentralize because principles are clear and consistently applied. Control becomes less necessary because coherence is embedded. This reduces overhead and increases adaptability.

For founders, integrity begins internally. It requires acknowledging limits, honoring boundaries, and acting from clarity rather than compulsion. This internal discipline expresses itself externally as reliability. Others sense when leadership is grounded. Trust grows not through charisma, but through consistency.

Integrity cannot be installed after the fact. It must be built continuously through small, ordinary choices. Each alignment reinforces the structure. Each compromise weakens it. Over time, these accumulations determine whether the enterprise endures.

Invisible architecture matters more than visible scale. When integrity is present, systems breathe. When it is absent, no amount of design can compensate.

Designing for Coherence, Not Control

Control is often mistaken for order. Founders facing complexity respond by tightening oversight, adding approvals, and increasing monitoring. These measures can create short-term stability, but they rarely scale well. Over time, control-based systems become rigid, slow, and exhausting to maintain. Coherence offers a different path. It relies less on enforcement and more on alignment.

Designing for coherence begins with clarity of intent. When purpose, values, and priorities are understood consistently, behavior aligns without constant supervision. Individuals make decisions that support the whole because they understand the logic governing the system. Control becomes unnecessary because deviation is less likely. The system regulates itself through shared understanding.

Control-heavy designs assume mistrust. They prepare for failure rather than enable competence. This assumption becomes self-fulfilling. People comply minimally. Initiative declines. Innovation stalls because risk is punished rather than contextualized. Coherence-based designs assume responsibility. They provide structure that supports judgment rather than replaces it.

Coherence does not mean absence of boundaries. It requires clear roles, defined decision rights, and transparent processes. The difference lies in purpose. Boundaries exist to guide action, not to constrain it. When people understand why limits exist, they respect them. When limits feel arbitrary, they invite circumvention.

This approach reduces cognitive load. Individuals do not have to navigate contradictory instructions or shifting priorities. Effort is applied more efficiently because direction is stable. The organization moves with less friction because fewer resources are spent correcting misalignment.

For founders, designing for coherence requires restraint. It means resisting the impulse to intervene unnecessarily. It involves trusting systems to function once alignment is established. This trust must be earned through careful design and consistent leadership. When coherence is present, intervention becomes exceptional rather than habitual.

Coherence also enhances adaptability. Systems grounded in shared logic can adjust to new conditions without reengineering control mechanisms. People understand what to preserve and what to modify. Change becomes contextual rather than disruptive.

Control demands constant energy. Coherence conserves it. Enterprises designed for coherence endure because they are easier to inhabit. They require less force to sustain and offer greater stability as complexity increases.

Structure That Breathes: Systems as Servants

Structure is meant to support life, not replace it. When systems are designed without regard for human rhythm, they become oppressive. Processes multiply. Flexibility disappears. People begin serving the system rather than being served by it. This inversion signals a failure of design. Structure should carry weight so that people do not have to. When it does the opposite, exhaustion follows.

A breathing structure is one that adapts without losing integrity. It expands when demand increases and contracts when pressure eases. It allows for variation without collapse. Such systems recognize that consistency does not require rigidity. They preserve essential functions while permitting adjustment at the edges. This balance allows the organization to remain responsive without becoming chaotic.

Systems serve best when they are simple, visible, and purposeful. Complexity should arise only where necessary. When rules exist solely to manage exceptions, they often obscure intent. Breathing structures clarify what matters most and leave room for judgment elsewhere. This design trusts people to operate within clear parameters rather than forcing uniform behavior.

When systems become servants rather than masters, energy is redistributed. Decision-making accelerates because fewer approvals are required. Accountability improves because responsibility is clearly located. People engage more fully because they are not navigating unnecessary friction. The organization feels lighter, even as it grows more capable.

Founders play a critical role in preserving this quality. Under stress, the instinct to harden systems returns. Temporary measures become permanent. Exceptions are codified. Over time, the structure loses its capacity to flex. Maintaining breath requires vigilance. It demands periodic simplification and removal of controls that no longer serve.

A breathing structure also acknowledges limits. It does not demand constant performance at peak capacity. It allows for recovery, learning, and recalibration. This allowance increases longevity. People remain effective longer because the system supports human cadence rather than overriding it.

Systems that serve do not disappear. They function quietly. When they work well, they are barely noticed because they reduce friction rather than create it. This quiet effectiveness is a mark of mature design.

Self-Alignment as Business Strategy

Alignment between self and structure is often treated as a personal concern, separate from strategic thinking. In reality, it is foundational. A founder's internal state shapes decision quality, risk tolerance, and the capacity to sustain effort. When inner life is disordered, strategy compensates through overcomplexity. When inner life is aligned, strategy simplifies. Clarity replaces force.

Self-alignment begins with coherence between values, behavior, and ambition. The founder knows what matters, acts accordingly, and resists pursuits that fracture attention. This coherence reduces internal negotiation. Decisions are made faster and with less regret because they are anchored to a stable center. Over time, this stability compounds into strategic advantage.

Aligned founders design better systems because they are not managing internal conflict through external control. They do not need to dominate or over-insulate structures. They can tolerate uncertainty without panic and change without reactivity. This emotional regulation translates into organizational resilience. The enterprise responds to pressure with adaptation rather than defensiveness.

Self-alignment also affects timing. Founders who are internally coherent recognize when to act and when to wait. They do not confuse urgency with importance. This discernment improves capital allocation, talent decisions, and growth pacing. Fewer resources are wasted on reactive initiatives. Effort concentrates where it matters most.

There is also a signaling effect. Teams sense alignment quickly. Trust increases when leadership behaves consistently across contexts. Communication simplifies because intent is stable. This trust reduces friction and accelerates execution. Strategy benefits not from brilliance alone, but from reliability.

Self-alignment is not static. It requires ongoing attention. As the enterprise evolves, new tensions arise. Alignment must be renewed. This renewal is part of leadership practice, not a one-time achievement. Founders who neglect it gradually reintroduce fragmentation into the system.

Treating self-alignment as strategy reframes leadership development. It is no longer about acquiring techniques, but about maintaining coherence. This coherence supports everything else. When the founder is aligned, the structure follows. When the founder fragments, no amount of strategy can compensate.

Business built from integrated self and structure endures because it rests on a unified logic. The work moves forward without tearing the one who carries it.

Chapter 23

Wealth as Stewardship, Not Possession

The Myth of Ownership

Ownership is one of the most persistent illusions in modern entrepreneurship. Builders speak easily of *my company*, *my capital*, *my people*, as though time, talent, and energy could be fixed in place through legal or financial means. This language creates a sense of control, but it obscures a deeper truth. Nothing essential can be owned in the way the word implies. Everything that gives a business life is in motion.

Enterprises evolve beyond their founders. Teams change, disperse, and regenerate. Capital circulates through markets, hands, and generations. Even ideas, when they are alive, refuse containment. They adapt, replicate, and eventually exceed the vision of those who first articulated them. The myth of ownership persists because it promises permanence in a world defined by impermanence. But building as though permanence were guaranteed produces rigidity rather than strength.

This illusion has consequences. When founders believe they own what they are meant to steward, fear enters the system. Control tightens. Delegation feels dangerous. Succession becomes threatening rather than natural. The builder begins defending territory instead of tending growth. What was once creative becomes protective. What was once generous becomes guarded. The enterprise may continue to function, but its vitality diminishes because care has been replaced by possession.

Recognizing the limits of ownership does not weaken authority. It clarifies it. The founder's role becomes custodial rather than imperial. They are responsible for direction, integrity, and continuity during the season in which the work passes through them. This responsibility is serious precisely because it is temporary. Knowing that nothing ultimately belongs to them sharpens attention. Decisions are made with greater care because they affect something that will outlast personal involvement.

Stewardship accepts impermanence without collapsing into detachment. The founder does not withdraw interest or commitment; they deepen it. They act knowing that what they are shaping will one day move beyond them. This awareness disciplines ego and steadies judgment. The work is approached as something to be prepared for transfer, not defended as identity.

The myth of ownership asks the builder to prove worth through accumulation. Stewardship asks them to demonstrate care through alignment. One clings. The other tends. Enterprises built on stewardship endure longer because they are designed to circulate rather than ossify. They remain adaptable because they are not anchored to a single ego or moment.

Wealth, in this frame, is not something claimed. It is something carried. And carrying something well requires attention, restraint, and humility; qualities ownership alone cannot provide.

Wealth as a Tool, Not a Trophy

Wealth is often treated as a symbol rather than an instrument. It is displayed, compared, and admired as evidence of success. In this framing, money becomes a trophy; a visible confirmation that effort was worthwhile and status has been achieved. This treatment distorts its function. Wealth ceases to serve the work and instead begins serving the ego. When this shift occurs, judgment degrades and responsibility narrows.

As a tool, wealth exists to enable action. It funds capability, absorbs risk, and creates optionality. It allows systems to stabilize and people to focus on meaningful contribution rather than survival. Used well, it increases resilience. Used poorly, it amplifies distortion.

The difference lies not in the amount, but in the posture of the one holding it.

Treating wealth as a trophy introduces performative behavior. Spending decisions become symbolic rather than strategic. Resources are allocated to signal success rather than to strengthen foundations. Excess is justified as reward. Restraint is misread as limitation. Over time, this posture creates fragility. The enterprise becomes expensive to maintain and difficult to adapt because resources are locked into appearances rather than function.

Wealth as a tool demands precision. Each allocation is measured against purpose. Capital is directed toward what compounds capability, not what flatters image. This precision often looks conservative from the outside, but it is internally expansive. The system gains flexibility because resources are preserved for moments that matter rather than consumed for validation.

This approach also disciplines ambition. The builder stops asking what wealth proves and starts asking what it enables. Growth decisions are evaluated based on sustainability rather than spectacle. Opportunities are declined not because they are unprofitable, but because they distract from core capacity. Wealth supports coherence rather than acceleration for its own sake.

There is humility in this posture. The builder recognizes that money is inert until directed intelligently. It does not confer wisdom. It amplifies intent. When intent is clear, wealth becomes powerful. When intent is confused, wealth magnifies confusion. This awareness encourages restraint and reflection rather than indulgence.

Treating wealth as a tool aligns with stewardship. Tools are maintained, not worshipped. They are chosen carefully and used deliberately. Their value lies in effectiveness, not display. When wealth is held this way, it strengthens the enterprise quietly. It does its work without demanding attention.

A trophy demands admiration. A tool demands competence. Builders who understand this difference protect both their capital and their integrity over the long arc.

Abundance Without Inflation of Ego

Abundance tests character more subtly than scarcity. When resources are limited, restraint is enforced externally. When resources expand, restraint must be internal. This is where ego often enters. The builder begins to identify with scale, access, and optionality. Confidence drifts into entitlement. Judgment softens because consequences feel distant. What was once careful becomes casual.

Inflation of ego under abundance is rarely dramatic. It shows up as assumption rather than arrogance. The builder expects deference where dialogue once existed. Risk tolerance increases not through insight, but through insulation. Feedback is filtered because disagreement feels unnecessary. Over time, these shifts distort leadership. Decisions are made from comfort rather than clarity.

Abundance without ego inflation requires discipline. The builder must actively separate self-worth from resource availability. Wealth becomes a condition, not an identity. This separation allows abundance to be held without distortion. Capital expands capability without expanding self-importance. The builder remains attentive rather than complacent.

One marker of healthy abundance is listening. Builders who have not inflated with wealth continue to seek perspective. They remain open to correction. They understand that resources reduce friction, not fallibility. This openness preserves learning. The system stays responsive because leadership has not hardened.

Another marker is proportionality. The builder does not escalate lifestyle, scale, or risk automatically in response to increased means. Decisions remain anchored to purpose. Growth is paced according to capacity rather than appetite. This proportionality prevents overextension and protects long-term stability.

Abundance can either liberate or distort. When ego inflates, wealth becomes a shield against reality. When ego remains grounded, wealth becomes a platform for more responsible action. The difference lies not in numbers, but in posture.

Stewardship demands that abundance be carried lightly. Not minimized, but integrated without spectacle. When the builder can hold more without becoming more entitled, wealth fulfills its role as a support rather than a seduction.

The Responsibility of Resourcing Others

Wealth concentrates power. Whether acknowledged or not, access to capital shapes outcomes beyond the individual holder. Decisions about hiring, compensation, investment, and allocation determine whose work is supported, whose ideas are tested, and whose time is protected. This influence carries responsibility that extends beyond personal preference. To steward wealth is to recognize that resourcing others is not incidental; it is central.

Resourcing others well requires discernment. Capital should amplify capability, not dependency. It should strengthen systems rather than substitute for their absence. When money is used to bypass structure or accountability, it weakens what it intends to help. Short-term relief can produce long-term fragility. Stewardship demands that resources be paired with clarity, expectations, and support for sustainable contribution.

There is also an ethical dimension. Builders must consider not only efficiency, but impact. Who benefits from this allocation? What behaviors does it reinforce? What future does it enable? These questions slow decision-making, but they prevent distortion. Wealth deployed without reflection often entrenches imbalance. Wealth deployed with care redistributes opportunity without eroding standards.

Resourcing others also tests ego. Builders may seek loyalty, gratitude, or control in exchange for support. This transactional posture undermines trust. True stewardship does not demand allegiance. It offers resources in service of shared purpose and allows autonomy to remain intact. Influence is exercised through alignment rather than leverage.

At scale, responsible resourcing requires systems. Informal generosity becomes inconsistent and opaque. Clear criteria, transparent processes, and principled limits protect both giver and receiver. These structures prevent favoritism and ensure that support remains aligned with mission rather than mood.

Resourcing others well strengthens the ecosystem around the enterprise. Talent develops. Innovation deepens. Trust expands. The builder's influence multiplies because capability has been cultivated rather than extracted. This multiplication is quiet but enduring.

Wealth that does not resource others eventually isolates its holder. Wealth that does builds continuity. Stewardship recognizes that capital's highest function is not accumulation, but enablement; carried out with precision, humility, and restraint.

Money as a Mirror: What Capital Reveals

Money does not change character; it reveals it. Capital amplifies existing tendencies, making underlying values visible through action. When resources are scarce, choices are constrained. When resources expand, constraint shifts inward. What the builder prioritizes when options multiply exposes their true orientation far more clearly than what they claimed when options were limited.

Capital reveals relationship to fear. Some builders hoard, accumulating reserves far beyond strategic need, driven not by prudence but by anxiety. Others spend impulsively, using money to quiet insecurity or manufacture momentum. In both cases, money becomes a coping mechanism rather than a tool. The pattern was present before wealth appeared; capital merely gave it scale.

Money also reveals relationship to power. Builders who equate wealth with authority tend to centralize control. They confuse funding with wisdom and expect compliance in exchange for resources. Conversely, builders who understand stewardship use capital to distribute capability. They fund autonomy rather than obedience. The difference determines whether an enterprise becomes hierarchical or generative.

Capital exposes clarity of purpose. When intent is diffuse, money scatters. Investments chase novelty. Spending follows trends. The enterprise grows busy but incoherent. When purpose is clear, money concentrates. Allocation reinforces direction. Even modest capital produces disproportionate impact because it is aligned rather than reactive.

Money further reveals temporal orientation. Builders focused on immediacy seek quick returns, rapid validation, and visible wins. Those oriented toward endurance invest patiently, accepting delayed payoff in exchange for resilience. This distinction shapes risk tolerance, partnership choices, and growth pacing. Wealth magnifies whichever orientation already governs the builder.

Because money reveals rather than conceals, it offers feedback. Discomfort around spending, guilt around success, or compulsion around accumulation signal unresolved beliefs. Ignoring these signals leads to repetition. Engaging them leads to integration. The builder learns not only how to manage capital, but how capital is managing them.

In this way, money becomes diagnostic. It shows where alignment holds and where it fractures. Builders who pay attention use this information to refine posture rather than justify behavior. Wealth becomes an instrument of self-awareness rather than a distraction from it.

Capital will always reflect the one who holds it. Stewardship begins by being willing to look honestly at what is being reflected.

How Scarcity Distorts Power

Scarcity exerts pressure that reshapes behavior long before it reshapes outcomes. When resources feel insufficient, decision-making contracts. Fear narrows perception. Power becomes defensive rather than generative. In this state, leadership shifts from stewardship to survival, and the effects ripple outward through every system the builder touches.

Scarcity distorts power by encouraging control. The builder hoards authority because delegation feels risky. Information is withheld to preserve advantage. Decisions are centralized under the belief that fewer hands reduce error. In reality, this concentration increases fragility. The system becomes dependent on a single point of judgment, and resilience declines because adaptability has been sacrificed for perceived safety.

Scarcity also distorts ethics. When resources feel tight, compromises appear reasonable. Boundaries soften. Shortcuts are justified as temporary. Over time, these exceptions accumulate into norms. The builder may still speak the language of values, but behavior drifts. Trust erodes because people sense that principles are contingent on circumstance. What began as necessity becomes habit.

Power under scarcity often becomes extractive. The builder demands more from people than systems can support. Time, attention, and emotional labor are consumed without replenishment. This extraction may produce short-term output, but it weakens the foundation. Burnout spreads. Talent leaves. The enterprise survives, but it does so by depletion rather than renewal.

Even when scarcity is real, its distortion is not inevitable. Stewardship responds to constraint with prioritization rather than panic. The builder distinguishes between what is essential and what is merely urgent. Resources are allocated deliberately. Transparency replaces secrecy. Power is shared carefully rather than clutched instinctively. This posture preserves dignity and coherence even under pressure.

Scarcity becomes most dangerous when it lingers psychologically after conditions have changed. Builders who grew up under constraint may continue operating from fear long after abundance appears. Control habits persist. Trust remains limited. Power stays rigid. In these cases, wealth does not heal distortion; it amplifies it. The system becomes overbuilt and underlived.

Recognizing how scarcity shapes power is a prerequisite for releasing its grip. Builders must examine not only their current resources, but their historical relationship to lack. When this examination occurs, leadership relaxes. Power regains its proper function as a means of enablement rather than defense.

Stewardship restores power to its rightful role. It uses authority to stabilize systems, not to protect ego. It responds to scarcity with clarity rather than contraction. In doing so, it prevents temporary conditions from hardening into permanent distortion.

The Entrepreneur as Steward, Not Sovereign

Sovereignty implies dominion. It places the entrepreneur at the center of the system, exercising authority as ownership and control. In this model, power flows downward and legitimacy is derived from position or possession. Stewardship operates differently. It understands authority as responsibility rather than entitlement. The entrepreneur is not above the system, but accountable to it.

Viewing oneself as a sovereign encourages extraction. Decisions are framed around what can be taken, protected, or leveraged. Success becomes a matter of dominance. Over time, this posture isolates the builder. People comply rather than contribute. Feedback diminishes. The system obeys, but it does not thrive. What looks like strength is often fragility reinforced by fear.

The steward's posture is grounded in service to continuity. The entrepreneur recognizes that the enterprise is larger than personal ambition and longer-lived than individual involvement. Authority is exercised to preserve health, alignment, and adaptability. Power is used to set conditions rather than impose outcomes. This use of power stabilizes the system because it respects its complexity.

Stewardship also reframes decision-making. The question shifts from *What benefits me now?* to *What sustains this system over time?* This shift introduces patience. Short-term advantage is weighed against long-term consequence. The steward resists opportunities that offer immediate gain at the expense of integrity or resilience. This restraint protects reputation and trust, which are far more difficult to rebuild than capital.

There is humility in stewardship. The entrepreneur accepts that they are a temporary carrier of influence. This acceptance reduces defensiveness. Criticism is received as information rather than threat. Succession is considered early rather than avoided. The enterprise is designed to function without constant assertion of authority. These choices increase durability.

Being a steward does not diminish leadership. It clarifies it. Others sense when authority is exercised in service rather than self-interest. Commitment deepens because participation feels meaningful rather than coerced. The system benefits from shared investment rather than enforced compliance.

Sovereigns demand loyalty. Stewards cultivate trust. One concentrates power. The other distributes capability. Enterprises led by stewards endure because they are built to outlast individual control. Wealth, in this frame, is not a symbol of dominance, but a resource entrusted for careful use.

Value Beyond Valuation

Markets assign numbers. Valuations compress complex realities into figures that can be compared, traded, and optimized. This function is useful, but it is incomplete. Not everything that sustains an enterprise can be measured cleanly, and not everything that can be measured carries enduring value. When builders allow valuation to define worth, they mistake representation for reality.

Value beyond valuation includes elements that resist quantification: trust, reputation, cultural coherence, ethical credibility, and long-term optionality. These assets accumulate slowly and compound quietly. They rarely appear on balance sheets, yet they determine whether an enterprise can survive stress, attract principled partners, and adapt without collapse. Builders who ignore these forms of value often discover their absence only when crisis exposes it.

Valuation-driven thinking also distorts behavior. When numbers become the primary reference point, decisions skew toward what is legible to markets rather than what is necessary for health. Short-term gains are favored over foundational investments. Appearances are optimized at the expense of substance. Over time, the enterprise becomes impressive but hollow; highly valued yet internally brittle.

Recognizing value beyond valuation reorients strategy. The builder invests in systems that build resilience even when returns are delayed or indirect. They protect culture during growth rather than sacrificing it for speed. They preserve credibility by honoring commitments even when breach would be profitable. These choices may depress short-term metrics, but they strengthen long-term position.

This posture also stabilizes identity. Builders who equate worth with valuation experience volatility as personal threat. Numbers rise and fall, taking confidence with them. Builders who ground themselves in broader definitions of value remain steadier. They understand that market signals fluctuate, while integrity compounds. This steadiness improves judgment because decisions are not made under existential pressure.

Value beyond valuation also shapes relationships. Partners, employees, and communities sense when they are being treated as contributors rather than line items. Loyalty deepens. Collaboration becomes easier. The enterprise gains access to goodwill that cannot be purchased outright but proves decisive over time.

Markets will always measure. Builders need not surrender to that measurement as total truth. Stewardship requires holding valuation lightly; using it as information without allowing it to dictate identity or direction. When value is understood more broadly, wealth supports endurance rather than distorting it.

Withholding as Wisdom: When Not to Spend

Spending is often treated as evidence of momentum. Capital deployed signals action, confidence, and belief in growth. In entrepreneurial culture, restraint is easily misread as hesitation or fear. Yet some of the most consequential decisions a builder makes involve choosing *not* to spend. Withholding, when guided by clarity rather than anxiety, is an expression of wisdom.

Money spent prematurely distorts systems. It fills gaps that should have revealed structural weaknesses. It accelerates processes that have not yet stabilized. By solving problems with capital instead of design, the builder masks misalignment rather than correcting it. What looks like progress often delays necessary learning. When funds eventually tighten, the unresolved issues return with greater force.

Withholding preserves signal. Scarcity, when managed intentionally, reveals what is essential. Teams become more discerning. Priorities sharpen. Effort is directed toward what truly matters rather than what is merely possible. This discipline strengthens judgment. The builder learns which initiatives can survive constraint and which rely on excess to appear viable.

There is also a timing dimension. Capital is most effective when deployed at moments of readiness. Spending before readiness creates dependency; spending after readiness multiplies impact. Withholding allows capacity to mature. It gives ideas time to prove coherence before scale is applied. This patience reduces waste and increases resilience.

Emotionally, withholding requires regulation. Builders must tolerate the discomfort of not acting when action is available. This discomfort often arises from ego rather than necessity. The urge to spend can be driven by a desire to feel decisive, generous, or important. Restraint challenges these impulses. It asks the builder to trust process over appearance.

Wise withholding also protects integrity. Not every opportunity deserves funding. Not every request should be met. Saying no preserves alignment. It communicates standards. Over time, this selectivity builds trust because others understand that resources are allocated with intention rather than impulse.

Withholding is not hoarding. Hoarding stems from fear and creates stagnation. Wise withholding is temporary and purposeful. It holds capital in reserve until conditions warrant release. When release comes, it is decisive and effective.

Stewardship recognizes that money unused can be as powerful as money spent. Knowing when to hold is as important as knowing when to act. This discernment separates disciplined builders from reactive ones.

Letting Wealth Circulate Without Losing Integrity

Wealth that remains static degrades. Hoarded capital loses relevance, agility, and moral clarity. Yet wealth that circulates without principle corrodes trust just as quickly. The discipline of stewardship lies in allowing resources to move while preserving alignment. Circulation without integrity becomes noise. Integrity without circulation becomes stagnation. Enduring systems require both.

Letting wealth circulate begins with recognizing its purpose. Capital is meant to support life within the system; people, ideas, infrastructure, and continuity. When resources are released in service of these aims, circulation strengthens coherence. When they are released to chase influence, loyalty, or visibility, distortion follows. The difference is not subtle. It appears in outcomes that either reinforce trust or quietly erode it.

Integrity in circulation requires criteria. Resources move according to values, not pressure. Requests are evaluated against purpose. Opportunities are assessed for alignment rather than excitement. This selectivity prevents capital from being captured by trends or personalities. It ensures that movement remains meaningful rather than reactive.

There is also a boundary component. Circulation does not mean indiscriminate generosity. Stewardship respects limits. It recognizes that saying yes everywhere weakens the ability to say yes where it matters most. Boundaries protect both giver and receiver. They preserve dignity by preventing dependency and resentment. Wealth circulates best when it invites capability rather than obligation.

Letting wealth circulate also demands transparency. When allocation logic is opaque, suspicion grows. People begin attributing motive where none may exist. Clear rationale preserves trust even when decisions disappoint. Integrity is reinforced not by universal approval, but by consistency of principle.

Over time, disciplined circulation creates resilience. Capital flows toward competence and alignment. Waste diminishes. Systems strengthen. The enterprise gains a reputation for seriousness rather than spectacle. Partners engage with confidence because they trust the logic governing resources.

Circulation inevitably involves loss. Not every investment returns. Not every allocation succeeds. Integrity is preserved not by avoiding loss, but by absorbing it honestly. Learning replaces blame. Adjustment replaces defensiveness. Wealth continues to move because fear has not frozen it.

Stewarded wealth does not announce itself. It works quietly, precisely, and with care. It supports what endures and withdraws from what distorts. In this way, circulation becomes an expression of fidelity rather than indulgence.

Chapter 24

Witness, Not Warlord: Leading Through Presence

The Myth of the Hero-CEO

The modern entrepreneurial landscape still clings to an outdated archetype: the heroic founder who dominates by force of personality. This figure is imagined as singular, decisive, and relentless; someone who bends markets, people, and circumstance through sheer will. The myth persists because it flatters ambition. It promises that certainty equals leadership and that dominance produces order. In practice, it produces fragility.

The hero-CEO model assumes that leadership is an act of conquest. Authority is asserted rather than cultivated. Decisions are framed as victories. Dissent is treated as threat. This posture may generate short-term momentum, particularly in early-stage environments where speed matters more than coherence. Over time, however, it becomes unsustainable. Complexity outgrows individual control. Systems demand nuance rather than force. The heroic posture begins to crack under its own weight.

This model also imposes impossible constraints on the leader. The hero cannot rest without risking relevance. They cannot express uncertainty without weakening the myth. They cannot distribute authority without diminishing their central role. As a result, they isolate themselves. Feedback narrows. Judgment degrades. The leader becomes both indispensable and increasingly disconnected from reality.

Organizations built around heroic dominance develop predictable pathologies. Teams learn to defer rather than think. Initiative declines because outcomes are preempted by the leader's certainty. Risk is hidden rather than surfaced. Over time, the enterprise becomes dependent on performance rather than structure. When the hero falters, the system has no center to hold it.

Burnout is not incidental in this model; it is structural. The leader exhausts themselves maintaining the illusion of invincibility. The organization exhausts itself compensating for the absence of shared ownership. What appears powerful from the outside is often brittle within. Collapse may arrive suddenly or slowly, but it is rarely surprising.

The failure of the hero-CEO is not a moral judgment. It is a structural inevitability. Leadership that relies on domination cannot adapt to environments that require responsiveness, trust, and distributed intelligence. As enterprises grow more complex, leadership must become quieter, not louder. Presence replaces performance. Stability replaces spectacle.

The era of the warlord leader is ending not because it is unethical, but because it no longer works. What replaces it is not weakness, but a different kind of strength: the capacity to hold complexity without needing to conquer it.

Leadership as Presence, Not Performance

Performance-based leadership depends on visibility. The leader must be seen deciding, directing, and intervening. Authority is reinforced through action and display. While this approach can produce clarity in narrow contexts, it becomes costly as systems grow. The leader's presence turns into constant motion. Attention is consumed by signaling rather than sensing. Over time, performance displaces awareness.

Presence-based leadership operates differently. It does not require constant assertion to be effective. The leader's influence comes from steadiness rather than activity. By being fully attentive, they register shifts before they escalate. They notice tension without dramatizing it. Their responses are proportionate because they are informed by observation rather than impulse.

Presence reduces the need for control. When leaders are attentive, they can trust systems to function within defined parameters. They intervene selectively rather than habitually. This restraint strengthens rather than weakens authority. Teams feel trusted. Responsibility distributes naturally. The system becomes more resilient because it is not dependent on constant oversight.

Performance seeks validation. Presence seeks accuracy. The leader no longer measures effectiveness by how visible they are, but by how well the system operates without them. This shift requires ego discipline. Stepping back can feel like loss of relevance. In reality, it is an expansion of capacity. The leader becomes a stabilizing reference point rather than a bottleneck.

Presence also changes communication. Words carry more weight because they are fewer. Silence is used intentionally rather than avoided. Meetings become more focused because attention is not fragmented. The leader listens without rehearsing response. This quality of attention creates psychological safety and invites clarity from others.

In high-pressure environments, presence is particularly valuable. Performance escalates stress by amplifying urgency. Presence dampens volatility by absorbing it. The leader's calm signals that the system can withstand strain. This signal allows others to think rather than react. Stability spreads through the organization because it is modeled at the center.

Leadership as presence is not passive. It is active awareness applied with restraint. It replaces the need to control everything with the capacity to hold what matters most. Over time, this posture outlasts performance because it conserves energy and preserves coherence.

Listening as Leadership

Listening is often undervalued in leadership because its effects are indirect. It does not produce immediate action or visible command.

Yet sustained listening shapes direction more reliably than forceful assertion. Leaders who listen well develop accurate understanding. Those who do not operate on assumption. Over time, this difference compounds.

Listening as leadership requires more than silence. It requires disciplined attention without preemption. The leader does not listen in order to reply or to confirm existing beliefs. They listen to detect pattern, context, and tension. This kind of listening reveals what is not being said as clearly as what is spoken. It surfaces issues before they harden into crises.

When leaders listen consistently, information flows upward without coercion. Teams speak earlier and more honestly. Problems are addressed while they are still malleable. This early visibility reduces the need for dramatic intervention. The system corrects itself because feedback has not been suppressed.

Listening also redistributes power. It signals that insight is not monopolized at the top. Authority remains intact, but it becomes porous. Others are invited to contribute intelligence rather than simply execute directives. This invitation increases engagement because people feel their perception matters. The organization gains access to a broader range of insight.

Poor listening produces predictable distortions. Leaders misread signals. Decisions are based on incomplete information. Teams adapt by withholding complexity to avoid being dismissed or overridden. Over time, the leader becomes insulated from reality. What appears as confidence is often ignorance protected by hierarchy.

Listening does not require agreement. Leaders may hear perspectives they do not adopt. The value lies in comprehension, not consensus. Understanding opposing views sharpens judgment and reduces blind spots. Even when decisions go against input, being heard preserves trust.

Listening as leadership demands patience. It slows the impulse to decide prematurely. This delay is not inefficiency; it is precision. The leader acts later but more accurately. Systems benefit because fewer corrections are required.

Quiet attention is not weakness. It is the foundation of wise direction. Leaders who listen deeply lead systems that are more adaptive, more honest, and less prone to collapse under pressure.

Authority Without Aggression

Authority is often confused with force. Leaders raise their voices, escalate urgency, or assert dominance to demonstrate control. These behaviors may compel compliance, but they do not generate respect. Over time, aggression erodes authority by substituting intimidation for legitimacy. The system responds out of fear rather than alignment, and fear degrades judgment.

Authority without aggression is rooted in groundedness. The leader does not need to prove command because it is already established through consistency and clarity. Decisions are communicated calmly and carried through reliably. This reliability becomes the source of authority. Others follow not because they are pressured, but because direction is stable.

Aggressive leadership often arises from internal agitation. When leaders feel uncertain or threatened, they attempt to regain control externally. Volume increases. Posture hardens. These signals may temporarily reassert dominance, but they introduce volatility into the system. People focus on managing the leader's emotional state rather than the work itself. Attention is diverted from purpose to survival.

Grounded authority operates differently. The leader regulates themselves first. Emotional spikes are absorbed rather than transmitted. This containment stabilizes the environment. Others feel safe to think clearly and act responsibly. The leader's presence sets the emotional tone without needing to declare it.

Authority without aggression also respects boundaries. Expectations are stated plainly. Consequences are enforced consistently. There is no need for dramatization because structure carries the weight. When rules are clear and fairly applied, enforcement feels impersonal rather than punitive. Trust increases because the system behaves predictably.

This form of authority endures stress. Under pressure, aggressive leaders escalate further, compounding instability. Grounded leaders slow down. They assess before responding. Their restraint signals confidence rather than weakness. The system mirrors this steadiness and recovers more quickly.

Command that flows from groundedness is quieter, but it reaches further. It does not depend on proximity or constant reinforcement. It is carried through culture rather than imposed through force. Over time, this authority becomes self-sustaining because it is embedded in how the organization operates.

The Power of Unreactivity

Unreactivity is often misunderstood as detachment or indifference. In leadership, it is neither. Unreactivity is the capacity to remain present without being pulled into immediate response. It is the ability to absorb stimulus without reflexively returning it amplified. This capacity becomes especially valuable under pressure, when systems are most vulnerable to escalation.

Reactive leadership accelerates volatility. A sudden challenge provokes a sudden response. Emotion transfers rapidly from leader to system. Urgency multiplies. Decisions are made in compression, prioritizing speed over accuracy. While this may feel decisive, it often introduces error. The organization spends more energy correcting reactions than addressing causes.

Unreactive leadership interrupts this loop. The leader pauses long enough to register what is actually happening. They distinguish signal from noise. This pause does not delay action indefinitely; it refines it. Responses emerge proportionate to reality rather than proportional to emotion. The system stabilizes because escalation has been contained at the source.

This stability is a gift. Teams take their cues from leadership behavior more than instruction. When leaders react strongly, others brace. When leaders remain composed, others think. The leader's nervous system becomes a regulating force for the organization. This regulation increases collective capacity under stress.

Unreactivity also preserves authority. Leaders who react emotionally appear unpredictable. Even justified reactions can undermine trust if they are disproportionate. When responses are measured, authority feels secure. People know what to expect. Consistency replaces caution. Engagement improves because fear diminishes.

Developing unreactivity requires internal discipline. Leaders must become aware of personal triggers and habitual responses. They must practice containment without suppression. This practice is not about eliminating emotion, but about choosing when and how it is expressed. Over time, this choice becomes automatic.

Unreactivity does not eliminate urgency. It clarifies it. True emergencies still demand rapid action. The difference is that action is guided by assessment rather than impulse. The system moves quickly without losing coherence.

In environments defined by uncertainty, unreactivity becomes a strategic advantage. It reduces noise, preserves energy, and allows intelligence to surface. Leaders who cultivate it create organizations that respond rather than recoil, endure rather than exhaust.

Detachment from Applause or Attack

Leadership that depends on external reaction is unstable by design. When applause dictates direction, leaders drift toward performance. When criticism dominates attention, leaders become defensive. In both cases, judgment is compromised because action is calibrated to response rather than purpose. Detachment from both praise and attack restores sovereignty.

Applause is seductive because it appears to confirm correctness. Leaders may unconsciously repeat behaviors that generate approval, even when those behaviors are no longer appropriate. Over time, this reinforcement loop narrows decision-making. Risk is avoided if it threatens popularity. Necessary discomfort is postponed. The organization stagnates because leadership has become responsive to sentiment rather than reality.

Attack exerts a different pressure. Leaders fixate on opposition, interpreting disagreement as threat. Energy is spent rebutting rather than building. Decisions become reactive, designed to neutralize critics rather than advance mission. This posture grants outsized influence to dissenting voices and distorts priorities.

Detachment does not imply disregard. Leaders remain informed by feedback without being governed by it. Praise is acknowledged without becoming directive. Criticism is evaluated without becoming defining. This balance preserves clarity. The leader acts from internal alignment rather than emotional stimulus.

This detachment stabilizes the system. Teams sense when leadership is not swayed by mood. Confidence increases because direction remains consistent despite fluctuating response. The organization becomes less performative and more purposeful. Energy previously spent managing optics is redirected toward substance.

Detachment also protects integrity. Leaders who are not seeking validation are less tempted to compromise standards for approval. They can make unpopular decisions when necessary and accept delayed recognition. This patience strengthens long-term position even when short-term response is unfavorable.

Cultivating this detachment requires self-awareness. Leaders must recognize where approval or criticism triggers emotional reactivity. By observing these responses rather than acting from them, leaders reclaim choice. Over time, external reaction loses its grip.

Leadership grounded in purpose rather than validation endures. Applause fades. Attacks pass. What remains is the work itself and the steadiness with which it is carried.

Presence in the Everyday

Leadership presence is often associated with decisive moments; crises, negotiations, or public statements. Yet its most consequential expression appears in the ordinary. The everyday interactions, routines, and small decisions shape trust far more reliably than dramatic interventions. Presence that is consistent in mundane contexts creates a foundation others can rely on without hesitation.

In daily operations, presence shows up as attentiveness rather than intensity. The leader arrives prepared. They listen without rushing. They follow through on what they commit to, even when the commitment seems minor. These actions may appear unremarkable in isolation, but they accumulate into credibility. People begin to trust not because of charisma, but because of predictability.

Mundane consistency reduces anxiety. When leadership behavior is steady, teams do not spend energy interpreting mood or anticipating volatility. They can focus on the work itself. This focus increases efficiency without additional pressure. The system runs smoother because emotional friction has been minimized.

Presence in the everyday also communicates respect. When leaders treat routine matters with care, they signal that no part of the work is beneath attention. This signal elevates standards organically. People mirror the seriousness they observe. Quality improves not through enforcement, but through example.

In contrast, leaders who reserve presence for high-visibility moments create gaps. Day-to-day neglect breeds confusion. Important details slip. Relationships weaken. When crises arise, the leader's sudden intensity feels intrusive rather than stabilizing. Trust cannot be summoned on demand; it is built incrementally.

Everyday presence also disciplines ego. There is little spectacle in showing up reliably. No applause accompanies consistency. Leaders who maintain presence without recognition demonstrate commitment to substance over image. This commitment anchors culture more firmly than any campaign or announcement.

Over time, mundane consistency becomes invisible infrastructure. It supports resilience because it does not depend on exceptional effort. The organization can absorb stress because its foundation is familiar and steady. People know what leadership feels like on ordinary days, which prepares them for extraordinary ones.

Presence in the everyday is not glamorous, but it is decisive. It creates trust that cannot be manufactured quickly and coherence that does not require constant reinforcement.

The Company You Keep

Leadership is shaped as much by proximity as by intention. The voices a leader allows closest influence judgment, tone, and direction over time. This influence is often underestimated because it operates quietly. Yet the company a leader keeps; advisors, peers, confidants, and gatekeepers; becomes an extension of their thinking. What is heard repeatedly becomes normalized. What is excluded gradually disappears from consideration.

Wise leaders are deliberate about this proximity. They do not surround themselves with affirmation alone. Nor do they tolerate constant opposition for the sake of appearing open-minded. They curate environments that challenge without destabilizing, that offer perspective without agenda. This balance preserves clarity. The leader remains informed without becoming reactive.

When leaders keep only agreeable company, blind spots deepen. Feedback becomes sanitized. Reality is filtered to protect comfort. Decisions drift because dissent has been engineered out of the room. Conversely, when leaders keep adversarial company exclusively, energy is consumed managing tension. Direction fragments. The leader becomes defensive rather than discerning.

The most resilient leadership environments include voices that are principled, grounded, and independent. These voices are not impressed by authority nor threatened by it. They speak honestly because their position does not depend on approval. Such counsel stabilizes leadership because it interrupts distortion without demanding control.

Who is empowered matters as much as who is heard. Leaders signal priorities by whom they elevate. When individuals are promoted for loyalty rather than competence, culture shifts toward compliance. When influence is granted to those who embody judgment and restraint, coherence strengthens. The organization learns what qualities endure.

Leadership isolation is a hidden risk. As authority increases, candor often decreases. People hesitate to speak freely. Without intentional countermeasures, the leader's world narrows. Maintaining honest company requires effort and humility. It involves inviting correction and resisting the instinct to defend position reflexively.

The company a leader keeps shapes legacy more than strategy. Ideas change. Markets evolve. Relationships endure. Leaders who choose proximity wisely preserve clarity across changing conditions. Their authority remains grounded because it is informed by reality rather than insulated from it.

Replacing Charisma with Coherence

Charisma exerts immediate pull. It energizes rooms, commands attention, and accelerates momentum. In early stages of building, charisma can be effective. It rallies people around vision and compensates for incomplete structure. Over time, however, reliance on charisma becomes a liability. It demands constant performance and fades when attention shifts. Coherence endures because it does not depend on spectacle.

Charismatic leadership centers on personality. Direction flows from presence and persuasion. While this can inspire, it also concentrates influence narrowly. When the leader is absent, momentum stalls. Decisions wait. The system becomes dependent on individual force rather than shared logic. This dependency limits scale and increases fragility.

Coherence-based leadership operates differently. It distributes understanding rather than excitement. Purpose, values, and priorities are clear enough that action continues without prompting. People know how to decide because the logic governing decisions is consistent. Authority is embedded in structure rather than personality.

Replacing charisma with coherence requires discipline. Leaders must resist the temptation to intervene dramatically when clarity would suffice. They must invest in systems, language, and norms that carry meaning independently. This work is less visible and less immediately rewarding. It does not generate applause. It generates continuity.

Coherence also protects against distortion. Charisma can obscure misalignment because it persuades rather than resolves. Coherence exposes inconsistency because it relies on alignment over time. When values and actions diverge, the gap becomes evident. This visibility supports correction rather than denial.

Organizations led through coherence are steadier. They adapt more easily because they are not anchored to a single presence. Trust deepens because behavior is predictable. Culture stabilizes because it is reinforced structurally rather than theatrically.

Charisma may open doors. Coherence keeps them open. Leaders who shift from charm to consistency extend their influence beyond immediate reach. The organization continues to function with integrity even when the leader is not in the room. This continuity marks the transition from personal leadership to institutional endurance.

The Witness Who Holds the Center

The highest function of leadership is not domination, persuasion, or even direction. It is holding the center. The leader becomes a witness to the system as it moves, shifts, and strains. This witnessing is not passive observation. It is active steadiness. The leader remains present without needing to intervene prematurely, allowing the organization to reveal what it needs rather than imposing answers reflexively.

Holding the center requires restraint. The leader resists the urge to solve every tension personally. They allow processes to work, people to think, and systems to correct themselves where appropriate. This restraint is not disengagement. It is trust applied deliberately. The leader stays available, attentive, and grounded, intervening only when alignment or integrity is at risk.

As a witness, the leader sees patterns that those inside motion cannot. Distance combined with presence provides perspective. Repeated issues are recognized as systemic rather than personal. Noise is distinguished from signal. Decisions are informed by trajectory rather than momentary fluctuation. This perspective allows the leader to guide without micromanaging.

Holding the center also stabilizes emotion. In moments of uncertainty, the leader does not amplify fear or excitement. They absorb intensity without transmitting it unchecked. This containment allows others to regulate themselves. Calm becomes contagious. The system regains equilibrium because someone is not feeding its volatility.

Legacy emerges here. Leaders who hold the center shape organizations that outlast them. Their influence persists because it was embedded in rhythm, structure, and shared understanding rather than personal force. The organization remembers how to function because it learned how stability feels.

The witness does not withdraw from responsibility. They deepen it. By remaining present without compulsion, they preserve clarity. By acting without aggression, they preserve trust. Their leadership is felt not through constant assertion, but through the steadiness that makes everything else possible.

In this posture, leadership becomes less visible and more consequential. The warlord fades. The witness remains. And in that quiet endurance, the work continues with coherence long after the noise has passed.

Chapter 25

The Entrepreneur as Builder, Witness, and Gardener

The Builder: Crafting with Sacred Intent

To build is to translate intention into form. It is the act of giving shape to values that would otherwise remain abstract. Vision without structure does not mature; it decays. Ideas that are not embodied become unstable, vulnerable to distortion and appropriation. The builder's responsibility is therefore not scale, but integrity of form. What is built must be able to hold the intent that gave rise to it.

Structure matters because memory does not last. Words fade. Explanations blur. What remains are systems, defaults, and constraints. People live inside what has been built long after the builder has moved on. Processes teach more reliably than speeches. Incentives shape behavior more consistently than ideals. The builder's work becomes an externalized philosophy, whether consciously designed or not.

Sacred intent in building does not imply reverence or ceremony. It implies seriousness. The builder asks what this structure will train people to believe, prioritize, and tolerate. Every architecture implies a worldview. A system optimized for urgency teaches fear. A hierarchy optimized for control teaches compliance. A structure designed for clarity teaches responsibility. These outcomes are not accidental. They are embedded.

Building with sacred intent requires restraint. Not everything that can be built should be. Excess introduces noise. Complexity obscures meaning. Scale amplifies whatever logic is already present, whether healthy or distorted. The disciplined builder resists the impulse to add prematurely. They simplify before expanding. They ensure fit before speed. They understand that every addition carries maintenance cost and cultural consequence.

The builder also accepts that not all structures are inhabitable. Some impress from a distance but fail under daily use. Others produce output but erode those inside them. Sacred building asks whether people can work here with dignity, whether purpose can breathe through the system, whether coherence survives pressure. These questions precede metrics. They determine whether the work will endure.

In this sense, the work itself becomes formative. The builder is shaped by the structures they choose to create. A system built with care cultivates patience. A system built with aggression cultivates anxiety. The builder cannot remain untouched by their own design. Building is reciprocal. What you construct externally reorganizes you internally.

The builder's task, then, is not conquest but embodiment. To allow values to take form in ways that outlast explanation. To create structures that carry meaning forward without requiring constant defense. When building is done this way, scale becomes secondary. The structure stands not because it is large, but because it is aligned.

The Witness: Enduring Without Grasping

If the builder's role is to give form, the witness's role is to remain present without possession. Witnessing is the discipline that prevents construction from hardening into control. It allows the leader to stay engaged without becoming entangled, to observe what is unfolding without rushing to dominate its direction. This posture becomes essential once structures are in motion and life begins responding in ways no design could fully anticipate.

Enduring without grasping requires a fundamental shift in how leadership is understood. The leader stops treating outcomes as extensions of identity. Success is no longer proof, and failure is no longer threat. Events are held as information rather than verdict. This detachment does not weaken commitment; it stabilizes it. The leader can stay present longer because they are not exhausted by constant emotional negotiation with results.

The witness sees patterns that grasping obscures. When leaders cling to outcomes, they overreact to fluctuations. Minor setbacks provoke intervention. Temporary success invites overexpansion. This oscillation destabilizes systems. The witness, by contrast, tracks trajectory rather than moment. They distinguish between noise and signal. Their responses are slower but more accurate.

Witnessing also preserves agency in others. Leaders who grasp tend to intervene prematurely, robbing teams of the opportunity to learn and adapt. The witness allows space for completion. They tolerate discomfort long enough for intelligence to surface. This tolerance builds capability throughout the system rather than concentrating it at the top.

Enduring without grasping also protects ethics. When leaders identify too closely with outcomes, principles become negotiable. Justifications proliferate. The witness maintains distance sufficient to evaluate decisions against values rather than pressure. This distance safeguards integrity when temptation to compromise is highest.

The witness does not retreat into passivity. They remain accountable for boundaries, direction, and consequence. The difference lies in timing and posture. Action is taken when alignment is threatened, not when ego is unsettled. Authority is exercised cleanly, without emotional residue.

Over time, this discipline changes the texture of leadership. The system becomes calmer. Decisions feel less forced. Trust deepens because others sense they are not being manipulated to serve someone else's emotional needs. Endurance replaces urgency.

The witness allows the work to unfold without needing to own it. In doing so, they remain capable of guiding it long after the builder who grasps has burned out.

The Gardener: Tending What You Cannot Control

Where the builder gives form and the witness provides steadiness, the gardener accepts limitation. Gardening begins with an acknowledgment that growth does not obey command. Conditions can be shaped, but outcomes cannot be forced. This acceptance marks a turning point in leadership maturity. The entrepreneur stops confusing effort with authority and begins working in partnership with processes that have their own intelligence.

The gardener understands that cultivation is indirect. Soil is prepared, seeds are chosen, water is supplied, and boundaries are set. What emerges does so on its own timetable. Attempts to accelerate this process usually damage it. Pulling on growth weakens roots. Overexposure scorches what is still forming. Neglect starves potential. The gardener's task is not to hurry, but to remain attentive.

This posture stands in direct contrast to warfare-driven leadership. War assumes opposition and demands domination. Gardening assumes life and requires care. When leaders adopt a combative stance toward uncertainty, they exhaust themselves and their systems. They treat resistance as enemy rather than feedback. The gardener reads resistance differently. It signals misalignment, insufficient support, or premature expectation. The response is adjustment, not escalation.

Tending what cannot be controlled also reframes failure. In gardening, loss is not always error. Weather intervenes. Seasons shift. Some seeds simply do not take. These outcomes inform future action without indicting the caretaker. In enterprise, this perspective preserves learning. The leader does not collapse identity around results. They integrate experience without becoming brittle.

The gardener also practices withdrawal deliberately. Not all phases require intervention. Some require absence. Overwatering drowns roots. Constant attention disrupts natural calibration. Knowing when to step back is as important as knowing when to act. This restraint preserves vitality. It allows systems to self-regulate and develop resilience independent of constant oversight.

This role deepens patience. The gardener works on timescales longer than immediate reward. They invest in conditions whose benefits may not be visible for years. This long view alters decision-making. Short-term gains are evaluated against long-term health. Exploitation gives way to sustainability. The work becomes less extractive and more enduring.

By tending rather than commanding, the entrepreneur aligns with reality rather than resisting it. Growth that emerges this way is sturdier because it was not coerced. The gardener builds enterprises that can survive weather they did not anticipate because they were designed to adapt rather than dominate.

Multiplicity Without Fragmentation

As the builder, witness, and gardener mature within the same individual, a new challenge appears. These roles operate according to different logics. The builder seeks form and decisiveness. The witness prioritizes observation and restraint. The gardener works indirectly, accepting uncertainty and delay. Without integration, these modes can feel contradictory, pulling leadership in opposing directions. The task at this stage is not choosing one role over another, but holding all three without fragmentation.

Fragmentation occurs when roles are activated reactively rather than consciously. The leader builds aggressively when anxious, withdraws into witnessing to avoid responsibility, or defaults to gardening when decisiveness is required. These shifts feel disorienting to others because posture changes without explanation. The system experiences inconsistency not because leadership is complex, but because it is unintegrated.

Multiplicity without fragmentation requires a unifying center. The leader must understand when each role is appropriate and move between them deliberately. Building is applied when structure is missing or decaying. Witnessing is applied when clarity is required without interference. Gardening is applied when growth must be supported indirectly. Each role serves the same purpose: coherence over time.

Integration also requires identity stability. The leader does not derive self-worth from any single role. They are not attached to being decisive, calm, or nurturing as identity markers. These are functions, not selves. By releasing identification, the leader gains flexibility. They can act firmly without becoming rigid, observe patiently without disengaging, and tend carefully without losing authority.

When roles are integrated, leadership becomes legible. Others sense consistency even as posture shifts. Decisions feel contextual rather than erratic. The system learns that firmness, restraint, and care are not contradictions, but complementary expressions of the same intent. Trust deepens because behavior aligns with situation rather than mood.

This integration also reduces internal strain. Leaders who fragment exhaust themselves switching roles defensively. Leaders who integrate move fluidly. Effort decreases because internal conflict has been resolved. Energy is conserved for the work itself rather than spent managing identity.

Multiplicity without fragmentation marks a transition from reactive leadership to mature stewardship. The entrepreneur becomes capable of complexity without confusion. The work benefits because it is guided by a unified intelligence rather than a collection of competing impulses.

Rhythm Over Rigidity

Rigid leadership seeks consistency through sameness. It applies the same posture regardless of context, mistaking repetition for reliability. This approach simplifies decision-making but undermines responsiveness. Systems governed by rigidity fracture under change because they cannot adjust without breaking. Rhythm offers an alternative. It preserves coherence through movement rather than fixation.

Rhythm acknowledges that leadership operates in cycles. There are moments to build, moments to observe, and moments to withdraw. These phases are not failures of discipline; they are expressions of it. Just as breath alternates between inhalation and exhalation, leadership alternates between action and restraint. Attempting to remain in a single mode exhausts both leader and system.

In practice, rhythm allows the entrepreneur to move deliberately between roles. Construction intensifies when structure is needed. Observation deepens when signals are unclear. Withdrawal is embraced when integration must occur. These transitions are not random. They follow cues from the system itself; capacity, tension, pace, and alignment. The leader listens for these cues rather than imposing uniform behavior.

Rigidity often arises from fear. Leaders cling to fixed approaches because they feel safer than uncertainty. Yet this safety is illusory. When conditions change, rigid systems require force to maintain, increasing friction and error. Rhythm reduces this friction by adapting posture to reality. The leader expends less energy correcting misalignment because posture adjusts before misalignment hardens.

Rhythmic leadership also stabilizes culture. Teams learn that intensity will be balanced by recovery, urgency by reflection. This predictability reduces anxiety. People do not brace constantly for escalation. They trust that effort will be followed by consolidation. This trust increases endurance across the organization.

Choosing rhythm over rigidity requires confidence. The leader must resist external pressure to perform consistency at all costs. They must accept that thoughtful pacing may appear uneven from the outside. Internally, however, it preserves alignment. The work advances without tearing those who carry it.

Rhythm allows leadership to remain alive. It accommodates change without losing direction. Over time, this flexibility becomes strength. The enterprise does not merely survive shifts in condition; it moves with them, guided by a cadence that sustains both structure and people.

The Death of the Hero Founder

The figure of the hero founder persists because it offers a simple story. One person sees what others cannot, acts when others hesitate, and carries the enterprise forward through force of will. In early stages, this narrative can be functional. Scarcity demands intensity. Ambiguity rewards decisiveness. But what enables emergence eventually prevents endurance. The very traits that accelerate birth often obstruct maturity.

The hero founder myth collapses when continuity becomes the primary requirement. Enterprises outgrow singular intelligence. Complexity multiplies. Systems demand coherence rather than charisma. At this stage, leadership anchored in personal force becomes a bottleneck. Decisions slow because everything routes through one center. Risk increases because blind spots remain unchallenged. The organization survives by compensating for the leader rather than being supported by them.

Heroism also distorts culture. Teams organize around personality rather than principle. Loyalty replaces judgment. Initiative narrows because deviation feels unsafe. When the hero is present, momentum exists. When absent, paralysis follows. This dependency is not resilience; it is fragility disguised as devotion.

The death of the hero founder is not a loss; it is a transition. Leadership shifts from myth to method. Authority moves from persona to structure. Meaning is carried by systems, not stories. This transition is uncomfortable because it requires relinquishing identity. The founder must release the role that once defined their value. Yet without this release, legacy collapses into memory rather than continuation.

Enterprises that endure are not built on legend. They are built on clarity, rhythm, and shared understanding. The founder's influence persists not through reverence, but through embedded logic. People know how to act because the system teaches them, not because someone is watching.

Letting the hero die allows the work to live. The founder becomes less visible and more consequential. Their absence no longer threatens collapse because their intelligence has been distributed. This is not abdication. It is maturation.

Legacy depends not on being remembered as exceptional, but on leaving behind something that functions without applause. The hero demands recognition. The builder of continuity disappears into the work.

Shaping Culture by Who You Are, Not What You Say

Culture is not established through declarations. It forms through repetition. What leaders tolerate, prioritize, and embody teaches more powerfully than any stated value. Over time, these patterns crystallize into norms. The organization becomes a reflection of lived behavior rather than articulated intention.

Leaders often overestimate the influence of language and underestimate the influence of habit. Mission statements may declare openness, but if disagreement is met with defensiveness, caution prevails. Policies may promote balance, but if exhaustion is rewarded, overextension becomes standard. Culture absorbs what is practiced consistently, not what is proclaimed occasionally.

Who the leader is under pressure matters most. In moments of stress, behavior defaults to instinct. These moments reveal true priorities. Teams watch closely, even when leaders believe they are unobserved. A calm response signals stability. A reactive one spreads anxiety. Over time, these signals accumulate into a shared understanding of what is safe, valued, and expected.

Shaping culture through being rather than saying requires internal discipline. Leaders must align private conduct with public stance. Inconsistencies are noticed quickly. Credibility erodes when behavior diverges from message. Alignment restores trust because it reduces cognitive dissonance. People can relax into clarity when signals are coherent.

This influence extends beyond immediate interaction. Hiring choices, promotion criteria, and conflict resolution practices reinforce culture continuously. When leaders reward judgment over compliance, curiosity over certainty, and integrity over speed, these qualities propagate. Culture becomes self-reinforcing because it is embedded in consequence rather than rhetoric.

The leader's internal state also matters. Anxiety leaks. Resentment surfaces. Patience stabilizes. These internal qualities shape external dynamics even when unspoken. Culture becomes the residue of how leadership carries itself daily, especially when no one is watching.

In this sense, culture is not managed; it is transmitted. Leaders leave a fingerprint on time through the way they move through the work. This fingerprint persists long after specific words are forgotten. It defines how the organization responds to uncertainty, conflict, and growth.

Shaping culture by who you are demands accountability at the deepest level. It asks leaders to become what they hope to see rather than instruct it into existence. This demand is exacting, but it is also liberating. When being and building align, culture emerges naturally, without force.

Building for the Time You Won't See

Most building is oriented toward immediate reward. Results are expected within visible horizons. Recognition follows effort quickly or not at all. This orientation shapes decisions subtly but powerfully. Builders optimize for what can be demonstrated rather than what can endure. Yet the most consequential work often matures beyond the builder's involvement. Leadership that aims for continuity must operate on timelines it will never personally inhabit.

Building for a future you will not see requires humility. The leader accepts that their role is partial. They are one link in a longer chain. This acceptance changes posture. Decisions are evaluated not by how they reflect on the builder, but by how they position the system for those who follow. Short-term advantage yields to long-term coherence.

This perspective alters how success is defined. Instead of maximizing immediate output, the builder invests in conditions that support adaptability. Knowledge is documented rather than hoarded. Authority is distributed rather than centralized. Systems are designed to teach newcomers how to act without constant supervision. These investments rarely generate applause, but they preserve function.

There is also an ethical dimension. Building for unseen time resists extraction. It avoids burning resources, people, or reputation for temporary gain. The builder considers consequences that will be inherited by others. This consideration disciplines ambition. Growth is paced to preserve integrity rather than to inflate metrics.

Working on extended timelines also stabilizes emotion. Builders who measure themselves against distant horizons experience less volatility. Setbacks feel less catastrophic because they are contextualized within a longer arc. Success feels less intoxicating because it is understood as provisional. This steadiness improves judgment.

Planting trees whose shade you may never sit under requires trust. Trust that the work matters beyond recognition. Trust that continuity has value independent of attribution. This trust anchors leadership in purpose rather than validation.

When builders operate this way, legacy becomes implicit. It is not announced. It is discovered by those who inherit a system that functions with clarity and care. The future recognizes the work not through memory of the builder, but through the ease with which it continues.

The Business as Reflection, Not Refuge

Work has a way of absorbing whatever is unresolved in the one who builds it. When inner life lacks coherence, enterprise becomes a convenient refuge. The business fills space that should have been held internally. Activity substitutes for clarity. Expansion distracts from reckoning. In these cases, the organization is not an expression of wholeness, but a shelter from it.

Using business as refuge creates distortion. Decisions are made to avoid discomfort rather than to serve purpose. Growth becomes compulsive. Busyness masks emptiness. The enterprise is asked to regulate emotion, provide identity, and deliver meaning it was never designed to carry. Over time, this burden deforms structure. Systems become overextended because they are compensating for personal fragmentation.

When business functions as reflection instead, a different dynamic emerges. The work mirrors the builder's state rather than compensating for it. Clarity outside corresponds to clarity within. Boundaries are respected because the leader has internal boundaries. Pace is humane because the leader is not fleeing stillness. The enterprise becomes an extension of coherence rather than a defense against its absence.

This reflective relationship demands honesty. Builders must ask whether their drive arises from vision or avoidance. Whether urgency reflects necessity or discomfort with pause. Whether expansion serves the work or shields the self. These questions are uncomfortable, but they prevent projection. Without this examination, the business absorbs pressure that belongs elsewhere.

Reflection also reveals misalignment early. When internal tension increases, external friction follows. Meetings feel heavier. Decisions become harder. These signals invite correction at the source. Rather than forcing the system to adapt, the leader returns inward to restore alignment. The work stabilizes because the builder has.

A business built as reflection does not promise escape. It does not rescue the leader from uncertainty or pain. It amplifies whatever is present. This amplification can feel demanding, but it is also clarifying. The work becomes a teacher rather than a hiding place.

When the entrepreneur allows business to reflect rather than refuge, leadership matures. The enterprise gains integrity because it is no longer carrying unresolved weight. What remains is work that expresses the builder's wholeness rather than compensating for its absence.

Legacy as Living System

Legacy is often imagined as a fixed achievement: a brand, a building, a name that endures. This image tempts leaders to pursue permanence through monument. Yet monuments do not adapt. They preserve form but not life. A living system, by contrast, changes while retaining coherence. It survives because it was designed to evolve, not to remain intact.

A living legacy is one that continues to learn. It holds principles rather than prescriptions. Those who inherit it understand how to think, not merely what to replicate. This understanding allows the system to respond to new conditions without losing alignment. The original builder's influence persists not through replication, but through continuity of intent.

Designing for living legacy requires relinquishing control over outcome. The builder cannot dictate how future generations will interpret or apply what was created. They can only embed logic that guides adaptation. This requires trust. Trust that coherence will outlast personal oversight. Trust that others will act responsibly when given clarity rather than constraint.

Living systems are resilient because they are not frozen. They permit renewal without collapse. They incorporate feedback without defensiveness. When parts decay, they are replaced. When conditions shift, posture adjusts. This flexibility preserves vitality. The system remains relevant because it was not designed to be final.

Legacy as living system also reframes success. The measure is not longevity of form, but continuity of function. If the work continues to serve, to adapt, and to generate value with integrity, legacy is intact. Attribution becomes secondary. The builder's name may fade, but the influence remains embedded.

Leaving a living system is an act of humility. It acknowledges that the builder is temporary, while the work may not be. This humility liberates leadership from the need to be remembered. Focus returns to care rather than credit.

The entrepreneur who builds this way leaves no monument. They leave conditions for growth. What persists is not a frozen achievement, but a garden that continues to evolve long after the gardener has stepped away.

Conclusion

Sacred Creation: Business as a Candle in the Chaos

The world will always offer the same instruction: build by force, expand through domination, secure your place by burning brighter than those around you. This logic is old, persistent, and persuasive. It promises certainty through conquest and remembrance through spectacle. Many accept it without question, only later discovering the cost hidden beneath its intensity. You have seen that cost. You have watched what happens when unchecked fire consumes not only competitors, but the one who carries it.

Somewhere between collapse and rebuilding, you made a different choice. Not a louder one. A quieter one. You chose steadiness over brilliance. Endurance over display. You chose to carry a flame rather than wield a weapon.

This book was written for that choice.

Sacred creation does not reject ambition; it disciplines it. It does not abandon power; it reorients it. The entrepreneur who walks this path does not enter the market to conquer, but to contribute. Business becomes a practice rather than a battlefield. A form through which internal clarity is tested, refined, and made visible in the world.

When approached this way, enterprise is no longer armor or identity. It is not proof of worth or a refuge from uncertainty. It is a structure that reflects the builder's internal order. Where there is coherence within, there is coherence without. Where there is restraint, there is resilience. Where there is humility, there is endurance.

The chaos does not recede because you chose this path. Markets remain volatile. Systems still fracture. Cycles of expansion and contraction continue. This book never promised immunity from collapse. It offered something more durable: a way to endure collapse without becoming bitter, reactive, or lost.

You now understand withdrawal as discipline, not defeat. Stillness as structure, not escape. Non-attachment as strength rather than indifference. You know how to return without grasping, to rebuild without proving, to grow without inflation of ego. This is mastery not because it prevents loss, but because it integrates it.

Every decision you make going forward carries weight beyond efficiency. Structures teach. Systems declare values. What you build trains others in how to move through uncertainty. In this sense, work becomes liturgical. Each policy, each hire, each design choice expresses a belief about what matters and what endures.

The sacred entrepreneur does not chase scale for its own sake. They consecrate structure. They steward attention. They circulate resources with care. Their work does not shout. It persists. In a world addicted to noise, this persistence becomes a quiet form of leadership.

This book does not conclude with an ending, but with a transfer. You are not handed answers. You are entrusted with a flame. What you illuminate with it will depend on your restraint as much as your courage.

The fire does not need to be loud to change the world. It needs to be steady. And in an age defined by speed, confusion, and collapse, the builder who walks calmly, plants deliberately, and tends without force is not behind the times.

They are building the time to come.

Carry the candle well. The chaos will return. Let it find you already lit.

Index

I. ON INFLUENCE AND INTELLECTUAL LINEAGE

This work stands within a lineage.

It does not attempt to replicate classical Stoicism, nor to modernize it for convenience. It draws instead from the enduring clarity of Stoic thought: that perception shapes action, that discipline preserves freedom, and that internal order precedes external stability.

The reflections on withdrawal and contraction are indebted to contemplative traditions that recognize rhythm as structural, not sentimental. The concept of deliberate withdrawal echoes the Kabbalistic notion of tzimtzum; not as theology, but as principle. Space must exist before form can stabilize. What expands without contraction fractures.

The emphasis on stewardship over ownership is not new. It appears across religious, philosophical, and civic traditions that distinguish possession from responsibility. Wealth, influence, and authority are framed here as burdens of care, not proofs of worth.

Systems thinking also informs this book. Structures behave according to internal coherence. Misalignment produces strain. Feedback ignored compounds. These are not spiritual ideas; they are observable ones.

None of these sources are quoted at length because this book does not aim to comment on them. It aims to apply them. Where they appear, they do so as structural influences rather than arguments.

If the tone feels spare, it is intentional. The ambition of this book is not to persuade. It is to clarify.

The reader is invited to recognize echoes without requiring citation. Influence acknowledged is influence respected.

II. CONCEPT LOCATOR